Land, Politics and Nationalism
A STUDY OF THE IRISH LAND QUESTION

Land, Politics and Nationalism
A Study of the Irish Land Question

Philip Bull

GILL & MACMILLAN

Gill & Macmillan Ltd
Goldenbridge
Dublin 8
with associated companies throughout the world
© Philip Bull 1996
0 7171 2190 9 hard cover
0 7171 2191 7 paperback

Index compiled by Helen Litton
Print origination by *Deirdre's Desktop*
Printed by ColourBooks Ltd, Dublin

1   3   5   4   2

To Sheridan and Alexandra

Contents

Acknowledgments

This book is based in part on research undertaken over a number of years, and in its course I have been greatly assisted by the staff of many libraries and archival repositories. The principal manuscript collections consulted in Ireland are those held in the National Library of Ireland, the Library of Trinity College, Dublin, the Library of University College, Cork, and the National Archives, Dublin (formerly the State Paper Office). In Britain manuscript work was undertaken primarily in the British Library, the Bodleian Library, Oxford, the Public Record Office and the House of Lords Record Office. To the staff of all these institutions I express my deepest gratitude for their patience and willing assistance. I am also indebted to the University Library, Cambridge, where I have periodically been able to take advantage of its incomparable facilities for more general research. I am most deeply grateful to my colleagues on the staff of the Borchardt Library at La Trobe University, who provide so excellently the library support essential to a scholar undertaking research and writing.

The publication of a first book provides an opportunity to acknowledge some longer-term debts. At the University of Adelaide I was given an excellent foundation for my later work in history, and I wish particularly to thank Hugh Stretton, Trevor Wilson and Peter Phillips. My doctoral research and writing at Cambridge was supervised by the late Nicholas Mansergh, and it would be hard to imagine a supervisor who combined so well the qualities of kindness and consideration with astute criticism and firm guidance. I remain immensely appreciative of his help and interest. My greatest professional debt is to Oliver MacDonagh, who first introduced me to Irish history and who has been a continuing source of encouragement and help. I thank him most sincerely for all of this.

The idea for a book on the land question generally, rather than on the narrower period in which I had previously worked, came from Fergal Tobin of Gill & Macmillan, and I am most grateful for his encouragement and persuasion in bringing it to publication. Colm Croker as copy-editor has helped improve the written presentation and made a number of most useful suggestions on matters of detail. The author of a book of this kind is inevitably in the debt of those historians who have written more specifically on particular aspects of the subject, and I readily acknowledge this.

The opportunity for research and writing by an active university teacher depends upon the necessary institutional support, and I wish to acknowledge the periods of research leave granted to me by La Trobe University. I am especially grateful to my colleagues in the School of History who have provided an environment which has always been intellectually and professionally stimulating. I especially thank John Salmond for reading a draft of this book and making useful suggestions for improvement. I also thank Trinity College, Cambridge, for giving me an academic home in 1987–8, during which time I undertook research and writing which has been accommodated in this book, as well as for providing in earlier years the studentship which made possible my doctoral research.

Many friends and colleagues in Australia, England and Ireland have given encouragement and assistance to me over the years, and provided hospitality to me. I especially wish to thank Alison and Bill Church and Michael and Patricia Bull, and their families, for extended hospitality in their homes while I undertook research in London. My greatest debt is acknowledged in the dedication of the book.

Philip Bull
Melbourne
March 1996

Introduction

This book is a history of the Irish land question. Its parameters are readily defined. As a major issue in Irish and British politics the question of the land tenure system in Ireland assumed increasing significance from the middle of the nineteenth century, with important political and social ramifications down to the present. It is on the land question as a political issue that this book is focused, although it also seeks to give an adequate background to, and account of, the economic, social and legal context of agricultural land occupancy in Ireland during this period. It is not, however, a study of land and society in a more general sense. It can perhaps best be seen as a successor to R. Barry O'Brien's *The Parliamentary History of the Irish Land Question* (1880)[1] or J. E. Pomfret's *The Struggle for Land in Ireland* (1930),[2] rather than as attempting the more comprehensive task of social analysis as undertaken in a volume like J. S. Donnelly's *The Land and the People of Nineteenth-Century Cork* (1975).[3] The book, however, benefits from, and draws substantially upon, the burgeoning of historical studies in Ireland during the past quarter of a century, of which Donnelly's book is but one example, and its principal justification is its attempt to provide a more general history of the land question which takes cognisance of the impressive body of more recent literature. Indeed, it should be noted that Pomfret's book, perceptive and illuminating as it is, predated even the establishment of the journal *Irish Historical Studies* some fifty years ago, an event from which the evolution of a modern, more professional historiography of Ireland is often dated.

In many respects the Incumbered Estates Acts of 1848 and

1849 marked the beginning of active intervention by parliament in the problems of land tenure and management in Ireland. It followed not long after James Fintan Lalor, through his articles in *The Nation,* had first given publicity to the notion that the land question should take priority over the national question, which indeed it came largely to subsume. The conjunction was little more than coincidental. What began with the Incumbered Estates Acts was a phase in which remedies for Irish land and agricultural problems—so devastatingly manifest in the Great Famine—were seen by parliament to lie in measures designed to help landlords assert themselves more strongly as the providers of capital and the promoters of prosperity and order in the countryside. Insofar as it marks the first major recognition by parliament that there was a legislative role to be played in the resolution of Irish land problems, it is an important turning-point, but it was preceded by major evidences in Ireland both of serious defects in the law and practice of land tenure—highlighted in the monumental work of the Devon Commission in the mid-1840s—and of practical and impassioned proposals for change. The first two chapters of the book are designed to locate the emerging land question in a wider context and to indicate the lines along which proposals for reform were being drawn.

If the first phase of parliament's involvement was marked by a concern with the role of the landlord, the second saw a significant shift in the assumptions on which legislative intervention was based. From 1870 onwards tenant farmers, rather than landlords, became the focus of parliament's attention and an ever-increasing preoccupation of governments in administering the affairs of Ireland. A product of two decades of varied and persistent agitation in Ireland, and of changing perceptions in Britain as to where responsibility for Irish land problems lay, this approach was to lead to significant changes in the law governing the relations of landlord and tenant. These legislative developments were in turn to alter Irish perceptions as to where legitimacy lay in the endemic conflict between the two sides, strongly reinforcing beliefs and myths about traditional principles and practices of land occupancy.

The effect of these changes, largely Liberal measures, was to alter the law in ways which compromised accepted British principles of property to the point where Conservative policy-makers began to look to a transfer of ownership from landlord to tenant through land purchase schemes. As well as being more attractive to Conservative concepts of property, land purchase had the advantage of fulfilling some long-term aspirations of the tenant movement. This approach culminated in the Wyndham Land Act of 1903, which brought about a revolution in land tenure in Ireland, the end of landlordism as an institution, and the effective removal of the basis on which the land question had assumed its political importance. This did not, however, entirely remove the issue from the political arena, for it continued to have a residual influence on Ireland's political, social and economic life. This occurred both through a continuing identification of Irish nationalism with the ethos and ideas engendered through land agitation and through continuing cultural and other influences attributable to the longstanding nexus between national identity and the interests of the small farmer. This book attempts to make some general assessment of the longer-term implications of the political dominance of the land issue in modern Ireland's evolution to nationhood.

While tracing the evolution of changes in land tenure, it has been one of the purposes behind this book to set the narrower issues in a broader context in relation to differing Irish and British perceptions, to the changing political environments in both countries, and to the varied pressures being applied to those representing and articulating specific interests in the land. The book is, therefore, an attempt to set the land issue in a framework which makes conflict more explicable from the perspectives of those on either side of what became the major divide in Irish social and political life.

While this is a book which relies extensively on the secondary literature, as a general work of this nature must do, it draws substantially on original research in two areas. Firstly, detailed research on the development and character of the United Irish League in the years between 1898 and 1903, while important in its own right, also makes possible the drawing of a more complete picture of land agitation in general. The documentation available for this later agitation, fuller than for the Land League or the Plan of Campaign, enables more extensive conclusions about the character of such agitation, and of the demands which lay behind it. The second area in which a significant element of original research influences the shape and character of the book is in relation to the impact of the 1903 Land Act on the subsequent course of nationalist politics. While it has been readily acknowledged that this act marked the end of landlordism in Ireland, sufficient weight has not generally been given to its political implications, either in the loss of momentum ideologically for the nationalist movement or in the changes it brought to the outlook of those on whom the nationalist movement had depended in the past for its support. These two areas of more specialised research have significant implications for the development of the book, and the insights derived from them influence interpretations which underpin this treatment of the land question more generally. Thus, while covering much familiar ground, the book sets out to achieve two primary goals: to provide an overview of the history of the Irish land question in the light of the more recent literature in the field, and to sketch out a new perspective on how the Irish land question relates to major political developments in the modern era.

The principal argument around which the book is developed is that conflicting assumptions about the nature of land tenure relationships in Ireland were left unresolved to the point where the issue became so important in national life that it shaped the future of Irish nationalism and the shape of the society which emerged out of the nationalist struggle, creating between the issues of land and nationalism a nexus which was so strong that the one issue became effectively a metaphor for the other. It is suggested that out of this conjunction there emerged dichotomies in Irish national life which prefigured and helped to determine the breakdown of pluralism in modern Ireland; in this sense, an understanding of the course of the land question in the nineteenth and early twentieth centuries may help to provide an understanding of the basis of conflict and division within modern Ireland.

1

Landlords, Tenants and Agrarian Change

The question of tenure of agricultural land dominated the
political life of Ireland in the second half of the nineteenth
century and played a major part in shaping British perceptions
of the difficulty of governing Ireland. It is an issue which to be
understood must be firmly set in both an Irish and a British
context, for as a problem it is the product of the interaction of
two societies and two cultures. It has too often in the past been
seen, according to predisposition, as either an instance of
British injustice in the government of Ireland or as a manifestation of the intractability of the Irish and of their problems.
Neither of these perspectives allows an adequate understanding
of the real nature of the problem of land tenure. The characterisation by Sellar and Yeatman—that as the English (or more
specifically Gladstone) were 'getting warm' in their pursuit of an
answer to the Irish Question, 'the Irish secretly changed the
Question'[1]—contains a depth of perception, perhaps unconscious, of the failure of cultural communication between the two
societies. Nowhere is the confusion in the relationship of the
two countries so evident as in the land issue, where action by
British governments and parliaments which was intended to
resolve problems invariably resulted in no more than their redefinition. Fruitful as this process may in the longer term have
proved, it was more an illustration of incompatibilities of
outlook and values than a manifestation of effective political resolution of problems. The short-term consequences were
disappointment, frustration and anger. The complicated consequences of, and responses to, Gladstone's land legislation of
1870 and 1881 represent no more than particularly notable

instances of this. A new account of the Irish land question must shift the focus of this conflict in such a way as to bring out its significance in the evolving relationship between two separate but interlocking societies.

When Patrick O'Farrell chose the title of his book *Ireland's English Question*,[2] his object was, no doubt, to help reverse traditional images of the relationship between the two countries. Such a process helps to throw new light on old problems, but in the case of Ireland that reversal of perspective is more than usually important. There is little difficulty in comprehending the principles and objectives which determined British action in Ireland—the whole literature of British political and social theory and practice is to hand for that purpose—but if we are to understand the consequences of the impact on Ireland, we need to give priority to the Irish context, to an understanding of local tradition, practice and perspective. This is a more elusive task, and so requires a more conscious effort to capture the nature of the exchange, the areas of non-communication, the consequences of unconscious, as well as deliberate, super-imposition. In India British administration evolved an earlier and more comprehensive awareness of the impact of alien institutions and ideas on the complexity of an indigenous system, but in Ireland there was little recognition of the match and mis-match of two systems. Whereas in India the relative suddenness of imperial control forced acknowledgment of pre-existing conditions, in Ireland long familiarity and the ebb and flow of conquest obscured the lines of demarcation between the native and the colonial and made possible the pretence that coalescence was achievable.

Coexistence, if not coalescence, was a possibility, not least because the Irish generally recognised the necessity of compromise if the particular dilemmas of their society and of their relationship with England were to be resolved. But a number of developments in the course of the first half of the nineteenth century were to obscure—and perhaps irrevocably to eradicate—that possibility of compromise, at least within the framework of the Union of 1801, the context to which British policy had been so fully committed.

The first of these developments was the failure of the British government to effect the full political emancipation of the Irish Catholics which had been understood to be part of the process of union. This vitiated any possibility that Irish political and institutional life could be absorbed into the 'normality' of British politics. As unlikely as that might in retrospect appear, given the pan-Protestant nature of the British state, the impact of Enlightenment ideas and the fears generated by revolutionary ferment in Europe gave a better chance of this process beginning at this time than previously. The failure of the British government to bring about what it had itself recognised as a political and constitutional necessity, together with the unsuccessful attempts of Catholics, in a spirit of co-operation with the state, to achieve what they had been led to believe would occur, and—perhaps most importantly of all—the means by which Catholic Emancipation was finally achieved in the 1820s, finally and indelibly marked Irish Catholics as a race apart, a nation in waiting. This had far-reaching implications not only for the Union but also for the position and fate of the Protestant minorities, not least for the landlords and for their role and status in rural Ireland.

The second development which affected the possibility of accommodation between Britain and Ireland within the framework of Union was the Great Famine of the late 1840s. As a consequence of the social, economic and demographic devastation that then occurred, and the inevitable attribution of responsibility, whatever readiness had previously existed among the Irish majority to be responsive to British interests and concerns was largely dissipated. Nor were the effects of the Famine restricted to that part of the population, the Catholic majority, most devastated by it. Presbyterian tenant farmers in Ulster were sufficiently affected, and their economic position undermined to a degree, that they became uncertain as to the security they had traditionally enjoyed and distrustful of the intentions of a landlord class with which they had previously worked relatively well. For the landlords generally the Famine had far-reaching consequences. It undermined their credibility with the British ruling class, of which they had previously considered themselves a part, and bred among them a resentment that they had been held largely responsible by the British government for providing the support necessary to sustain the population, even though the assumption that underlay that expectation was of a poor-law ideology largely alien to Irish tradition and took little account of the manifest lack of resources in Ireland for coping with the scale and extent of the devastation resulting from the Famine. The Famine also added an international dimension to the relationship between Britain and Ireland. Through the creation of an Irish 'nation' abroad, most particularly in the United States of America, the Irish established a substantive continuing context within a foreign nation, thus fundamentally altering the balance and ambience of their relationship to, and sense of dependency on, Britain. The Famine had thus struck at some of the most important political and cultural assumptions underlying the structure of the Union.

A third development which made more difficult any accommodation within the framework of Union was the steady consolidation of *laissez-faire* as the official ideology of the British state. In this respect the Great Famine was again crucial. It has been argued 'that the efficacy of *laissez-faire*, and by extension political economy, of which it was seen to form an intrinsic part, was most searchingly and most dramatically questioned as a result of the Great Famine of 1846–7'.[3] The consequence of this questioning was that an economic ideology which to the British ruling classes—and especially the increasingly important middle classes—comprised a set of principles with universal application was increasingly seen in Ireland as peculiarly English and as an instrument of domination. This constituted a formula for conflict and disruption, ensuring that the central discourse on economics, especially insofar as it related to problems of land tenure in Ireland, was one in which there was little common ground and which served to accentuate and escalate polarisation. This was a contest especially unfavourable to the Irish landlords, in whose service the prevailing principles of political economy were being applied. Whereas the English landlord ascendancy had ridden the storms of agrarian enclosure and the destruction of the old paternalist order without undermining their social and economic pre-eminence, the Irish landlords had neither the resources nor the opportunity to exploit the new capitalism. Moreover, their title to their land lacked the sanction of custom and tradition which attached to that of their English counterparts. The replacement of a paternalist ethic by an economic one made more overt the latent conflict between landlord 'colonisers' and 'native' occupiers. The latter, as R. D. Collison Black has pointed out, did not reject the new *laissez-faire* principles because of ignorance as to their efficacy, but because they believed in an 'alternative system, the essence of which was [that] ... Rents should be fixed not by competition but by an independent valuation, and as long as the tenant paid the rent so set, he should be entitled to undisturbed occupation of the soil.'[4]

The old paternalist order allowed for some fudging of the nature of the landlord–tenant relationship, obscuring the rival claims to absolute rights of possession behind a concept of social function. With the advent of a concept of 'free trade in land', with its concomitant right of the landlord to dispose as he willed, these rival perceptions could no longer be submerged. Not only did this set the scene for an ever-widening ideological divergence between 'English' and 'Irish' ideas of land tenure in Ireland, but it caught Irish landlords on the horns of a dilemma: should they adhere to the new ideology which enhanced their power economically, or should they continue to recognise, as many of them had, the ambivalence associated with their title to the land and allow this to temper their relationship with their tenants? The cost of the former was an increasing alienation from their tenantry and the risk of greater conflict and violence; the latter course was likely to create an appearance of weakness in a context of a polarisation largely created outside the control of individual landlords.

Even without these changed circumstances, the relationships on the land in Ireland were historically complicated and confused. Rival perceptions of legitimacy were never far below the surface. These were in large part a consequence of conquest and its legacy, and as such were not fundamentally different from other instances of the same phenomenon. Irish landlords had never proved a very efficient medium of control and subjection from London's viewpoint, but nonetheless they could not in the context of their own estates ever fully lose their identity as usurpers. Moreover, for those who were now their tenants, lingering resentment at displacement inevitably influenced the tone and character of the relationship; this was based not only on individual and family memories of displacement from a more absolute control of their land, but also on a sense of communal denigration. Thus even the best endeavours of exemplary landlords and conciliatory tenants were bound, in the broader scheme of things, to be judged not in terms of their own overt standards, but by reference to these two rival perceptions of legitimacy. In this context, even minor discord was likely to end not in discourse and orderly settlement, but in driving a more serious wedge between the two sides. Landlord generosity was often interpreted as weakness and defensiveness—subconscious compensation for conquest—and lack of appreciative response by tenants to landlord initiatives was viewed as incorrigible failure to perceive their own interests rather than resentment at what was seen to be the landlord's assumed authority. It is no accident that the stereotypes of landlord and tenant in Ireland are of the rapacious and arrogant landlord and the greedy and violent tenant, even though modern research shows these to have been far from typical. These stereotypes have a lasting appeal because they were representations of an inescapable reality in rural Ireland, and they were forceful points of reference to which more ordinary experience was often subordinated.

This book is about land tenure as a political issue in the nineteenth century, and as such it is about the process of polarisation between two classes, landlords and tenants, and two perceptions of the place of each in rural society. That process involved the destruction of the fragile elements of consensus which governed the conduct of many—perhaps most—landlords and tenants attempting to make the best of their respective roles, attempting to treat the past as a *tabula rasa* rather than a chronicle of conquest and spoliation. The destruction of what there was of a *modus vivendi* was in part a consequence of the developments which, it has been argued, were also crucial to the fate of the Union with Britain; but deep weaknesses were inherent and pervasive in the very nature of landed relationships in rural Ireland.

Two separate and largely incompatible models of the landlord–tenant relationship vied with each other and undermined the possibilities of social stability in the Irish countryside. One of these models was an imported one. It represented the philosophy and practice of the ruling elites, and most especially the landlord class. The other model is a far more difficult one to define; it is less anchored in historical structures and more a product of reactions and responses to the imposition of landlord and government expectations. It should be assumed to be informed by recollection of conquest on the part of the farming population of Ireland; and that is an assumption which can help the formulation of better explanations of developments in the Irish land question and can sustain a more constant awareness of the native perception of that issue. This might be called the indigenous model, and an important purpose of this book is to show how it took shape in the clash and interplay of traditional practice, historical perception, myth, and the impact of contemporary political and social forces.

The social and political model which embodied the perspective of the ruling elites, both British and Irish, is—at least in its more traditional manifestations—a simple one to define and explicate. In this model, the 'owners' of the land are indeed its owners in absolute terms, with the right to sell or lease as they pleased and at whatever price allowed by the market. Any interference with these 'property rights' was anathema—property being central and sacred both to the 'old society' and to the new capitalist order emerging in its place. But the centrality of property in the 'old society', as manifested in English rural society, was matched by the equally important attribute of paternalism. It was a society of vertical relationships in which the ownership of property was associated not only with duties but also with the necessity of operating within a society held together by complex systems of patronage.[5]

Thus the absolute rights of property were significantly circumscribed by tradition and strong social convention as to how those rights were exercised. With the *laissez-faire* revolution of the late eighteenth century, the importance of property was entrenched, now as a means of production in a capitalist economy, but patronage was replaced by competition. The breaking of the nexus between property and paternalism increased, potentially, the real power of the owners of land, given the economic criterion which now, in theory at least, was the sole measure by which their efficiency was to be judged. Indeed, in Ireland this more capitalist environment began to facilitate the transfer of property from debt-encumbered landlords to new owners, thus further breaking the element of continuity so fundamental to a paternalist social system.

While officially paternalism as a social ideology had been made redundant by industrial and ideological change in Britain, many features of it persisted, despite the absence of specific economic purpose. Expenditure by landlords on the improvement of their estates was now more likely to be perceived as an economic function of maximising investment, but there continued to be an expectation of deference towards the old elite, reinforced by what were little more than residual fragments of patronage, now divorced from a commitment to a protectionist social order. That expectation was to a degree acknowledged by a rural population which by and large still recognised the social hegemony of the landed elite. In this way in Britain, and particularly in England, the outward forms of an organic rural society were to some extent sustained. But this was not so in Ireland. There the more the new ideology impinged on the relationship of landlord and tenant, the greater the discrepancy between rival perceptions of the nature of land tenure emerged. Whereas the model of the paternalist, improving landlord had been integrated into the new British economic structures—indeed, made more viable by the industrial and agricultural changes which were both cause and product of a developing market economy—in Ireland the lack of new capital, the absence of alternative occupation for the rural population, and the ideological undermining of the values of a paternalist system set the scene for a conflict which was eventually to destroy the landlord system. This model of landlordism, derived from English experience, was much more than a passive factor in the development of an Irish alternative. The pressure, evident particularly by the 1830s and 1840s, for Irish land tenure practices to conform to English ones served as a powerful stimulus to clarify an Irish model, to which popular attitudes were more able to relate. It is important, therefore, to understand the remedies that were being proposed for Irish problems in terms of that traditional English model.

In the writings of English travellers and commentators the expectations for improvement in Irish agriculture and rural life are clear and consistently enunciated: it is for the landlord to reform his estates in terms of a traditional paternalist role, modified by new capitalist motives. The critique of Irish agrarian life evident in many of these writings is one of sympathy, strongly tinged with condescension, for the Irish tenants, who are seen as having little power over their fate, and of condemnation of their landlords for not acting more decisively to modernise and rationalise their estates in terms of the needs of a modern, capitalist economy. For example, T. C. Foster, sent by

The Times as its special correspondent in Ireland in the aftermath of the Devon Commission on land tenure in Ireland, was clear in his views of the nature of the Irish 'problem'. There was, he thought, a cycle in which excessive population on the land consumed a disproportionate part of the product of the land, with the consequence that 'wealth cannot increase, nor capital accumulate, to afford other means of employment', thus further binding the population to the land.[6] An earlier traveller, H. D. Inglis, had made the same point in 1834: 'Men who are unable to turn to any business but agriculture, will agree to pay any rent, so long as want of employment prevails to so enormous an extent.'[7] Social disturbance and agitation was, in Foster's view, an understandable consequence of this, and he saw such disturbances as originating in 'the body of the people', and 'not to be attributable to a few worthless individuals':

> They are the outbreak of a strong pent-up feeling, which is almost universal, because the cause which produces it is almost universal—namely, want of employment and consequent starvation and discontent; and that this is at the bottom, and is the true cause, of 'Ribandism', under whatever name it assumes.[8]

The solution was equally clear: that landlords had the responsibility—and Foster assumed they had the power—to restructure their estates as more efficient agricultural units, in which farms were made more compact and investment secured more profitable farming conditions. That this had not been done was due to lack of will on the part of landlords. He compared the condition of many of the rural poor of Ireland with the starving poor of the London streets, and—naming the Marquis of Conyngham as an example—declared that 'To him who permits it, the odium of having such a tenantry and an estate so managed rightly attaches.'[9] Finally, that hoary old scapegoat of rural Ireland, the absentee, was brought to the service of Foster's analysis, illustrating the ultimate in landlord negligence. The absentee landlord was an important factor in this analysis of Irish affairs, not because absenteeism was necessarily incompatible with an effective economic role, but because it was the most extreme abrogation of the paternalist function, as exemplified in its modified nineteenth-century form. For Foster, the landlord's presence on his estate was absolutely essential, since he was 'the example, teacher, arbitrator, helper, friend of the poor, and the patron of every good work'.[10]

Commentators such as Foster pointed to the existence of rundale field systems in Ireland as an example of the backwardness of its people and its agriculture, and they saw the resistance of tenants to enclosure proposals as a chronic incapacity to perceive their own interests. Rundale, or strip farming, was the Irish equivalent of the English open-field system. Like its English counterpart, it involved both an allocation of fields to individual farmers and common rights to the use of uncultivated land, waste and mountain land for grazing and fuel collection. In Ireland this type of farming was accompanied not by the English manorial village form but by a cluster of farm-houses known as a 'clachan'. Foster referred, as did so many others, to the notable achievement of Lord George Hill on his Gweedore estate in overcoming opposition to the removal of this system by enclosure, and in introducing other reforms, thereby surmounting the chronic difficulties of inefficiency and conflict which characterised Irish agriculture.[11] Similarly, Mr and Mrs S. C. Hall—also observer-travellers in Ireland—took the estate of Sir Charles Style at Glenfin in County Donegal as another example of a reforming landlord sweeping aside the old rundale system, 'a state of things which paralyses all improvement' and 'in which semi-barbarous state large portions of the country still exist'.[12]

Analyses such as these embodied both a misconception of the nature of the Irish rural situation and a miscalculation as to what was socially acceptable for the Irish peasant population. Setting aside practical questions of comparability of land and other physical conditions for agricultural production, these views also involved a false analogy with what had happened in England over the preceding century. Rundale can be taken as an example. These writers were right in seeing this system of scattered fields, where each tenant's land was intermingled with that of others, as unconducive to modern, capitalist agriculture, but their absolute views of its evils and their formulations for its abolition took little account of how similar agrarian practices had been reformed in England. There landlords had enjoyed the benefit of acts of parliament to assist the process of enclosure, but even then they had to face the storms of objections and resistance from those who believed that their traditional rights to the occupancy and use of land were being eroded or destroyed. Often very substantial compensation had to be paid for the commutation of these rights, and resort had sometimes to be made to the processes of the law to subdue resisters. Moreover, in England enclosure was occurring in the context of a massive rural exodus, much of the population being attracted or economically forced to the new industries of the towns and cities. Driven as it was by the force of a new ideology by which parliament and the ruling classes had been gripped, this process was one of enclosure the easy way. Even so, up to a mere decade or so before these writings on Ireland were being published there were still cases of violent conflict in England over enclosures. On Otmoor, a mere five miles from Oxford, there had been frequent rioting and civil resistance from the time of the first attempt in 1801 to institute an enclosure scheme. As late as 1830 there were major riots, with the yeomanry brought in to impose order. So extensive was the sympathy for the opponents of enclosure that those arrested were recaptured and set free by the crowd in the streets of Oxford as they were being conveyed by the yeomanry to the jail.[13]

Struggles such as these were in essence no different from those of rundale occupiers in Ireland, or indeed those of many small tenants on 'squared' farms endeavouring to maintain what they saw as their traditional right to security on their land. The analogy drawn with the modernisation of agriculture in England was used to denigrate as 'barbarous' farming practices in Ireland which were not dissimilar to those recently in existence in England; indeed, as late as 1864 one agricultural writer was 'puzzled and shocked' to find fields still lying open in parts of Hertfordshire.[14] But in Ireland landlords, in conjunction with their understandably reluctant tenants, were—generally speaking—being expected to carry through this revolution with no system of parliamentary enclosure acts, without any due process for consideration and appeal in relation to compensation, without the capital available to the English landlord from his involvement in the new buoyant market economy, and without any means of reducing the population dependent on the land. The pressure on landlords to apply, and occupiers to accept, these new conditions in a different and fundamentally unfavourable economic and social environment played a part in creating a more systematic defence of traditional rights and practices. Moreover, this assault on older practices was counter-productive in other respects. Lacking the facilitators and incentives for enclosure which had driven the process in England, the coexistence of the two systems was in any case bringing about a different kind of remedy in Ireland, with each system adopting attributes of the other and thus creating a distinctive and dynamic evolving pattern of land settlement.[15] Furthermore, there were cultural strengths inherent within this evolution, for in the northern areas the rundale/clachan system accommodated Scottish Presbyterian tradition as well as that of the Gaelic Irish.[16]

The attempt to impose on Ireland the English model of land tenure, as it had evolved after the agricultural revolution, failed to take account not only of the special circumstances in which English agriculture had been so comprehensively reorganised, but also of a number of deep-seated differences between the two cases. At a quite fundamental ideological level, the basis did not exist in Ireland for the role the landlord played in English rural society. In England a framework of religious consensus had, not without friction, helped to hold together diverse classes in the countryside and to give a higher sanction to the role of the squire. Behind this lay residual elements of an even older tradition, to a degree metaphysical, in which the landlord on his estate, like the monarch on the throne, constituted an earthly representation of heavenly authority. While the continuing force of this cosmology should not be overplayed, it is nonetheless true that the cultural and social practices of the countryside, together with the religious hegemony of the Church of England, did much to sustain the paternal and authority role of the English landlord through an era of massive ideological and social change. It has been suggested that 'the most effective weapons of all for the maintenance of landowner power were probably ideological' and that 'the commonest such ideology in the European context has without doubt been the Christian religion'.[17]

In Ireland there was an absence of such mechanisms for 'reconciling rural populations with their subordinate lot',[18] making the relationships on the land very different from those in England. This was the product of history; as Judge Mountifort Longfield wrote:

In both countries the law is based on the feudal system, which gave the landlord a certain superiority over his tenants. But the feudal relation, with its reciprocal rights and duties, never existed in Ireland. Here the landlord never led his tenants into battle; if they fought on the same field, it was on different sides. They had no traditions of common victories or common defeats.[19]

Landlords generally were of a different religion to that of their tenants, and there was thus a line drawn between them which represented a cleavage of fundamental significance in terms of the functioning of a paternalist social system. If the model of English rural society is represented in the form of a pyramid, with strong vertical attachments, in Ireland the pyramid is an autonomous one within the indigenous Catholic population, to which the landlord is an outsider. Just as in English society the place of the landed gentry is well secured within the popular cultural life and festivities of the community, in Ireland those elements of popular culture assert the exclusion of the landlords. The legacy of conquest and displacement in the popular consciousness played a continuing role in this respect, but the landlord's status as an outsider had also been to a great extent 'sanctified' by religion. Not only did the religious differences between landlord and tenant undermine the possibility of a socially cohesive society, but the claim to a universal legitimacy and a longer tradition by the church of the tenants further diminished the aspirations of the landlord to be the centre of authority. The effect of this ultimately, as K. Theodore Hoppen has pointed out, was that Irish landlords were not able, as their English counterparts were, 'to contain [their] farmers within a species of broad cultural hegemony according to which the latter continued to accept landlordism as a "normal reality . . . " '.[20]

Paradoxically, it was the Roman Catholic Church which in the early nineteenth century held out the best prospect to the Irish landlords of establishing for themselves a modern role in the agrarian life of the country. The turmoil caused throughout Europe by the French Revolution had thrown the church fiercely onto the side of established institutions and state structures, even when these were Protestant. Increasingly the British state was being seen by the papacy as a force for stability in Europe, and by many churchmen in Ireland as a bulwark against social disorder and a potential source of patronage for the church. Even though much of the social and political unrest in Ireland was among the church's own flock, there was a readiness—even eagerness—to work with the state after the dismemberment of the penal laws, and with the signs of recognition evident in measures such as the Maynooth grant. In 1798 the Catholic Archbishop of Dublin had attributed the many advances Catholics had achieved to their loyalty, to 'submission to the constituted authorities', to their 'peaceful demeanour' and to 'patience under long sufferings' and warned them against 'rebellion, insurrection, tumult, or seditious clamour' if they hoped to secure the removal of their remaining disabilities.[21]

This represented an opportunity for the landlords to link their own futures with the interests of their tenants and the church to which their tenants generally belonged, to follow the path being mapped out by the British government as patrons of the religion which had previously been seen as the enemy of social and political stability. To some extent this opportunity was seized, but in the end it was destroyed by the failure to grant full Catholic Emancipation and the consequent closer identification of the Catholic Church with popular agitation. In addition, the failure to resolve the problem of tithes collected for the support of the Established Church further polarised the relationship of landlord and tenant, although even this issue was not one on which the Catholic Church as such mobilised itself as it had done with the Emancipation campaign. The shift in landlord ideas in line with the change in official ideology from paternalism to *laissez-faire* was one which further reduced the prospect of a positive relationship between landlords and a church whose philosophy on economic and social issues was largely pre-capitalist. Thus the recognition which was essential to landlords if they were to perform an effective role in Irish agrarian life, either in the economic sense or as figures of social and political authority, largely eluded them.

In accounts of Irish history in the nineteenth century, as in much other literature, images of 'good' and 'bad' landlords constantly recur. The 'bad' landlord—the 'rackrenter', the 'absentee', the 'evicter', the 'spendthrift'—is the characterisation which traditionally predominates. More recent research and writing, on the other hand, gives a higher profile to the 'good' landlord and suggests that he may have been a more typical figure in the Irish countryside than has usually been acknowledged. But what was a 'good' landlord? The images of this person are deeply confused between differing conceptions of the landlord's role and function. Sometimes the image is of the old-fashioned, easy-going paternalist, not unduly troubled by questions of efficiency, sensitive to the religious and cultural traditions of his tenants, and with a sense of the need to win a degree of personal acceptance in order to counteract lingering resentments at his usurpation of the land. The other side of this coin may, of course, be the lazy, indifferent and probably heavily indebted landlord, upon whom is heaped so heavily the blame for the crisis of landlordism in Ireland. Such a view of him is taken, in particular, by those who conform to yet another image of the 'good' landlord, that of the improving, modern capitalist, the investor who wishes to rid his estate of rundale, to create compact, effective, competitive farms, and to stimulate alternative employment for the excess population dependent on the land. Some recent work, including that of Dr W. E. Vaughan,[22] suggests that the 'good' landlord is one possessing characteristics in common with the classic 'bad' landlord, the rackrenter and exploiter of the tenants. In this view, it is the landlord who is clear-headed and ruthless enough to extract an appropriate market rent from his tenants who deserves commendation. It is this landlord who could capitalise on prosperous times in order to invest in agricultural improvement and be in a position to sustain his tenants through depressed seasons. A product of new economic analyses, such as that of Barbara Solow,[23] which suggests that Irish tenants—or a significant proportion of them—paid well below a fair market rent, this interpretation presents the real interests of Irish agriculture in terms of maximum capitalisation. In this view, it was the pusillanimity of landlords afraid to extract reasonable rents who put at risk the interests of the whole agricultural sector, including both other landlords and the tenants.

In the mid-nineteenth century, in English and official opinion, as well as in much Irish ascendancy opinion, it was the improver and moderniser who constituted the best landlord. Lord George Hill in Gweedore or Sir Charles Style at Glenfin or Colonel Henry Smith in County Wicklow[24] represented the ideal of much contemporary opinion in their attempts to modernise

Irish agriculture along the lines of what had happened already in England. However, looked at from the viewpoint of the tenants, these were the landlords responsible for maximum interference. For example, a high priority for these modernisers was the abolition of rundale cultivation, but that system, for those who still farmed by it, represented not only traditional practice, but also an important means of achieving community equity, each occupier securing a balance of good and bad land as well as sharing the use of non-cultivated land for grazing and other purposes. Likewise, the 'Ulster custom' especially common in many of the northern areas of the country was also under attack by many landlords, for it involved, in terms of the outlay by an incoming tenant to his predecessor, a payment well in excess of what could be attributed to the value of improvements; it was thus a drain on the resources and the efficiency of farming. But for tenants who enjoyed this practice it was an important acknowledgment of traditional rights of occupancy. Historians have tended to generalise Ulster custom as a practice prevailing among the Presbyterian tenantry, with an implication that it represented to a degree an acknowledgment of the distinctive religious culture of this society, but E. Estyn Evans has suggested that it 'may have had its origins in the rights of clansmen in pre-plantation days'.[25] This notion is reinforced by recent work which suggests that during the seventeenth-century plantations it was the Celtic Highland Scots, especially those from the south-west border region of Scotland, rather than the more anglicised Lowland Scots, who were most successful in establishing themselves in rural Ulster because they found there an existing social and economic framework in which they were able immediately to fit.[26] It could well be, therefore, that in the Ulster custom we can observe a practice formalised in the Norman-derived landlord system in order to preserve rights that existed generally within an earlier Gaelic social system. In fighting for it, even against economic rationality, tenants were defending what they saw as the legitimacy of their occupancy of the land against the claim of landlords to the right of its disposal. This is further confirmed by the widespread belief throughout the country, whether the Ulster custom was practised or not, that such a right to security was a general and fundamental one, a belief amply attested to throughout the minutes of evidence of the Devon Commission.

These two examples, rundale and Ulster custom, reflect the

strength of native custom which was under attack by landlords instilled with the fervour of *laissez-faire* economic ideas or commitment to the kinds of agricultural and social reform which had characterised the agricultural revolution in England. Michael Beames has shown that much of the Whiteboy violence of the two decades before the Famine was provoked by improving landlords who breached the 'moral economy' (the universally understood and accepted conventions by which social relationships had been traditionally governed) in their attempts to instil greater agricultural efficiency.[27]

The onslaught on traditional practices and rights by reforming landlords represented a significant change from the situation under the more casual, unreformed and unimproving landlord of the pre-capitalist era. While his presence in the countryside might have seemed superfluous to a tenantry which retained some sense of an older, more autonomous agrarian social structure, often he did not intrude very heavily on the tenants' lives. The rent he collected, while a grievance, had to a degree been naturalised into the culture and, if not too high, could be tolerated as an encumbrance not easily removed. In any case, what the tenant paid in rent was often significantly less than what was set, and there were a range of community 'sanctions' which discouraged landlords from having recourse to eviction. Insofar as such landlords exercised a paternalist role, it was most probably of a rough-and-ready kind, not heavily laden with moral imperatives and with some sensitivity to the culture and religion of the tenantry. This role had already been partly undermined by the sharper sectarian issues which emerged after the establishment of the Orange Order in 1795 and the 1798 rebellion, as well as by the greatly reduced level of landlord investment after 1815 in estate improvement and general economic activity.[28] It has also been argued that during the 1790s, in part because of the collapse of Protestant morale and confidence, there was a breakdown of the older 'moral economy', as a result of which the Irish peasantry saw their interests as having been abandoned by the gentry.[29] The advent of the reforming landlord of the nineteenth century brought further change. Now tenants found themselves the subject of the landlord's reorganising zeal, their traditional practices under attack, and—perhaps most irksome of all—their lives and those of their families subject to the endeavours of the landlord and his wife to improve their quality and moral purpose.

Elizabeth Smith, Scottish by birth and upbringing, was the wife of Colonel Henry Smith, a County Wicklow landlord. Her journals, between 1840 and 1850, chronicle her day-by-day responses to life on their Irish estate after their return there from India, and her judgments as to what was required to lift Irish agricultural life both economically and in its moral and social direction. It would appear that she and her husband were relatively successful in improving the efficiency of the estate, including redrawing of farm boundaries, and establishing a positive relationship with their tenants. They were hostile to the activities of Protestant proselytisers among the Catholics, and showed respect for the religion of their tenants, attempting to work as co-operatively as possible with the Catholic clergy. They were in no way adherents of pure *laissez-faire* ideology, and Elizabeth Smith was bitterly hostile to English responses to the Famine, specifically to Trevelyan's Treasury policies, and to the mixture of indifference and charity which they displayed.[30] But the Smiths believed in the new-style capitalist farming and made a major commitment to applying its principles on their estate. It is evident, however, that their well-intentioned, careful and sympathetic management of their estate never gained them the degree of acceptance and authority which they believed it should have done. While the tenants and their families fell in line with the reforms and there was a general improvement in efficiency and well-being, there is an underlying sense in the journal of a spirit of reluctant co-operation.

For Elizabeth Smith, this was attributable largely to the character of the Irish people, and the culture and outlook by which they had been shaped, including what she saw as the past 'haughty bearing of the *aristocracy* by birth', which had resulted in the cutting of the 'links which used to connect the different ranks of society together':

> There was nothing struck me so remarkably when I first came here as the tenants marrying their children—setting them up in different trades, etc., without ever saying one word about it to their landlord. It went through their whole conduct—we were to them only the receivers of a much grudged rent.[31]

In this reluctance on the part of the tenant the reader may

rather detect a resentment at so interventionist a role in their lives by those who were essentially outsiders to the farming community. While the Smiths emerged comparatively well from this clash of cultures, their endeavours were assisted by the relative prosperity of their part of the country. Lord George Hill in Gweedore was the subject of much more bitter controversy, adulated as a self-sacrificing benefactor by those who supported his reforms, but vilified by many others, his efforts at improve-ment for his tenantry characterised as 'improving them off the land'.[32] A distinguished liberal Irish landlord, Viscount Monck, referred in 1846 to tenant suspicion which saw improvement as 'inseparable from dispossession'.[33] Indeed, what landlords and Englishmen saw as 'improvements' may have differed dramati-cally from the things which represented improvement—in status and convenience, for example—for the tenant.[34]

The contrast between the Smiths and Lord George Hill alerts us to a further dimension of the Irish land question which is important to an understanding of its development as a political issue. Levels of agricultural prosperity differed dramatically in Ireland according to region. Thus the term 'tenant farmer' is applied at one extreme to prosperous farmers, already largely operating within capitalist principles, and at the other extreme to poverty-stricken holders of small fields; the former were more likely to be found in the eastern half of the country, the latter along the western seaboard. In these differing economic zones there are, in any real economic or social sense, quite different 'land questions'. But, in political and agitational terms, there is one Irish land question, with virtually universal application across the whole country, even in the Protestant areas of Ulster, despite its expression there in more muted terms and its more occasional activation. Later, when organisational expression is given to the land issue, it is in a form which combines large and small, rich and poor tenant farmers, although Ulster Presbyterian farmers (except on two occasions) remain outside this mobilisation. The reason for this unison between farmers of such disparity of economic and social interest is that, in three crucial respects, all of them relating to the landlord system, they cohere as a unity.

Across the whole range of Irish tenant farmers the landlords were seen as an excrescence to an indigenous system of land occupancy, making a claim for absolute ownership which was totally at variance with the perceptions of the occupiers of the land, who lived their lives on the basis of traditions and assumptions of a proprietorial interest in their farms. This was the first respect in which tenant farmers, both rich and poor, could identify with each other and conceive of their interests as common. This was less a factor in Ulster, where many of the tenants were themselves descendants of colonists of relatively recent origin, but there Presbyterian egalitarianism provided a somewhat similar basis for antagonism to the pretensions of landlords. The second respect in which common interest transcended the diversity of condition among tenant farmers was in the religious divide between them and their landlords, marking an historical experience which encompassed discrimination and persecution. In Presbyterian Ulster the same phenomenon existed, but without the same historical force as existed among the much vaster numbers of Catholic farmers. But in both cases fundamental religious difference made impossible the relationship with landlords on which the system of landlordism ultimately depended for its effectiveness. Finally, and closely related to both the questions of legitimacy of land occupancy and religious difference, there were the underlying distinctions of race which were a product of conquest. These were kept alive by the sense of grievance related to the other two elements, and with them helped to secure as a recurring factor a sense of common, nationwide purpose which frustrated the aspirations of landlords to establish a hierarchical sense of local cohesion. These forces were ultimately to play a vital role in shaping a sense of Irish national identity, but they also created out of the very disparate interests of differing categories of tenant farmers a single Irish land question.

If on the tenant side diverse interests were being drawn together in a common perception of themselves, this cohesion was being strongly reinforced by developments within the world of landlordism. Often, since the attempted introduction to Ireland of the Norman landlord system, the survival of the colonising 'planters' had depended more on their capacity to relate to the people with whom they had to coexist than to represent the interests of London, but this tendency to 'turn native'—an important integrative force—was subject periodically to the countervailing impact of a 'colonising mission', a product of more intense purpose at the heart of British action in

Ireland. Cromwell's campaign in Ireland had been such a case. Now, in the middle of the nineteenth century, three separate forces—each of them in its own way a 'colonising mission'— were drawing landlords towards interventionist policies the unintended effect of which was to reactivate a consciousness of the alternative, indigenous model of land tenure. These three forces were: *laissez-faire* economic ideology, with its requirement that the operations of agriculture should be subject to market considerations; British imperialism, to the interests of which the Irish economy was being increasingly related; and the process of acculturation to English norms, facilitated by linguistic anglicisa-tion, and which increasingly led landlords and the rural elite to which they belonged and the organs of government to attempt to impose on the tenant class and the rural population in general English customs and values. This was paralleled by the growth of virulent Protestant proselytism in Ireland; and even though such activities were more often than not condemned by landlords, they had the effect of further accentuating for the peasantry a sense of attack on their culture and institutions.

The indigenous response is evident from the 1820s onwards. It is, of course, highlighted by the Emancipation campaign. This very significant mobilisation of the rural Catholic population, while not overtly raising social and land issues—indeed, had it done so, the support of the church would have been much more ambivalent—represented the undermining almost totally of that most sensitive area of landlord influence, electoral politics. It is not surprising that a number of supporters of the Emancipation campaign were from the landlord class—and being Protestant they were able to stand for election in its support—for identifica-tion with that cause represented the best chance for landlords to maintain some semblance of leadership in their communities. But such involvement was too little to affect the overall consequence, which was that the rural Catholic population, together with their urban counterparts and in the context of widespread support throughout the United Kingdom, had brought into reality their separate and autonomous political identity. This enabled much greater effect to be given to their other grievances, most immedi-ately that of tithes, but in the longer term those which were related to the conditions of land tenure. It also removed most of the residual constraints of a patronage/deference social system, thereby making it more likely that the agrarian issues dividing landlord and tenant would be raised and vigorously pursued. From this time the lines of conflict between landlords and tenants took shape in much the same terms in which the subject of land tenure was to develop as a major political issue. The Great Famine enormously intensified the passion and the desperation surrounding the issue, but it added little to the definition of the problem. In the first half of the nineteenth century the clash between a landlordism driven to justify itself by reference to new economic and cultural orthodoxies and a tenantry reacting against this in order to preserve their own conception of the nature of their tenure of the land had been clarified and brought more into the open. What the Famine did was to etch in stark relief the imperatives driving each side and the incompatibility of their interests as they currently conceived them. From this the Irish land question emerged to dominate the political life of Ireland for the next fifty years and, to an extent, beyond.

2

Pressure for Reform

The emergence into political and economic discourse of an alternative model of land tenure is evident from the 1830s onwards. If this manifestation of the tenant demand is to be properly understood, then the form in which it is expressed should be set alongside wider cultural assumptions. While the defenders of the tenant interest sought to articulate their appeal in the context of ideas which held the centre of the stage in the public political arena, the tenants whom they represented were probably more influenced by ideas and beliefs inherited within the context of their own particular cultural and social milieu. These influences are very much harder for the historian to identify and define. It might, however, be useful to our understanding to assume, as a point of reference, that tenant attitudes were to some degree informed by an awareness of conquest. In 1830 it was only 150 years since the Williamite land settlements, little more than 200 years since those of James I, and less than 300 years since the Elizabethan plantations. As those familiar with other examples of colonisation are aware, the memory of conquests so recent is a strong and enduring one, despite endeavours by the colonisers to wipe it out. And in Ireland it was a majority memory, and one kept alive not only by persecution but also by religious continuity and a strong indigenous culture.

One of the definitive explorations of social and economic discourse on Ireland in the nineteenth century is R. D. Collison Black's astute and penetrating *Economic Thought and the Irish Question, 1817–1870.* In the early part of that book the author explores the emergence of models of land tenure based on a belief in an alternative system to that projected by English capitalist ideology, and he summarises the 'essence of the Irish view on landlord–tenant relations in this period' in these terms:

> The right of the landlord to his property was not called into question, nor his right to receive a fair return for its use: on the other hand, the tenant, by virtue of his cultivation of the soil, possessed a right to its undisturbed occupation which the landlord should not be entitled to challenge as long as he received its rent.[1]

The various proposals adumbrated during this period conform fairly closely to this description, but it should by no means be assumed that because proposals for tenant reform were couched in terms within these limits, they necessarily reflected the 'essence of the Irish view on landlord–tenant relations'. The position and perspective of the advocates of the proposals need to be identified and allowance made for the degree to which they were mediators for the tenants rather than directly representing their views. When that is done, there seems to be no compelling evidence that the aspirations of the tenants themselves were limited in the way described, even though for practical purposes it may have seemed politic to accept the parameters laid out for them.

One of the earliest and most robust proponents of the tenants' case was William Conner. The author of a number of speeches and pamphlets in defence of the tenants, Conner was a stickler for clarity of analysis on the land tenure issue, and was a fierce critic both of landlords who assumed concepts on land tenure alien to Irish custom and culture and of politicians, O'Connell for example, who constructed policies on the issue without relating them to the realities of the tenants' conditions and perspective. Conner's analysis of the problem of Irish land tenure is succinctly stated in an 1846 pamphlet[2] as:

> Exhorbitancy of rent, producing the poverty, and insecurity of tenure, leading to the outrages, of Ireland have their source in the undue competition for the non-increasing and scarce land.[3]

While weaknesses in Conner's economic analysis may be discerned,[4] for him treating the non-renewable resource of land as a commodity lay at the heart of the Irish problem, since it involved violent offence to native perceptions of the occupier's relationship to the land. Conner, a landlord, saw peace on the land as impossible so long as this disregard of the reality of social and agrarian tradition persisted. His remedy, in a phrase which became the hallmark of his ideas, was 'a valuation and a perpetuity'. Independent valuation for determining rent, combined with the right of the tenant and his successors to occupy the land subject to the payment of the rent so fixed, offered, in Conner's view, the only means of adjusting the law of land tenure to accommodate both indigenous beliefs and the reality of a landlord system derived from outside. It recognised the permanent interest of the tenants in their land, while ensuring that rent levels could not be used to force them out of that permanency. It was a compromise, but one which was in part devised to secure a role for the landlord on the basis of acceptance rather than conflict. While it involved for the landlord the abrogation of his more absolute rights over his property, it opened up the possibility of an accommodation with the society within which he was placed. But just as very few landlords had seen support of Catholic Emancipation as being in their own interest, so also very few could see the reform proposed by Conner other than as threatening both to their property rights and their social and political role.

An early follower of Conner was James Fintan Lalor. The two men were eventually to quarrel, and to do so very publicly. Like Conner, Lalor had identified the rights of the occupiers of the land as the central issue, not only in settling the conflicts over land tenure, but in Irish life more generally. While Lalor shared Conner's view of the rights in perpetuity of the tenant farmers, he went further than Conner in constructing an alternative concept of authority. While in English law all land was ultimately vested in the crown, in Lalor's view this made impossible any compromise over Irish land tenure within the limits of English legal definitions. Returning, as David Buckley has shown, to the foundations on which English law had itself been built, Lalor established a new authority in 'natural law' and 'social contract'.[5] This enabled him to establish an alternative basis of authority, 'the people', as the ultimate source of sovereignty, a means of legitimating the continuing rights of the occupiers of the land; that it also embodied a basis for Irish nationality was testimony to Lalor's view of the singleness of these two facets of the Irish problem. Like Conner, Lalor saw the claim of the tenants to rights of occupancy as antecedent to British land settlement, but unlike Conner he could not envisage those rights being accommodated within the existing structure of landlordism. Lalor, however, had been greatly affected in his views by the Great Famine and, as Buckley emphasises, for him this cataclysm had swept away any pre-existing 'social contract' in Ireland and had removed any legitimacy attaching to the landlord class as such.[6] Landlords, like everyone else, had now to pursue their own place within a newly defined social contract, the basis of which had to include both traditional rights of occupancy and the reality of Irish nationality.

It was the English philosopher John Stuart Mill who first placed the question of Irish agricultural land tenure in a wider context embodying not only Irish cultural and social factors and English legal assumptions but also the general principles of political economy as then understood. In his *Principles of Political Economy*, first published in 1848, Mill argued for a proposition almost identical, as he acknowledged, to that of William Conner. Like Conner, Mill saw the solution of the difficulty in two propositions: a perpetuity of interest for the tenant, and the removal of competition as the determinant of rent. Appealing to the necessity, even in pure economics, of taking account of 'the influence of imagination', he asserted that there is 'a virtue in "for ever" beyond the longest term of years'. 'Besides', Mill continued,

> while perpetual tenure is the general rule of landed property, as it still is in all the countries of Europe, a tenure for a limited period, however long, is sure to be regarded as something of inferior consideration and dignity, and inspires less of ardour to obtain it and of attachment to it when obtained.[7]

On the second proposition, the removal of competition in determining rent, Mill was equally adamant. Basing his case on the nature of cottier[8] tenure in Ireland, he distinguished between farming for profit and what is essentially the use of land as a form of labour. 'Peasant rents', he wrote,

ought never to be arbitrary, never at the discretion of the
landlord: either by custom or law, it is imperatively necessary
that they should be fixed; and . . . reason and experience
recommend that they should be fixed by authority: thus
changing the rent into a quit rent, and the farmer into a
peasant proprietor.[9]

Concerned, unlike Lalor, about the implications of this for the
landlords, Mill nonetheless argued that the public interest
required that parliament should make 'the whole land of
Ireland the property of the tenants, subject to the rents now
really paid (not the nominal rents), as a fixed rent charge'.[10]

By the 1852 edition of his work, Mill acknowledged that the
Famine had to a degree removed the impoverished cottier class,
and he described with considerable irony the manner in which
this change had occurred. But he also warned that, while for the
landlords 'it may be very convenient that the bulk of the inhabitants . . . should seek on another continent that property in land
which is denied to them at home', parliament ought to regard it
differently:

> When the inhabitants of a country quit the country *en masse*
> because its Government will not make it a place fit for them
> to live in, the Government is judged and condemned. It is the
> duty of Parliament to reform the landed tenure of Ireland....
> Justice requires that the actual cultivators should be enabled
> to become in Ireland what they will become in America—
> proprietors of the soil which they cultivate.[11]

These were very forceful statements at the time, especially by an
Englishman, and Mill's views on land tenure were to make him a
seminal voice in the emerging debate both in Ireland and in
Britain. In particular, we can identify three contributions made
by Mill which were distinctively his own. In the first place, Mill
reconciled the Irish aspiration for control of the land by its
occupiers to the principles of political economy. He did this by
demonstrating the essential difference in economic role
between the Irish agricultural tenant and the English tenant
farmer, showing that in the Irish case the same capitalist role
could not be attached to the tenant unless recognition could be
given to the reality of the tenants' effectual property interest.

Secondly, and especially in his post-Famine editions of *Principles of Political Economy*, Mill introduced a moral imperative to the question of land reform, a dimension given particular potency because of its English formulation. He thus laid the basis for what was to emerge as a distinctively liberal English perspective on the problem of Irish land and prepared the ground for a significant section of English opinion to reconcile Irish land reform with its belief in property rights. Thirdly, he recognised the primacy of Irish native custom as the determinant of the conditions of land tenure in Ireland, and thereby helped to restore confidence, validity and form to Irish definitions of land tenure principles.

The extent of Mill's sensitivity on this issue is not fully evident until the publication in 1868 of his *England and Ireland*, in which he asserts the entirely contrary character of Irish society to that of England:

> Before the Conquest the Irish people knew nothing of absolute property in land. The land virtually belonged to the entire sept; the chief was little more than the managing member of the association.... In the moral feelings of the Irish people, the right to hold the land goes as it did in the beginning with the right to till it.[12]

Even in his earlier work Mill created a broader context for this tradition in Ireland by setting it, uncharacteristically for English writers, in an international context by drawing out the parallels between Ireland and some continental European societies, as well as by making the comparison with the very different way in which British administrators had recognised, even if inaccurately, distinctive native land tenure principles in India. Mill's influence was a major one in preparing English liberal opinion for land reform in Ireland which went beyond the limits of normally accepted English principles, but he also contributed substantially to a renewed assertion in Ireland of instinctive and inherited beliefs about land occupancy.

Conner, Lalor and Mill formed a distinct tradition of analysis of the Irish land question. All of them looked to solutions in a political sense in order that social cohesion and stability might be secured, as well as justice. What all three had in common was an analysis of the Irish land tenure system based on a recognition that what the tenant farmer of Ireland was defending was totally at variance with the principles and practice of those administering and sustaining the system, namely the landlords, parliament and the government. For each of these analysts, the tenant had — through custom and history — a right to the land which was of the nature of an 'ownership', a right which precluded the 'absolute' rights of ownership claimed by most of the landlords and increasingly identified as essential to the working of the principles of political economy. What all three of them claimed, each in his own distinctive way, was that those principles could only be effectively applied, given the particular cultural and social traditions of Ireland, by a recognition that the economic benefits accruing from a permanency of interest in the land would only ensue in Ireland if substantive ownership were vested in the cultivators. As Mill asserted, the logic of changing the nature of tenancy in Ireland led inexorably to the concept of peasant proprietorship. Collison Black directly correlates Conner's 'a valuation and a perpetuity' with the concept of 'dual ownership',[13] which came into effect through the provisions of the 1881 Land Act and which in turn laid the basis of the peasant proprietorship brought in progressively through the various land acts from 1885 onwards. Thus, while the analysis which underlay the views of Conner, Lalor and Mill is ultimately vindicated in terms of the solution towards which parliament was inexorably drawn, it is not the analysis which dominated discussion of the issue in the two decades between the Famine and Gladstone's Land Act of 1870.

There has been some recent debate about the consistency of Mill's views on Irish land tenure, and in particular E. D. Steele has shown that Mill appears to qualify and even contradict his commitment to fixity of tenure both elsewhere in the *Principles of Political Economy* and in other writings.[14] And yet this does not seem to be a sequential development in his ideas, for his strongest statement for such recognition appears in his controversial *England and Ireland* of 1868. Other scholars have suggested ways in which the consistency of Mill's views can be charted through these apparent changes.[15] Perhaps what emerges most clearly from this debate among scholars is what might be called a consistency of intent in Mill's views on Ireland. As a radical in English politics he was concerned that justice should be done to Ireland, but that it should be done within a framework which preserved both Union and Empire, English power being for Mill, as for so many other English radicals of the period, a force for liberty within an international context. The Famine may have incited Mill's anger as a liberal, but it also encouraged his aspirations as an Englishman. Like other commentators, both English and Irish, Mill saw Irish farming apparently settling into a pattern after the Famine which suggested that the problems of Irish land might be resolvable more readily than had previously been expected. The reduction of population and the consequent increase in the size of farms, together with the apparent lessening of demand in Ireland for radical land reform, had encouraged Mill and others to believe that differentiation in law between the tenure systems of the two countries might no longer be necessary. Insofar as he had resiled from a belief in a more extensive recognition of the proprietorial rights of Irish tenants in their land, it was because as an Englishman and a politician he jumped at any chance for a lesser solution. Events late in the 1860s had shown how mistaken he had been in that optimism. The reversion in 1868, in language seen by many of his contemporaries to be intemperate, to the position which he had earlier espoused was the product of belated recognition that lack of action had now brought into question not only conformity in land law, but the very survival of the Union between England and Ireland. He may be seen as reflecting in the 1850s and early 1860s an optimism in English opinion as to the prospects for Ireland as part of the United Kingdom which had by 1867 been rudely shaken. It is relevant to an understanding of that English optimism to look back at how Irish political opinion had itself been articulating the land issue during that period.

From the late 1840s the phrases which most abound in the political discourse on the Irish land question are not 'a valuation and a perpetuity', nor 'peasant proprietorship', but 'fixity of tenure', 'tenant right', 'compensation for improvements' and 'Ulster custom'. Closer analysis of these terms reveals both fluctuating meanings and incompatibility with the analyses of those like Conner, Lalor and Mill for whom recognition that a substantive degree of ownership rested with the occupiers was an essential part of any solution. The terminology confused even Mill himself. He wrongly identified his own demand for perpetuity of tenure with the 'fixity of tenure' advocated by the Repeal

Association,[16] even though the essence of that body's proposed reform was the institution of long leases; this had been the ground on which Conner had opposed the Repeal programme on land reform.[17]

After the Famine it was 'tenant right' which became the catchcry of the land reform movement. This was an altogether lesser concept than 'a valuation and a perpetuity', for it left largely untouched the question of control of rent, upon which ultimately both the security and the economic viability of the occupying tenant depended. All that tenant right, as publicly advocated in this period, represented was the creation in law for all tenants of what already existed for some in 'Ulster custom'. The demand for this reform is particularly identified with the Ulster landlord reformer William Sharman Crawford. It is instructive to explore the form of Ulster custom, its meaning in the understanding of the tenants, how it shaped the agenda of land reform as associated with Sharman Crawford, and how it thus became so central to the statement of the tenant case in the 1850s and 1860s.

The minutes of evidence taken by the Devon Commission are the most comprehensive record of the nature and incidence of what is variously known as Ulster custom or tenant right. Appointed 'to inquire into the state of the law and practice in respect to the occupation of land in Ireland' in 1843, the commissioners discovered that the practice of tenant right, while it varied in form enormously from estate to estate and area to area, was practised very widely throughout the whole country, not only in Ulster. Its essential attribute was the making of a payment to a vacating tenant by an incoming one. While a normal condition of the practice was that it had the approval of the landlord, who retained the right to select the new tenant, the commission found that it often happened without the landlord's knowledge, in this case the sanction for its use being the fear of reprisal for an incoming tenant who failed to comply. The amount of this payment varied enormously, but it appears that it was nearly always determined by a formula related to the value of the rent rather than on the basis of a variable factor, such as the value of improvements made by the outgoing tenant. The practice, therefore, best correlates to the sale of an interest or of goodwill. But it had a possible meaning beyond this. If the practice was a relic of an earlier system of land tenure, then the attachment to it of the tenants may have represented belief in a property right in the land beyond that encompassed in a normal contract of tenancy. Thus, in much of the commentary on Ulster custom the tenant right payment is often coupled to a principle of fixity of tenure; but rather than seeing these as distinct rights, it may be more accurate to consider the tenant right payment as a symbol and token of a perpetuity of tenure, as indeed a shorthand in popular perception for Conner's 'a valuation and a perpetuity'. If this were the case, it would help to explain the acceptance by the tenants, and the consequent political dominance, of the tenant right concept, but without implying that tenants accepted the limitations created in the process of defining it as a political slogan and as the basis of legislation.

It is the practice of tenant right, but without any explicit iden-tification of a right to perpetuity of tenure, which provides the essence of the land reform movement first identified with Sharman Crawford. While his actions may have been based on a belief that tenant right would achieve a 'practical fixity' for the tenant,[18] his intent was to secure legal recognition of the custom with which he was familiar in many parts of Ulster (and its equiv-alent elsewhere) for all tenant farmers throughout Ireland, whether they were already beneficiaries by custom or not. To this end he introduced bills in the House of Commons in the years 1835, 1836, 1843, 1845, 1847, 1848, 1850 and 1852. Further bills with the same end in view were introduced in 1852 and 1858, the general oversight of the issue in parliament having by then passed to William Shee. But it was not until Gladstone's Land Act of 1870 that recognition of Ulster custom, and related provisions for other farmers, was incorporated into law. That legislation was the culmination of a long campaign which had dominated the Irish political debate on the land question, focusing it directly on the single demand for tenant right, essentially defined as the legalisation of Ulster custom. That act did not, however, satisfy the aspirations of the tenant farmers; indeed, the translation into a specific legislative reality of what had long been accepted as a general aspiration revealed how wide of the mark that campaign had been in the identifica-tion of the issues affecting the tenant population.

When the legislation proposed by Sharman Crawford is examined and the speeches given in support of it analysed, it is found that the intention of the legislative proposals lacks the

variable and open-ended quality which seems to have characterised Ulster custom in practice and accommodated in it a
meaning more suggestive of traditional rights of occupancy. In
reality, the object of these bills was to secure what was defined,
in Shee's terms, as 'the Irish Tenant's right to enjoy, or be com-
pensated for, on eviction, those permanent and durable
improvements, without which a remunerative cultivation of the
soil is impossible, and which, in Ireland, are always or almost
always, provided at the tenant's expense'.[19] When enshrined in
such legislative form, the aspirations of the tenants had been
reduced to no more than securing minimum justice in terms of
the Irish practice of improvements being made by the tenants
rather than by the landlords. This was certainly an object
demanded by justice; but this did not mean that it represented
the substance of what the tenant farmers wanted. That even so
modest, rational and just a reform did not gain the approval of
parliament until as late as 1870 reflects an inability on the part
of British legislators to appreciate the Irish dimension of the
issue; it may also be a comment on the manner in which that
issue was articulated from within Ireland.

There were three principal reasons why Ulster custom, interpreted as 'compensation for improvements', became the focus
of the whole land reform movement in Ireland in the two
decades following the Famine. First, it was a product of the
specific interests and aspirations of the Ulster Presbyterian
tenant farmers, who were the most significant group benefiting
from the existing custom and for whom there were very particular apprehensions at the beginning of the period in question.
Secondly, for reasons that have little to do with the land issue
itself, it served the purposes of the proponents of Irish nationalism to build upon the tenant right demand as it had been
presented by Sharman Crawford and others. Thirdly, a concentration on what could be explained and justified as
'compensation for improvements' made easier the task of reconciling Irish reform to British interpretations of political
economy and thus helping to persuade British legislators of the
need for a law in Ireland which in England would be seen as
both unnecessary and objectionable. These three reasons will
now be examined in greater detail.

The Great Famine, as disastrous as it was both to landlords
and peasantry, gave to the former an opportunity to attempt the

transformation of their estates into a form more consistent with the expectations of contemporary English *laissez-faire* agricultural principles. The dramatic reduction in population, by death and emigration, made possible a consolidation of farms and the creation of conditions in which farmers had more of a hope of evolving into capitalist farmers in the way that had happened in England since the extensive enclosures of the late eighteenth and early nineteenth centuries. To make the most of this new opportunity, however, landlords embarked on a wave of evictions to clear more of their land, thus removing many of those tenants who had managed to survive the ravages of the Famine; while some sweetened the bitter pill with schemes of landlord-assisted emigration, many—as J. S. Donnelly has shown —cruelly turned tenants in their thousands out on to the road without offering any alternative.[20] The landlords' actions, as human finishers of what famine had begun, did little to enhance their standing in Irish society. More significantly, because this particular attempt to establish the ground for proper political economy was done with capitalist even-handedness, it revealed to the Presbyterian tenant farmers that in modern economics they were no different from their Catholic counterparts, thus paving the way for them to become more aggressive defenders of their interests than they had been in the past. Already alarm had been spread in Ulster by the overwhelming defeat in the House of Commons—by 112 votes to 25—of Sharman Crawford's 1847 bill to legalise tenant right. While reservations about putting into law what had previously been done by custom no doubt played a part in determining this defeat, it was inevitably interpreted in Ulster as hostility by the legislature to the custom itself. The wave of evictions which followed during 1848 and 1849 served to activate the Ulster tenant farmers into forming tenant right associations along the lines of the tenant leagues which had already been established in the south of the country.[21] Their involvement was to reinforce within this wider movement the strong focus upon Ulster custom and a preoccupation with securing its central feature in legislative form.

Secondly, as a factor linking the Ulster custom to a developing nationalism, it was from the Ulster tenant right associations and the various tenant protection societies and tenant leagues in the south of the country that the new national Tenant League was formed in August 1852. This new body, together with the

Catholic Defence Association, was to provide the basis for the Independent Irish Party as it emerged in the 1852 general election.[22] In fact that party was to define itself very particularly in terms of the Ulster tenant right movement, devising a pledge for its members which bound them to oppose any government not introducing a bill 'embodying the principles of Mr Sharman Crawford's bill'.[23] This identification of a national party so closely with the terms of the campaign of the Presbyterian tenants of the north was reinforced by circumstances which had more to do with nationalism than with the land issue as such. The later account of the Independent Irish Party written by Charles Gavan Duffy was entitled *The League of North and South*,[24] and this reflected the romantic hope of some of those involved in the party that this new combination between tenant farmers might presage co-operation on the question of nationalism as well. Such hopes were soon to be destroyed, but the fact that the first national party to identify its cause with that of the tenant farmers had turned Ulster tenant right into a synonym for the land question shaped the way in which opinion, both in Ireland and in England, envisaged the demand of the tenant farmers. What that meant was that the term 'tenant right' came to acquire meanings that differed according to varying interests; it did not mean that the terms of Sharman Crawford's proposed legislation encompassed the aspirations of the majority of tenant farmers.

As we have seen, the third reason that Ulster tenant right became the focus of the whole land reform movement in Ireland after the Famine was the ready way in which it could be translated into what was not only the most minimal demand of the tenants but the reform most reconcilable with the principles of political economy as then widely preached. It was precisely for this reason that the term 'compensation for improvements' became the most common interpretation of what Ulster custom or tenant right was. Pragmatic politics dictated that the advocates of the tenant cause should attempt to define their objective in the terms most likely to win support in the House of Commons. While Ulster custom, or the 'tenant right' which it characterised, was unknown as a practice in England and contrary to English perceptions of the rights of property, it was evident to any informed opinion that tenant farmers should not be deprived of the value of their own investment in permanent improvements. As Irish landlord practice, unlike that of English landlords, did not involve responsibility for such improvements, justice demanded that either that practice should be changed or some means found to compensate the tenant. As William Shee characterised Sharman Crawford's mission, it was 'a steady adherence to the principle that no man's claim could be admitted to call anything his own which he had not purchased or inherited, or produced by his skill, capital or industry'.[25] The obstacles to legislating differentially for Ireland were so considerable, and the change proposed so inappropriate in an English context, that the only chance of success lay in projecting the reform in terms of 'compensation for improvements', even though that reflected something less than was actually involved in the popular attachment to the idea of tenant right. Thus a concept which represented, on the one hand, the actual practice of one category of farmers and, on the other, symbolised a deeper belief in the rights of the occupiers of the land had become defined in a legislative form which significantly circumscribed the meaning it had for those on whose behalf it was advocated. Even so limited a proposal, despite the substantive redefinition to appease English sensibilities, was to prove unattainable within British parliamentary politics, at least in the context of the tenant movement which had emerged out of the Famine experience. By the time it was attained it was already redundant in terms of Irish politics.

With the collapse of the Independent Irish Party of the 1850s, and the abandonment for the time being of the concept of a parliamentary party linking the land issue to other Irish concerns, the 1860s saw the advent of a new dualism in Irish politics in which the most pressing concern of the largest category of the population was submerged within political structures in which it had only a secondary significance. Fenianism, which dominated the political atmosphere of the 1860s, represented a shift away from the attempt to build on the land issue for nationalist purposes, and for many Fenians the land issue was a diversion from the more important nationalist objective. The National Association, intended in part as a counter to Fenianism, and largely dominated by middle-class and ecclesiastical interests, attempted to give the land issue a place, alongside other concerns, within a body committed to what was essentially political lobbying rather than agitational politics. But land was not to be so easily sidetracked, and the issue shaped the fortunes of these two movements in ways which eluded those attempting to direct them.

The attitude of many Fenians, and certainly of the movement's organisational structures, to the land issue had been in part influenced by the experience of the Tenant League and of the Independent Irish Party to which it had been so closely related. The supposed undermining of that venture by the attractions of office and influence at Westminster, redolent as it had been of some of the features of O'Connell's Whig alliance so hated by the Young Irelanders, provided for the new Fenian movement its most potent point of reference. Pursuit of reform necessarily involved engagement with parliamentary politics, and that for Fenians had become the ultimate evil. Preferable to that was deferring settlement of the land griev-ances of some of their natural supporters until after the accomplishment of independence, and—in the interim—that did not preclude a degree of complicity with the renewed Ribbon agrarianism which, at least in some localities, shared a constituency with Fenianism.[26] However, the reality of the land issue was in practice inescapable for Fenians, whose rank and file were inevitably drawn into the maelström of any political activity focused on an aggressive pursuit of land reform; and this, from time to time, assumed a major role in some electoral contests. The Tenant League earlier and the Land League later identified the fundamental importance of the land question to any expression of nationalist politics, and the attempted abjura-tion by the Fenians of this crucial matter was bound to be undermined. Indeed, the absence in the 1860s of any effective expression of land agitation made it all the more certain that Fenianism would become a very important vehicle for translat-ing the land grievance into political form. Thus the overt intent of Fenianism became in practice suborned to the imperative of this most pervasive of issues in Irish politics.

The National Association was committed to the pursuit of three objectives: the disestablishment of the Church of Ireland, the advance of Catholic educational interests, and 'to secure by law to occupiers of land in Ireland compensation for all valuable improvements effected by them'.[27] This simultaneous advocacy of a number of aims contributed to an inherent weakness in the organisation; E. R. Norman has suggested that it ought to 'have concentrated on one point only, and used it as a focus of the discontent expressed also in others'.[28] The wisdom of this view is attested to by the history of other political organisations in Ireland, both preceding and following the National Association. But more seriously still, it was the standing of the land question within this trinity which proved especially destructive of the purposes of the National Association. In the first place, ecclesiastical dominance—and especially that of Archbishop Cullen—meant that respect for the perceived rights of property played a similar role within the Association in suppressing the interests of the tenant farmers as in the House of Commons;[29] this is evident in the definition of the land issue as a question of 'compensation for improvements'. Secondly, the same dominance, and the associated fear of popular agitation, ensured that priority was given to those issues of most concern to the hierarchy and of more relevance to middle-class Catholics. Finally, the combination of these factors opened the way to dissidence within sections of the National Association where the land issue was the paramount concern and provided the opportunity for Fenians to reassert their influence in that area. Thus, in the most notable example of this effect, a section of the Meath clergy connected with the Association were gradually alienated from it and developed their own local tenant right movement in order to maintain their local leadership and influence.[30] This failure by the National Association to grapple with the issue of land left a vacuum in Irish constitutional politics from which Fenianism was the most obvious beneficiary.

While the land as an issue was not overtly at the forefront of the declared policies and objectives of either of the organisations dominating Irish political life in the 1860s, its impact upon both was sufficient to establish its pre-eminence as a determining influence on the course of politics. Not only was Fenianism at the local level dominated by attitudes and aspirations relating to the land, but its growth in membership was increasingly concentrated in the western counties of Connacht and Ulster where it represented predominantly the hopes of the small-farmer class for ownership and redistribution of land.[31] In the case of the National Association, its failure to give priority to the land question doomed it as a vehicle for Irish political loyalties at a more popular level. The message emanating from these experiences was not entirely lost on British governments and politicians.

The view that land tenure in Ireland was as elsewhere in the United Kingdom, simply because it was thus represented in law, was a myth that should by this time have been eradicated in the consciousness of British governments. The very creation in the early 1840s of the Devon Commission, with its wide-ranging brief to inquire into the law and practice of land occupation in Ireland, was itself a product of the gradual impact on government of agitation and unrest in Ireland and the persistent efforts of Irish members, such as Sharman Crawford, to change the law. The weight of the Devon Commission was not, however, sufficient to shift parliament in the direction of support for the practice of tenant right, and in particular no recognition in law was given to that practice, despite several unsuccessful bills, including that of E. G. Stanley in 1845. When parliament did move, it was to attempt to reform the institution of landlordism rather than clarify the rights of tenants. The Incumbered Estates Act of 1848 was an attempt to restore the capital liquidity of Irish landlordism by facilitating the transfer of the ownership of estates from effectively bankrupt owners to those with the capital resources to perform the role of landlord as exemplified in the English model. However, the desired rejuvenation of land-lordism did not ensue—if anything, the accretion to its ranks of many new, more capitalistic owners, more often Irish than British, consolidated the shift to a more ruthless pursuit of economic efficiency, further accentuating the lines of conflict between the claims of the tenants and the aspirations of the landlords. One important step had, however, been taken with that attempted reform. There had been a practical acknowledgment that the relationship of landlord and tenant, and the rights and status of each, were not immutable and that intervention by parliament was an option available for moderating the conditions and circumstances of land tenure. This coincided with an increasing acknowledgment by commentators, including English ones, that landlordism in Ireland was not sanctioned by history in the way it was in England—nor, indeed, in most other European societies. An institution which had been so recently implanted by conquest could not, ultimately, avoid debate about its nature and function.

Despite these signs of changing attitudes, the British government's first venture into Irish land legislation was more an effort to hold the tide back than respond to the pressure for reform.

The fundamental purpose of Deasy's Act of 1860, the first major Irish land act put through parliament, was to declare that what was coming increasingly to be seen as the reality of Irish land tenure was in fact not so. Confronted with the evidence which had been accumulating over the years, given expression not only through Irish agitation but also from the minutes of the Devon Commission, that a belief existed in Ireland that a right of property lay with those who were tenant farmers, the object of Deasy's Act was to declare unequivocally in legislation that this was not the case. The act made explicit in law the assumptions of English landed society, restating the absolute rights of ownership vested in the landlord, clarifying the contractual nature of the relationship with the tenant, and strengthening the powers of the landlord in relation to eviction. This measure was accompanied by Cardwell's Act, which sought to recognise that Irish tenants, not their landlords, generally carried out improvements, and which made provision for landlords to compensate tenants for such improvements; but this was not made obligatory, and the act was largely ignored. These complacent measures, opposed as they were to the realities of Irish land tenure, were only possible because of the depleted morale and vitality of Irish farmers in the aftermath of the Famine, the degeneration and finally collapse of the Independent Irish Party, and the lack of any popular or parliamentary pressure for reform of Irish land tenure. They were also products of the truculent determination of the new Liberal Prime Minister, Lord Palmerston, to take preventive action against what he described as 'landlord wrong'. Palmerston did allow, in 1865, a select committee to inquire into the working of Cardwell's Act, but without any expectation of change resulting from it; that lack of expectation was fully realised.

Deasy's and Cardwell's Acts were intended to close for all time the question of differential land laws in Ireland to accommodate the strength of traditional native assumptions about occupancy rights; they were to complete the process, characterised in a number of minor Irish land acts between 1801 and 1840, by which the absoluteness of the landlord's ownership was secured and obstructions—in the form of status and custom—to 'free contract' removed.[32] In retrospect, however, these two pieces of legislation can be seen as the 'last hurrah' of the confident English assumption that the spirit of Irish native culture could be subdued to the letter of British law and the tenets of British economic ideology. The Russell/Gladstone administrations which followed Palmerston's death in 1865 were to find that the question of Irish land tenure was to be at the heart of the governmental and legislative process; as early as 1866 the government had attempted, unsuccessfully, to pass a bill to grant compensation to tenants for improvements.

While Palmerston's departure facilitated a more open look at the question of landlord–tenant relationships in Ireland, it was events in Ireland which put the matter back on the British political agenda. Agricultural depression in Ireland in the early 1860s had reawakened a sense of insecurity among the farming class, making the tenant farmers conscious of their lack of political representation since the demise of the Tenant League of the 1850s. New tenant associations had begun to emerge, and agitation on the land question had resumed. The lack of any national political movement to articulate these concerns meant that, as has been seen, the emerging Fenian movement drew much of its local political sustenance from this issue, giving both a new vitality and a more formidable and threatening character to land agitation. The rising incidence of Fenian activity, reaching its crescendo with the shooting of a policeman in Manchester and the Clerkenwell explosions, brought home to English opinion the degree of Irish disenchantment. Nor had the contribution of the National Association been insignificant in educating political opinion in England as to the continued sense of grievance felt throughout Ireland in relation to the terms in which the country had been brought into the Union; both through its conservative methods and its definition of an Irish reform programme it had alerted at least more sensitive and liberal opinion in England to the reality of Irish views. But there was also an important context within English opinion which made this impact greater. The further extension of the franchise, embodied in the Reform Act of 1867, together with new currents of thought—such as new ideas of socialism emerging through the First International—was making the English ruling elites more aware of the dangers of social revolution and of the possibility of a conjunction of forces against 'property' in Ireland with those in Britain. Thus, as a consequence of all these factors, a ruling class and a legislature which had as recently as 1865 been so clear as to the principles of property which should be applied to Irish land were now seriously debating proposals for Irish land legislation involving significant departure from those principles; and by 1870 parliament had actually legislated in terms contrary to what had been declared to be those principles.

The process by which this change came about is extremely informative both of the British political process and of Irish agrarian politics. In a penetrating and impressive piece of historical analysis, E. D. Steele has traced the interaction between Irish and British ideas and politics, the influence of ideas on the development of policy on the Irish land question, and the complex intellectual and political process by which the leaders of opinion, especially in Britain, shaped their ideas and evolved their decisions on Irish land.[33] What emerges from this analysis is a picture of a society in which a concern about perceived injustice was matched to a sense of apprehension about social stability to create a crisis which inexorably drew leaders of parties and opinion to a position which had only a few months, or even weeks, earlier been totally unacceptable to them. And at the heart of this development was the extraordinary contribution of no ordinary individual. Being drawn by the perception of necessity ahead of his own view of what was desirable, William Ewart Gladstone led others subtly and persuasively towards an acceptance that there had to be some acknowledgment in Ireland of a right of property residing with the native occupiers. How that could be done without encroaching too far upon the rights of the landlords as owners and without creating a precedent which would unsettle concepts of property in England and Scotland became the essence of the debate. The parameters within which this debate developed were very wide indeed.

The starting-point for most British opinion was the inviolability of the rights of property, together with an assumption that in Ireland the only legally discernible extant proprietorial right was vested in the landlords, albeit as a consequence of earlier conquest. Compensation for improvements had been a difficult concept to relate to this because it involved an assumption not only that the property-owner had been negligent but also that the improvements could have been legitimately carried out without his consent. However, the extensive debate in late 1869 and early 1870 showed that most people had by then recognised the distinctiveness—unattractive as it was—of Irish practice and accepted the need for a change in the law to allow the tenant to recover his investment. This was, after all, good capitalist principle, even though applied in an unusual manner. But it was equally evident that by 1869 this was no longer anywhere near sufficient to meet the demand being made in Ireland, a point made increasingly forcefully through political agitation, agrarian outrage and the various manifestations—such as the success in a Tipperary by-election in November 1869 of a Fenian prisoner, Jeremiah O'Donovan Rossa—of a more revolutionary fervour in Ireland. Under this pressure, more of the leaders of political opinion came to entertain the idea of legalising Ulster custom where it existed, and extending it by law elsewhere, in the hope that this would go further towards settling discontent in Ireland. This was, however, in the last resort more than could be swallowed in Britain.

At the opposite extremity of this debate was a perspective formed from a recognition of the grievance of displacement by conquest and the development of an 'idea of restitution'.[34] Interestingly, it was the Prime Minister himself who was most affected by this dimension, and its influence on him appears to have shaped his conduct of the discussions more than he was to admit publicly and more than was reflected in the form of the final legislation. Increasingly Gladstone came to see the issue in terms very similar to the view put by tenant advocates in Ireland, that the right of occupancy could not be separated from the historical circumstances of the conquest of Ireland and that the continuous association of the tenant class with the land was of such a character as to constitute a right to something very akin to 'fixity of tenure', the phrase in which the tenant demand was by now mainly couched. Ironically, it was some of the Irish landlords who offered least resistance to Gladstone's mode of thinking, for—while deeply unhappy about the practical conclusion likely to be drawn from it—many of them remained acutely sensitive to the view of the past on which it was based. In particular, Gladstone enjoyed strong support from a small cohort of Irish landlords active as liberals, most notably Lords Bessborough and Monck and the Duke of Devonshire;[35] in February 1870, for example, Monck had stressed the need to face the fact of enmity between the Irish people and British law.[36] The awareness that such ideas were influencing

Gladstone's mind, however, had a profoundly negative effect on a wide range of opinion within the circles in England, and not least within his own cabinet, upon which his legislative success depended. While radical opinion—exemplified within the cabinet in John Bright—was ready enough to attack the bastion of landlordism in Ireland, or indeed in England if opportunity were to arise, it remained staunchly attached to the rights of property. Moreover, many radicals grounded their opposition to much of the traditional structure of landlordism on a belief in the introduction of free trade in land; what tenant leaders in Ireland were now demanding was a further departure from that principle to insulate tenants even more fully than landlords from the influence of the market. Likewise, both Liberal and Conservative leaders remained bitterly opposed to what some of them were in the habit of calling 'giving what belonged to one man to another man', wishing to concede—if anything had to be conceded—the absolute minimum. It was not surprising, therefore, that Gladstone's desire to embody in the debate a dimension characterised by one of his critics as 'tribal right' did not enter the public arena.[37]

The Land Act of 1870, which was eventually enacted in very much the same form in which it had been introduced by the government, represented—needless to say—a compromise. Uncontroversially—so far had opinion moved—it gave in the province of Ulster the protection of law to the custom as practised there, but disappointingly for Gladstone it did not extend that custom as law throughout Ireland, the basis on which he envisaged a possible recognition and partial satisfaction of native claims to permanency of occupation rights. Where such custom could be established as existing in the other provinces, similar protection was given in the event of the tenant's occupancy being disturbed by the landlord. Elsewhere—and bitterly controversially—the act provided for compensation to the tenant if disturbed by the landlord. This latter was the most that Gladstone could achieve in terms of establishing that in Ireland, unlike England and Scotland, a right of occupancy for the tenant existed, even in the absence of customary practices sanctioned by landlords; this, however, violated fundamentally the rights of property being defended by most of Gladstone's colleagues as well as by his Tory opponents. As was argued at the time, if a tenant-at-will could be compensaed for a displacement which did not breach any contractual rights, why not similar compensation for an English tenant farmer vacating his land, or a residential tenant being evicted, or a worker being 'disturbed' from his employment?[38] These alternatives may not seem so unthinkable with a hindsight informed by subsequent developments leading up to the welfare state, but Dr Steele's surmise may be noted, that 'It was no accident ... that the trickle of collectivist legislation passed to cope with the pressures of a growing industrial and urban society started to broaden into a stream from the year 1870.'[39] The provision for 'compensation for disturbance' was in the end only carried by the sustained success of Gladstone in establishing that the failure of the bill would herald the possibility of a later measure devised in circumstances of an even further deteriorated situation in Ireland. He did this despite not being able to use the argument, that of the traditional rights of Irish tenants, which explained his commitment to this provision, for—again in Dr Steele's words—'Those rights were too strong an argument in relation to the bill that he had to explain.'[40]

What Gladstone—and he alone among his colleagues—had glimpsed in the 'idea of restitution' was an alternative path to the resolution of the Irish land question from which the necessities of politics had forced him to turn aside. That alternative, dormant as it remained, is most important in understanding the development of the Irish land question, for it represented what may retrospectively be seen as the only means of achieving through the legislative process then being undertaken a lasting reconciliation with Irish aspirations, the objective which formed an important part of the argument upon which the 1870 act depended for its passage. Because that perspective could not be accommodated, not only were the arguments for the 1870 legislation necessarily weakened, but its effectiveness was fatally compromised. The conditions for 'compensation for disturbance' in the act were so circumscribed as to make it difficult for the advocates of 'fixity of tenure' to see it as a substitute for the extension of Ulster custom, which might possibly have satisfied them that some acknowledgment was being made of the tenants' traditional rights. Lord Devon, son of the chairman of the earlier Devon Commission, had shrewdly warned Gladstone of the need to quote native custom as the reason for compensation which went beyond recompense for improvements.[41] While this would certainly have helped contain the idea within Ireland, it might also have served to conciliate Irish opinion and secure a more sympathetic hearing for the act, at least as an interim measure that testified to a British acknowledgment of the fact of usurpation.

The potential of Gladstone's alternative becomes more evident if we examine the views of a man whose influence on the Prime Minister appears to have been very considerable. George Campbell manifested a scepticism towards the shibboleths of English property ideology, in this reflecting changing ideas associated with economists like J. S. Mill and J. E. Cairnes.[42] This detachment perhaps derived in part from his Scottish origins, but was more directly a product of his experience as an administrator in India. His perspective was refreshingly open and succinctly stated:

> Those who argue that there is no room for compromise, because the landlords having everything—that is, absolute and unconditional property in the soil—have no occasion for compromise, and the tenants having no rights have no basis for compromise, take the very narrowest and the most English-lawyer view of the question. It is hardly possible to approach the subject without first realizing this—*viz.* that in Ireland a landlord is not a landlord, and a tenant is not a tenant—in the English sense.... The whole difficulty arises from our applying English laws to a country where they are opposed to facts, and to those 'αγραπτοι νομοι' which are written in the hearts, and find expression in the customs of the people.[43]

Campbell proceeded to establish his point that 'In Ireland there are two sets of laws—the English laws, and the laws or customs of the country, which, enforced in a different way, are as active and effective.'[44] He explained the sanctions by which it had become impossible for the landlord to break with impunity these alternative laws, and he illustrated the force of that customary law in the language and practices of the people. He noticed in his travels in Ireland that the language tenant farmers normally used was of 'owning a farm', 'selling his farm', 'having bought a farm', 'having inherited a farm'. He noted, as with concern did participants in the British discussion on the form of legislation, that Irish tenants disposed of farms at their death by will, charged them with fortunes for daughters, and in every respect dealt with them as if they were their property. The problem which had to be solved, he contended, was how 'the law of the land and the custom having the force of law may be brought into harmony and made to work together'.[45]

Historically, in Campbell's view, the 'cardinal mistake' had been the 'introduction of English laws and of purely English courts', and the failure of English judges to 'bring themselves to administer Irish law', which was eventually deemed 'nothing but "lewd customs"'.[46] In this view he had some contemporary English legal opinion on his side, in the form of no less a person than the Lord Chancellor, who—in the House of Lords debates on the land bill—'traced the need for legislation to the failure of the courts in Ireland to adapt English law to Irish custom and circumstances'.[47] What Campbell developed was a sense of a potential for an integration of native customary law with English law. That was something which Irish opinion could accommodate. The various formulae which had been evolved for a settlement of the land question, Conner's 'valuation and a perpetuity', 'Ulster custom', 'tenant right', the 'three Fs', were all constructed to establish a recognition of customary property rights reconciled to the continued existence of landlordism. What Gladstone's exploration of the question of Irish land tenure had produced was a recognition by him of this potential, but a political inability either to bring it about or to move—as an extension of Ulster custom as a legal right to the whole of Ireland might have done—in a direction compatible with it.

There is, here, an interesting contemporary parallel to be drawn which might help to illustrate this potential. A judgment of the High Court of Australia in 1992 decreed that a native occupier, Edward Mabo, whose antecedents had enjoyed a continuous association with the land since before European settlement, had legal title to that land. This reversed the assumption hitherto held that native title had been extinguished by European occupation. The result is that the search for a mechanism of 'restitution', a means of fulfilling an aspiration to give 'land rights' back to the indigenous population, has been made much easier. No longer need parliament attempt a process which can be represented as 'taking one man's property and giving it to another' by legislative act; instead legislation can be restricted to defining the process by which a legal claim to title can be established. There are, of course, many differences between the circumstances of this case and the recognition of 'traditional rights' which Gladstone would have liked to have informed his legislation on Irish land, but clearly the absence of any mechanism for judicial recognition of those rights made his task the more difficult. And whereas, in the Australian case, the potential conflict between claimants to native title and other title-holders (although not crown leaseholders) has probably been diminished by the court to the point of non-existence, in Ireland every claim by a tenant farmer to proprietorial right would have necessarily involved a diminution in the rights attached to another person's title. None of this, however, diminishes the analysis of the problem as mapped out by Campbell and taken up and envisaged by Gladstone; the failure to make a political reality of this perspective greatly weakened the potential of the 1870 Land Act as a contribution to the final settlement of the question of land tenure in Ireland. And while it would be erroneous to identify in a specific sense present occupiers as direct inheritors of those displaced by conquest, it was certainly the case that recognition of perceived traditional rights would have had a significant reconciling effect in an ethnic or racial sense.

While the concession of what Sharman Crawford had sought in the 1840s might have gone a long way towards conciliating Irish opinion at that time, the creation of something very close to it was no longer acceptable to Irish opinion in 1870. Indeed, with the failure of the attempt in 1866 of the Irish Chief Secretary, Chichester Fortescue, to put through a compensation bill for which he had considerable support in Ireland, Irish opinion moved to a more intransigent position. Thus, before the terms of the 1870 bill had even been settled in cabinet, the demand in Ireland was more stridently than ever before for the 'three Fs': fair rent, fixity of tenure, and free sale (i.e. freedom to sell the tenant's interest in a farm). The 1870 act had gone some way towards meeting the last of these, but the terms in which it was conceded further heightened the absence of the other two. In particular, the absence of any device for controlling rent meant that gains intended for tenants by the 1870 legislation could be circumvented in various ways, and that there remained ample scope for occasions of conflict. Control of rent now assumed the foreground of Irish agrarian grievance.

None of this is to say that the 1870 act was without significance. While it did very little indeed to satisfy the Irish tenant's claim for recognition of his right of occupancy, by making so substantial an incursion into the normal principles of the English law of contract and property on his behalf it went some way towards vindicating that claim and thus encouraging its further pursuit—as indeed many of its opponents had warned it would. From another angle, a hurdle had been jumped, and English political leaders could hardly claim the impossibility of its being jumped again. The act also contained a pointer to the future direction of the Irish land question. Disenchanted with what he saw as the cabinet's abandonment both of the rights of property and the hope for free trade in land, John Bright reconciled himself to the process by securing within the act the provisions which came to be known as the 'Bright clauses.' These opened the way, although with little practical facilitation, for tenant farmers to purchase the freehold of their farms. While little came of these clauses, this idea increasingly gained momentum as the only way ultimately of restoring the ownership of the land to the native occupiers. For Bright—and more importantly for Conservative policy-makers—it also represented a way of restoring established principles of property-ownership, compromised as they now were by the 1870 act and as they were to be even further by subsequent Gladstonian legislation in 1881.

Some of the urgency which had impelled cabinet and parliament to work so hard at finding a basis for legislation in 1870 was the perception and fear that if the land grievance were not removed, it would fuel and feed the more virulent nationalism emerging in Ireland, of which Fenianism was the most immediate indicator. Insofar as that hope was involved in its passage, the 1870 act was in vain. Indeed, it was to foreshadow a new and more potent linking of those two dynamic forces.

3

Land and Nationalism

The 1870 Land Act marked the beginning of a new era in the relations of Britain and Ireland. For one thing, it had demonstrated for the first time the willingness of British political leaders, members of parliament and a wider circle of opinion-formers to grapple with an Irish problem within the context of a sustained and systematic attempt to understand distinctively Irish perspectives. Moreover, the outcome had involved a significant shift in British attitudes, resulting in a change to Irish land law which breached in a fundamental sense British conceptions of property law and rights. A politically neat assessment of this achievement would be to ascribe it to the political interests of Gladstone and the elements of British society whom he represented. What surer way of gratifying radical opinion, hostile in any case to the whole institution of landlordism, than to assault the bastion, remote and shaky though it was, of Irish landlordism, just as English Nonconformist opinion had no doubt been gratified by the disestablishment of the Church of Ireland, removed though that also was from the immediate context of Nonconformist grievance. Such an analysis, however, not only does less than justice to the conscientious pursuit of a solution by Gladstone and others, but it also belies the reality of what was achieved. The violation of traditional property concepts deeply offended not only conservative, but also liberal and radical, views. Despite this, the legislation secured support, reluctant though it was, both from conservatives and radicals. An explanation based on British partisan interests ignores the very real extent to which ultimately the passage of the act was a consequence of a deep and wide-ranging debate which transcended the normal party divides. It was a process which engaged to an unprecedented degree the energies and minds of those seriously concerned with the place of Ireland within the United Kingdom.

What was given away by the British parliament was no small thing. The concept of the United Kingdom, brought into being by the Act of Union between Great Britain and Ireland in 1800, was of a fully integrated nation. While it is true that the rulers of this new entity made their own contribution to weakening that concept, especially through failure to grant Catholic Emancipation and the retention of colonial administrative forms in Dublin Castle, and also through the treatment of Ireland as an impoverished colony during the Famine, the thrust of policy was very strongly towards the elimination of differences between the various components of that United Kingdom. The Land Act of 1870, like the Irish Church Act of the preceding year, marked a significant departure in the opposite direction, and as such struck at the heart of British conceptions of the state. Perhaps most significant was the extraordinarily high ideological sensitivity of the area in which this concession was being made. The rights of property as understood in English law had long been central to the whole basis of authority within English society and had—at least in a rural context—provided much of the underpinning of the social order. The changes now being made in the Irish land law not only introduced a new principle of differential legislation between parts of the United Kingdom, but also offended many of the most cherished values of traditional society, especially as they were understood by the ruling elites. But over and above all this there is another major ideological dimension to be considered. The Union of Britain and Ireland had also been carried through simultaneously with the *laissez-faire* revolution in economic philosophy, and was to a degree influenced by it. The idea of a single market, a political unit which could operate as a cohering and potent economic force, was an important part of the evolving concept of the state, and clear, simple and uniform principles of property-ownership were essential to it. Irish land reform in 1870 struck a significant blow at that concept, and was as such a very large concession by parliament to Irish pressures.

The explanation of the British willingness to make such a sacrifice can be attributed to two very closely connected factors, both of which made the British political nation more than usually defensive about its position in Ireland. The first of these was a growing self-awareness in relation to the British role in Ireland in the past, a record increasingly perceived as crudely ineffective as well as oppressive. The fact of conquest itself, more widely appreciated in a society accommodating itself to very extensive recent imperial growth, was beginning to be seen as undermining the liberal aspiration for a common nationality with the Irish. The loss of the American colonies in the eighteenth century had engendered new and very different attitudes to the relationship of metropolis to colony, and reliance on autocratic power was neither as acceptable morally as it had once been nor seen as efficacious. In the retrospect so formed, and in the context of new attitudes shaped by the French Revolution and its aftermath, the oppression characterised by the penal laws applied against the Irish Catholic population was now seen to have left a fateful legacy. Likewise, the failure to grant Catholic Emancipation at the time of the Union and the devastation allowed to happen in the Great Famine had consolidated this retrospective view of political ineptitude in attempting to create out of the Union an effective single political and economic entity. The other factor behind the willingness to go so far in the direction of reform in 1870 was the sense of apprehension that, partly as a consequence of this historical record, the Union itself was at risk on account of the growing lack of consent within Ireland for its continuation. O'Connell's Repeal movement and the more radical demands of the Young Irelanders had raised very large questions about the prospects for the Union. More substantial evidence of the withdrawal of Irish support was revealed in the increased Fenian activity of the 1860s, although it was the growing signs of frustration with British government on the part of more moderate sections of political opinion in Ireland which seemed even more forcefully to drive home that point.

As has already been suggested, in this context the 1870 Land Act was largely in vain. Not only was the measure too little too late to satisfy the grievance over the land, but the evidence is that the process by which the primary issue was becoming nationalism rather than land had very considerably advanced in the four years preceding 1870. In part that transition was directly attributable to the handling of the land question. A quarter of a century after the early efforts of reformers like Conner and Sharman Crawford to highlight the problems of land tenure in Ireland no measures to address the concerns of the tenant farmers had been implemented. It should be remembered that the urgency of the appeals made by these reformers arose not only from the plight of the tenants themselves but also out of apprehension as to the stability of the Irish social and political arrangements. Likewise, the analysis of J. S. Mill arose largely from a recognition of the fundamental instability, in an economic as well as political and social sense, of the Irish land tenure system. Nor had the government and parliament been untouched by these concerns. The Devon Commission had undertaken one of the most extensive governmental inquiries of the first half of the nineteenth century, had acknowledged the need for reform, and yet had resulted in no significant legislation. The Incumbered Estates Acts and Deasy's and Cardwell's Acts had all shown an awareness on the part of parliament of the existence of a problem, but had all been premised on the notion that the solution was to be found in improving the viability of landlordism. By the middle of the 1860s even the government, however, had become sufficiently concerned to introduce legislation of its own, in the form of the 1866 bill for compensation for improvements introduced by Chichester Fortescue, only to have it fail in parliament. There had thus been a pattern of response to this most significant Irish issue which demonstrated a combination of recognition of the need for reform and apparent inability to do anything about it.

In a report commissioned by Chichester Fortescue in 1866 W. Neilson Hancock had been particularly direct as to parliament's equivocation. Commenting that 'After a discussion of twenty-five years, Parliament admitted that the law as to Tenants' Improvements was in an unsatisfactory state, and required a legislative remedy', he asserted that 'When a principle of this kind is once conceded . . . it is useless to say that the legislature is powerless to deal with the causes of complaint':

> The character of the ruling classes as rulers is at stake upon providing simple and effective means for carrying out the principles conceded. For, when a just principle is not denied, but its operation is defeated by the legislative machinery which proposes to grant it turning out costly, cumbrous,

mistaken, and inoperative, the strongest elements are laid for
discontent and disaffection to the Constitution.[1]

In the aftermath of the Great Famine, and with a growing
tendency to explain that tragedy in terms of government indifference and ineptitude, it is not surprising that the specific issue
of land reform began to be submerged within a more general
sense of disaffection with the existing constitutional arrangements. The stages by which that more general sentiment became
a settled attitude can be traced in a number of developments
and phenomena during the 1870s: the complex relationship of
the revolutionary Fenian movement to wider social and political
issues of the era; the role of Isaac Butt in creating a new institutional structure embodying a convergence of national and land
issues; the rural crisis of the late 1870s and the associated mobilisation of national and agrarian opinion through the Land
League; the effective exploitation of that crisis by a new political
leadership, more broadly based and more subtle in its handling
of diverse elements of Irish society than had been its predecessors; and the impact on Irish politics of Gladstone's return to
office and the passage of the 1881 Land Act, which served both
as a vindication of the demands made in the past and a justification of the course upon which Irish nationalist leaders had now
so fully embarked.
     An early notable expression of this new nationalist sentiment
can be found in the Limerick Declaration of 1867, made by a
gathering of Catholic priests, advocating repeal of the Union.
The declaration was organised by the Dean of Limerick, and sig-
natures were invited from as many clergy as possible to make
this a substantive statement of clerical opinion. Widely publi-
cised in the British press, it drew a close connection between
Fenianism, both in America and at home, and disaffection in
Ireland:

> Take away the *appui* that Irish American Fenianism finds in
> Irish disaffection here in Ireland and you at once and for ever
> remove the plea and the danger of foreign interference. . . .
> Without a removal of the combustible matter in this country,
> a spark at any moment may spread a devouring conflagration.[2]

The declaration was firmly anchored in the legacy of history, showing in some detail how oppression, neglect and poor government in the past made it impossible for the consequences to be handled within the existing form of the Union with Britain, within which the Irish had become too disadvantaged to be equal partners:

> There is no use in saying to such a man that he is free to run the race of manly competition with the Englishman, unless, indeed, such freedom be understood in the sense that an invalid rising from the bed of infirmity is 'free' to enter the lists with the athlete.[3]

It was only through a restoration of her nationality that Ireland could rectify this legacy:

> The very nature of the remedies required to make Ireland rich and contented renders it impossible for a British Parliament to adopt and apply them; and, besides that, home aspirations and the plea for Irish intervention from abroad can never be met unless by restoring Ireland her nationality—re-establishing the Sovereign and the Lords and Commons of Ireland.[4]

This closely reasoned and extended statement from so respectable a quarter, linking as it did both the dangers to England and Ireland of disaffection and a conservative statement of the form of the remedy, demonstrated the sharp movement in Ireland towards a response to Fenianism which accommodated its central demand within a framework which could secure broad support in Irish society. It was both a warning and a rallying-point which had its roots in an understanding of the connections which were being made between groups which had not normally enjoyed a close affinity. It demonstrated the extent to which grievance had gone beyond the reach of amelioration, arguing that the demand for nationality could no longer be merely a device for forcing reform, but was now a demand in its own right which could not be ignored.

The Fenian movement had effectively exploited this shift from a politics based on the demand for reform to a more generalised articulation of grievance about the whole form of Ireland's political and social condition. As far as the tenant farmers were concerned, so little had come of the sustained effort to get a modest reform which acknowledged—even though minimally—their own perceptions of their rights, that they were now easily tempted into political identifications which were more displays of anger and disenchantment than focused attempts at practical change. The ability of the Fenians to make the most of their opportunities, in elections, commemorations and funerals, and especially through the demand for amnesty for the Fenian prisoners, was greatly enlarged by the fact that— as R. V. Comerford has established—'Fenianism was no longer a bogey for the farmers and the prisoners had come to symbolise all popular grievances including those of the tenants'.[5] The particularity of specific grievances was thus transmuted into a stronger perception that it was the general issue of Ireland's form of government that was at the heart of all Irish problems. While there are, of course, longer-term historical perspectives and experiences—and not least the impact of the Great Famine—which must be taken into account in understanding this change, it was the lack of any kind of legislative response to the long exposed and articulated issue of land tenure reform which created the most substantial basis for this more nationalist frame of reference. Even the lesser reform of compensation for improvements, had it been granted in an effective and universal form by the mid-1860s, might have limited this development. Alternatively, an act in 1870 more informed by Gladstone's 'idea of restitution' might have stemmed its impact. As it was, the shift from reform to nationalism in the late 1860s became entrenched. This is not to suggest that this development marks the beginning of some inevitable onward march of nationalism (an interpretation rightly condemned by Dr Comerford),[6] but rather to indicate that the terms of political discourse change at this time in a way which significantly shaped the future.

It was not, however, a future cast as the Fenians had envisaged it. No matter what the depth of tenant farmer disenchantment with British parliamentary process as it affected Ireland, and no matter how ready the identification with transient Fenian theatre, the primary objectives of the tenant farmers appear to have been firmly based upon their tangible interests as occupiers of the land. In this sense the Fenians were relatively passive agents in what was happening, and had at this time little of value to offer the farmers, particularly given the secondary importance for the Fenian organisation of land reform and the abjuration by them of parliamentary action. What this political environment did create, however, was a substantial opening for a quite new political development. This was filled by the new Home Rule movement under the leadership of Isaac Butt, a Conservative and a Protestant with a background uniquely suited to an attempt to find a new basis for an Irish nationalism able to transcend some of the endemic divisions of Irish political and social life.

Isaac Butt's re-entry into political life in the late 1860s, as David Thornley has shown, was in part attributable to the Fenian troubles and to his involvement with the legal defence of the Fenian prisoners. In Butt's past, however, there was ample evidence of the wide ambience within which his views about Irish politics were formed.[7] In his new venture he embarked for the first time on the overt advocacy of nationalism, but in a form compatible as he saw it with wider British imperial and political interests. His astute handling and balancing of the diverse issues engaging Irish attention—Disestablishment, land reform, education, Amnesty, nationalism—established a basis for a political formation which was, for a time, almost unprecedented in the breadth of its support. The new slogan around which Butt organised his movement was Home Rule. In its more precise definitions it so protected imperial and Protestant interests that many of the Protestant elite, particularly disillusioned as they were at this time with British government in Ireland, were prepared to join and support Butt's movement. On the other hand, the concept was sufficiently vague that, when associated with Butt's defence of the Fenian prisoners, his involvement in the Amnesty movement and many of his more nationalist public statements, it could also seem attractive to more extreme nationalists.

Butt's new popularity in Ireland paralleled a diminution in that of Gladstone, whose disestablishment of the Church of Ireland in 1869 had appeared to herald a new British willingness to grapple with some of the more fundamental causes of Irish disaffection. The British Liberal leader's absolute commitment to disestablishment and disendowment of the Church of Ireland had engendered an exceptional enthusiasm for him and the Liberal Party among the Catholic majority in Ireland. This enthusiasm had dominated the 1868 general election, and the faithfulness of Gladstone to his promises on the church issue

brought such a consolidation of this sentiment that it seemed
for a time that Ireland was accommodating itself to the politics
of Liberal Britain. This was not auspicious from the point of view
of advanced nationalists, but it also represented dangers for the
tenant farmers. The greatest enthusiasm for Gladstone came
from the Catholic hierarchy, and their gratification at
Disestablishment turned their hopes immediately towards the
other item high on their agenda, the education question. On
the issues that mattered to advanced nationalists and tenant
farmers, the Amnesty question and land reform, the hopes
which Gladstone had raised were not fulfilled. Whereas there
had been a widespread expectation in Ireland that all the
prisoners would be released as soon as Gladstone came to
power, this did not happen. And, as has been seen, on the land
issue Gladstone was unable to carry a reform which met even his
own hopes. It was on these two issues that Butt's profile was at its
highest.

Amnesty and land represented crucial constituencies in Butt's
concept of a new Irish political movement. While he was far
removed from the characteristic profile of the more extreme
Irish nationalists, Butt shared with them a recognition and
respect for a distinctive Irish polity which could not be absorbed
within a solely British framework. The vigour and commitment
with which Gladstone addressed Irish issues in the late 1860s
had re-created a sense of confidence, especially among the
Catholic majority, but his failure to address adequately the two
issues which roused the most passion among the politically more
active sections of the rural population provided the platform
upon which Butt could build. And while Amnesty played a major
part in Butt's rise to political prominence, on the land issue he
was actually able to exert a significant impact on both the definition and direction of reform. Butt had himself been a significant
pamphleteer on Irish issues from as early as the late 1830s, and
this writing had included his views on the land question. By the
middle of the 1860s he had arrived at the position which put
him strongly in the tradition of those like Conner, Lalor and
Mill for whom the essence of the land question was the reality of
the distinctive Irish tradition. But more strongly than they had
done—and partly because of intervening developments—Butt
set the issue firmly in the context of nationalism.

In the pamphlet Butt published in 1866, *Land Tenure in*

Ireland: A Plea for the Celtic Race, his definition of Fenianism was not, as he admitted himself, one readily acceptable to its leaders, but it was revealing of Butt's own line of argument in relating the land and national issues:

> 'Fenianism' was not a political or even a national movement, but a social one. It may be said to be only the revelation of what has long been passing in the hearts and minds of the people. Whatever was political or national in its objects was subordinate to the social one—that of destroying land-lordism. Its war was upon all the institutions of landed property. Such a war assumed, it is true, a political and national form, because the power of England and the institutions of England uphold the present proprietary system in the country. But that which the Irish peasant feels as the real grievance of 'English domination', is not any wound to his nationality, but the land system which that 'domination' forced on him. In all previous Irish movements the national question had been put foremost; but the mass of the people understood the 'national question' in a sense somewhat different from that put upon it by their leaders. With them landlordism and the land system was the impersonation of English domination and misrule.[8]

This being the grievance, no mere meddling with what was basically an English system would resolve the problem, and Butt made clear his view that the extension of Ulster custom, as had been argued in the preceding decades, was no more than that:

> A mere legislative declaration that the custom of tenant right should be binding would be vague and indefinite. The enactment which would carry that custom *in its essential attributes* into legal effect, would be a law that every man now holding an agricultural tenement should continue to hold it as long as he pays a *fair* rent and conforms to the conditions which his landlord has any *moral* right to impose.[9]

Dismissing as matters of detail the methods of valuation and the need to allow for improvements made by the tenants, he declared that he did not 'wish to incumber with these discussions the assertion of the great principle of tenant right—that of fixity of tenure at a fair rent'.[10] This was essentially a restatement of Conner's principle of 'a valuation and a perpetuity', which had been submerged for two decades beneath the prevailing political campaign for 'tenant right', by which had largely been meant 'compensation for improvements'.

In restating in its positive form the view of Irish land tenure as it had earlier been argued, in particular by Conner, Butt also spelt out the negative implications for the landlords themselves, thereby answering many of the points raised against that view. First, he referred to the power of arbitrary eviction, of which in his view landlords should be deprived. His second point related to the application of supply and demand to the price of land, the fallacy which Conner had also so absolutely dismissed on the ground of land being a 'non-increasing' commodity. Questioning the view that 'in mutual competition prices find their level', Butt answered:

> that if political economy taught us any such thing as to the letting of land in Ireland, it would tell us that which, as a general rule, and applied to the great mass of the population, is contrary to fact, and would therefore be untrue. I believe it is not true of any old settled country, except Great Britain. Land is not an article for which the supply can be apportioned to the demand.[11]

Thirdly—and barely worth a mention in Butt's view—was the obvious, that 'the right to appropriate to the use of the landlord the property created by the industry of the tenant, is one that no one can seriously defend'.[12] It was this final point which had in fact become the sole focus of much of the movement for land reform in the preceding era, and Butt here effectively buried it as an issue of primary importance. He also addressed the view, an important and dominant one in a British perspective, that the needs of a single, capitalist market for the United Kingdom required the assimilation of Ireland into the agricultural districts of England and Scotland, creating a context in which 'large farms and capitalist farmers raise off the soil the largest amount of produce for the sustenance of man'. He had two answers to this. The first was 'that it involves the extermination of the people'. But, in case this was insufficient as a reason, he also argued the case put by other political economists, most notably

by Mill, 'that land divided into small farms in which the cultivators have a property, yields the most comfort to the largest
number of human beings'. In addition, he pointed to the virtual
impossibility of achieving such an assimilation given the
necessity of improving landlords incurring all at once 'the
expenditure which, in England, has been the slow and gradual
accumulation of a long series of years' and the manifest lack of
will for a necessary condition of the change, namely 'the extermination of the people'.[13]

The analysis here developed was much as Conner's had been,
and like his it was driven by a recognition that the existing state
of affairs was unsustainable. And like those earlier critics of the
land system, Butt came from outside the peasant world. He was a
lawyer, a Protestant, a conservative, but his understanding of the
realities of his own society transcended its sectional differences.
Moreover, he recognised—as Conner and others had done—
that the paternalist role expected of the Irish landlords required
that they themselves should recognise and respond to the world
which their tenants inhabited rather than to a theoretical
construct based on an English tradition and experience which
was radically different from the Irish one.

Replying to criticism of his opinions by landlords, Butt denied
any spirit of hostility to the Protestant and landlord interest:

> All my early recollections are associated with feelings not
> unfriendly to Protestantism or proprietary right. . . . But the
> more I cherish them [those recollections], the more grieved I
> feel that in the mind of a great, a generous and noble people,
> both Protestantism and proprietory right are associated with
> oppression and wrong. . . . I have shown how by a very little
> concession a huge mischief can be redressed, and a great
> feud reconciled. If the legislation I framed was 'cunningly
> devised', the whole device consisted in an effort to retain
> nearly all of proprietory right, and yet make the people free.[14]

This was, of course, not a plea for the abolition of landlordism,
but for its rescuing from the brink of disaster. It reflected not
only Butt's personal background, but also his attempt, still in the
future, to relate Fenian and Protestant conservative in a broad
coalition designed not only to achieve some form of self-government for Ireland, but to re-create 'bonds of society' distinctively

Irish in form. Resolution of the land question, in this context, was central to his wider political purposes. Pursuit of that issue was also a means of consolidating support in the country from both tenant farmers and Fenians, if handled in the right way. He did not, however, succeed in attracting significant Protestant and landlord support for his objectives.

Once Butt's efforts had resulted in the formation of a Home Rule Party, nominal though many of its members were, his political focus shifted towards the dual exigencies of holding together some kind of political alliance in Ireland and attempting to establish, out of most unfavourable materials, a coherent parliamentary strategy. This meant that the prominence given to the land question diminished and that it became for him a secondary issue to that of Home Rule. His contribution, however, to the restatement of the cause of the tenant farmers had been of substantial and enduring importance. He lifted the debate about land tenure out of a context in which it had been reduced to a question of minor adjustment to a system which would remain basically unchanged, reinvigorating the demand for a recognition that the traditional rights of the tenants included a proprietorial interest in their land and that to be viable any settlement of the land question had to accommodate that dimension. He had thus played a major part in preparing the ground on which the inadequacies of the 1870 Land Act could be established. Ironically, we now know that Gladstone had also privately come to terms with that larger dimension of Irish land, but had been unable to make of it a political reality. This development was not so private as to escape some acknowledgment by Butt himself, who wrote of the act:

> I am bound to say that, imperfect and inadequate as they are, I can trace in its provisions an earnest and sincere desire to protect the Irish tenant—a struggle to escape from principles by which the framers of the Bill believed themselves bound, but which, in favour of the Irish tenant, they made every effort to evade. I fear the result has been only an elaborate failure to do the justice which it was so elaborately attempted to work out.[15]

Butt's own practical efforts in parliament, represented by his land bills of 1875 and 1876, were modest attempts to improve the 1870 act, by establishing the reality of Ulster custom for all farmers and by attempting to close the loopholes by which landlords had been effectively circumventing what little protection tenants had been given by the act. But his most substantial contribution had been prior to that act, in helping to establish the parameters of a new discourse on the land question which would transcend the efforts and failures of Gladstone's measure and prepare the way for the further demands which would inevitably follow.

Butt's other contribution to the long-term development of the land question was to link it inexorably with the cause of nationalism. His attempt to create a political movement which drew its sustenance from a range of issues and embodied a re-creation of a distinctively Irish polity had lifted the land question out of the context of liberal reform and restated it not only in terms of its indigenous attributes as an issue, but also as a symbol and token of a distinctive Irish identity. This is not to say that Butt himself entirely shared such a perspective, although it is important to remember the extent to which many of his political constructions were intended to embody an Irish diversity which included the Protestant and landlord elements. Even in his own presentation of his views, however, there is a strong consciousness of the racial and colonial dimension of the land question; his major 1866 treatise on the issue had, after all, been subtitled 'a plea for the Celtic race'. But it is in the reality of what he helped to create that the identification of land and nationality find so strong an expression. In making the concept of Home Rule attractive as a focus for the aspirations of both tenant farmers and Fenians, he created a fusion of consciousness that was to shape the whole future of both the land question and Irish nationalism.

Many active Fenians had learnt two crucial lessons from the exploits of their movement in the 1860s. The first of these was that the more pure and theoretical of their principles had the effect of isolating them from open and active political involvements which potentially could advance their cause. Butt's distinctive identification of himself with the ideals of the Fenians, together with his construction of a political movement based on a broad nationalist aspiration, assisted many of these Fenians to break with the tradition of secrecy, conspiracy and violence and to participate in the development of an open nationalist movement. Finding his ideals attractive, and not least his appeal to Protestant sympathies, they saw the possibility of moving the Home Rule movement towards a stronger and more encompassing nationalism than had been possible within the constraints of Fenianism as previously understood. Accordingly, many active Fenians began to move into Butt's Home Rule movement, either as parliamentarians or as supporters in the country. This significant shift in Fenian thinking, T. W. Moody suggests, can be dated to the early 1870s and constitutes what he defines as the 'first new departure'.[16] It involved a decision by a number of prominent Fenians to be at least friendly towards Butt's movement, and at best actively to support it and, in the case of several, to jettison a cardinal principle of Fenianism and seek election to the British parliament as followers of the Home Rule movement. There were two broad reasons for the willingness of these individuals to temper their commitment to revolution with participation in constitutional politics. In the first place, they recognised that in the aftermath of their monumental failure at revolution in the 1860s the only alternative was political impotence. Secondly, there was a genuine respect for Butt and a sense that participating in his movement might in the long term serve to assist their own more advanced strategies. The effect of their actions, however, was to create some significant new antagonisms and personal conflicts within the ranks of more advanced nationalism, divisions which had to be confronted later in the 1870s before the full force of the 'new departures' could be realised.

The other lesson learned by many Fenians was that the most fertile ground for political activity in Ireland was to be found in the tenant farmers. The impact of revolutionary activity in the 1860s was probably much less than that of the electoral contests in which candidates known to be Fenians, although unlikely ever to have taken their seats, secured notable successes on the basis of tenant farmer support. Alone Fenianism posed the limited threat of occasioning violence, but linked to the land issue, even if only by association, it had the capacity to symbolise the claims of a wider Irish nationality. It is therefore not surprising that, as frustration with the 1870 Land Act increased, more and more Fenians became associated with political action in connection with the land tenure issue. In this, such Fenians were reacting in a similar fashion to that of many of their more eminent associates who were finding their way into Butt's Home Rule Party. Together they were helping to give a more nationalist character to Butt's movement and, while no doubt playing a role in frightening away Protestant and conservative support from Butt, contributing to a new sense of a political strategy which could be seen as Irish rather than sectional. They were also reflecting the change in attitude occurring among the Fenian elements of the American Irish. There the futility of past methods was causing increased frustration and there was a new awareness of other possibilities, both in relation to the exploitation of political opportunities in the United Kingdom—provided by political reform and a more forceful public opinion—and a more open political environment within which to address the grievances on the land, a matter of deep emotional importance to many American Irish.

The inadequacy of the 1870 Land Act became more evident as tenants and landlords experienced its practical application. The intent of the act to give tenants a greater security and interest in their holdings was easily circumvented by landlords through a series of devices, including pressure on tenants to sign leases and the inclusion of clauses in contracts which had the effect of the tenant abdicating his right to protection under the act. But, as had been predicted, the futility of a measure intended to give greater security without addressing the question of rent control very quickly became evident. Demand for further reform became more pressing, and resentment by many landlords at the intrusion of the law upon their rights of property tended even further to aggravate the relations between them and their tenants. Into these circumstances entered new economic pressures which were to precipitate the major and climactic confrontation between landlords and tenants—a conflict which very quickly came both to characterise and to dominate the relationship between Ireland and Britain.

The origins of the Land League are to be found earlier than the immediate events of 1879 out of which it more directly arose. Crucial to the development of the context in which the land war was to emerge was the existence of a number of tenants' associations throughout Ireland, but more particularly significant was the increased activity during the 1870s in the west, a region previously less politically active on the issue of tenant right, where the Land League was eventually to be born and nurtured. One of the most significant of these bodies was the Ballinasloe Tenants' Defence Association, formed in May 1876. Its initial meeting at Shannonbridge was acclaimed by the *Connaught Telegraph* as a 'most hopeful augury for the cause of Irish Tenant-Right'.[17] The meeting was structured around a number of symbols, emphasis being placed on Shannonbridge as being on the borders of Leinster and Connacht, and advantage being taken by one speaker of the proximity to the ruins of Clonmacnoise to declare that 'In vain did Elizabeth and Bloody Cromwell strive to destroy the ancient monuments of Ireland that we might forget our native greatness.'[18] The lesson in history was, however, mainly in order to focus upon the land and the alternative view of its use, drawing upon the view of Irish land tradition now well associated with the ideas of John Stuart Mill:

> The broad acres which were held in trust for the Irish people by the King and nobles, were taken and given to the followers of Elizabeth and Cromwell.... Behold, ye stiff necked landocracy, your bloody title deeds. For nearly 2,400 years . . . the Tanistry laws of Ireland, embodied in the Brehon Code, made every member of the sept the joint owner of land during his life. There was no rent during these long years; no power of eviction; no landlord; no tenant.... They [the people] know that there is no divine law by which King James could confiscate the property of the people and vest it in the landlord.[19]

The principal resolution of the meeting, for which this was all grist to the mill, was a protest at the state of the law which allowed landlords 'to evict their tenants and raise their rents at [their] own will and pleasure' and a pledge 'never to cease agitating until we secure to the tenant farmers of Ireland fixity of tenure, fair rents and free sale'.[20] These sentiments characterised an increasing number of such meetings in the later 1870s and underlay the foundation of a number of similar organisations, thus preparing the ground—especially in the west—for the Land League.

Of great importance in the laying of these foundations in the province of Connacht was the commitment of one particular individual, James Daly of Castlebar. In February 1876 Daly had purchased the *Mayo Telegraph*, which he turned into the

Connaught Telegraph,[21] a newspaper which very quickly became the mouthpiece of the cause of the tenant farmers in the west. In this weekly newspaper is chronicled the progress of the revived tenant right movement, extensive publicity being given to each meeting, with full coverage of speeches made, including many major speeches by Daly himself, and leading articles which presented the case for tenant organisation, political changes and reform of land tenure laws. But Daly's contribution to the revived land movement was much more extensive than the role of his newspaper. Gerard Moran has shown the extent to which Daly helped lay the basis of a new agrarian agitation through his astute handling of diverse political and social elements of the local community. His role was crucial in linking many local Fenians into the agitation while strongly asserting the commitment to lawful action. He also did much to establish the secular character of the movement and helped bring about the decline of clerical influence in local politics, this symbolised most dramatically in his role in the replacement in 1880 of a clerically favoured local MP by a Belfast Presbyterian cleric.[22] Moran also sees as crucial Daly's encouragement of the tenants in setting up their own meetings, rather than relying on leaders like himself, and suggests that 'this policy resulted ultimately in the formation and extension of the Land League'.[23] Daly was not, of course, on his own in this work. The latter years of the 1870s saw careful groundwork undertaken by a number of leaders in removing some of the dissensions and disputes among nationalists, especially among those who had been previously associated with the Fenian movement. Men like Matthew Harris, a founder of the Ballinasloe Tenants' Defence Association, Thomas Brennan, later to run the central office of the Land League in Dublin, and Michael Davitt worked closely together to prepare the ground, both in Ireland and America, for a new phase of nationalist activity. This they achieved by resolving many of the disputes and personality clashes which had marked the relationship of older nationalists during the 1870s,[24] some of them arising from the 'first new departure' early in the decade, as well as by reinforcing the attempts being made at another level by Davitt and John Devoy, the leader of the American Fenian organisation, the Clan na Gael, to achieve a more fundamental shift in Fenian attitudes towards the more active constitutional and parliamentary strategy associated with a small group of parliamentarians, including Charles Stewart Parnell.[25]

What was in reality being achieved through the combination of the revived tenant right movement and the political preparations among nationalists was the creation of an alternative focus to that of the Home Rule Party of Isaac Butt, the ineffectiveness of which had become increasingly evident. In particular, considerable attention was being drawn to the largely nominal nature of the commitment of many MPs to the nationalist cause, and also to the number of them who happened to be landlords; for example, in July 1876, the *Connaught Telegraph* argued that 'If Parliamentary representation is to be of the slightest service to this country (which we very much doubt) Irish electors must give their votes to men who are neither landlords nor place-hunting members of the legal profession.'[26] But accompanying this attack on the degenerate condition of the Home Rule cause in parliament was a continuous and sustained support from the tenant right movement for Isaac Butt's efforts to get the House of Commons to approve the land bill with which his name had become so strongly associated. Land agitation in Ireland, especially in the west, a shift among Fenians, both locally and in America, away from doctrinaire opposition to any form of parliamentary action, and a nucleus of MPs acting in a way which established a new model for involvement in the British parliament created a basis for building on the legacy left by Butt, especially in relation to analysis of the land issue, while superseding what had come to be recognised as a decaying leadership and a redundant parliamentary strategy.

There had thus been made a number of political and organisational moves in the region in which the Land League was to take root well before the onset of the economic difficulties with which its birth is associated. However, as is evident from T. W. Moody's account of these events, the deteriorating economic circumstances helped to force a priority for the land issue which greatly strengthened Davitt's intent to give a more open and practical character to the politics of Irish nationalism than existed within what had previously been his political milieu, the remnant of the Fenian movement.[27] These economic developments were not, however, unique to Ireland. The late 1870s was a time of crisis for agriculture throughout the British Isles. Bad seasons, falling prices and changing patterns of demand resulted in loss of income for farmers everywhere. While in Ireland bad seasons produced critical conditions for producers of the more traditional Irish agricultural products, especially potatoes and grains, changing market patterns also led to setbacks in the new areas into which Irish farmers had moved since the Famine. Economic recession in the manufacturing sector in Britain had led to changes in diet among the industrial population, adversely affecting the profitability of the beef and 'breakfast table' trade, especially the pork and dairy industries, which had developed so well in Ireland in the preceding decades. Underlying international factors, less evident at the time, were to turn this into a permanent trend. Increasing grain competition from North America, Australia and elsewhere was significantly depressing the price of the Irish product, and Irish butter was losing out in the British market to its Danish competitors. These factors played a crucial part in activating the conflict between landlords and tenants which built up from 1877 and reached its climax in the first phase of the land war between 1879 and 1881, but they do not of themselves form an adequate explanation of this conflagration.

Interpretation of the nature and significance of the Land League crisis of these years has long interested historians of Ireland. It formed the subject of a relatively early but highly professional study by an American historian, N. D. Palmer, in 1940.[28] This was followed in 1949 by T. W. Moody's seminal paper, 'The New Departure in Irish Politics, 1878–9'.[29] More recently a most impressive body of historical literature has been created through the further work of the late Professor Moody[30] and of a number of younger historians, James S. Donnelly,[31] Barbara Lewis Solow,[32] Samuel Clark,[33] Paul Bew,[34] and W. E. Vaughan.[35] Between them they have transformed our knowledge of this phenomenon in its political, social and economic dimensions, greatly enlarged our awareness of the detailed context within which these events occurred, and presented a range of overlapping, sometimes conflicting—but more often complementary—interpretations of them. This work must form the basis of any attempt to interpret the place of the Land League both in the longer-term evolution of the land issue in Irish politics and in the relationship of that issue to nationalist politics.

The National Land League of Mayo was established in August 1879, following on from the success of a large-scale demonstration at Irishtown in the previous April in defence of the tenants on a local estate who were being pressed, in the face of economic recession, to pay their arrears of rent. The Irishtown meeting, although receiving relatively little attention at the time, was of major importance in the development of the land question and in Irish politics more generally. There has been extended debate about the actual issue which prompted this meeting, and Professor Moody has come to the conclusion that the view, propagated especially by Davitt, that a Catholic priest, Canon Geoffrey Bourke, was the target of the meeting is 'highly questionable'.[36] Canon Bourke later denied the accusation that as the executor of the estate in question he had threatened to evict tenants for non-payment of arrears of rent, and in this denial he was supported by James Daly. However, it is worth noting the first announcement of the proposed meeting as early as February 1879 in Daly's own newspaper, in which praise is heaped upon 'the patriotic and spirited men of Irishtown and the neighbouring parishes [who] propose holding, at an early date, a monster meeting to give expression to the many griev-ances under which they suffer'. The perpetrator of the 'tyranny and oppression' practised on them is then described as one 'from whom better might reasonably be expected—one who should be the first to hold up to the scorn, which they deserve, all oppressors of the poor'.[37] These would certainly be the terms in which a Catholic priest would be described had his role been as depicted by Davitt, and it raises some doubt as to Moody's rejection of Davitt's claim—a claim made first in 1889 and, after being challenged, further repeated with corrections of detail in his *Fall of Feudalism* in 1904. Certainly the choice of a Catholic priest as the target of this major meeting from which sprang the Land League would have suited extremely well the strategy of Daly and his colleagues to distinguish clearly their new movement in secular and non-sectarian terms. It may be that Davitt's persistence of belief reflected a clear and accurate recol-lection of the general situation, and that others involved, such as Daly and Canon Bourke, had subsequently 'adjusted' their memory in line with changed alliances. It is certainly feasible that, whether personally culpable or not, Canon Bourke might well have been the focus of the Irishtown meeting.

The importance of the Irishtown meeting, as of that at Westport two months later, was that vast crowds, with all the theatre and panoply that a rural community could muster, had gathered together in 'monster meetings' as a demonstration of strength on matters of great public concern, and most notably on the vexed issue of land tenure. The formal creation of the Mayo Land League in August, and of the Irish National Land League into which it was absorbed in October, channelled that enthusiasm into a structure for which the foundations had been well laid by an astute leadership, both locally in Connacht and nationally. But the economic pressures around which these meetings were organised encapsulate the essential elements of the crisis of that time: tenant farmers experiencing a sharp economic reverse found themselves faced with landlords unwilling to concede any lightening of the burden of rent, and in these circumstances resorted to mass organisation and protest on a scale probably without precedent, at any rate since the time of O'Connell. In the conflict that ensued, and which rapidly spread throughout Ireland, farmers all over the country were prepared to subject themselves to considerable risks, including ultimately the loss of their farms, in order to force reductions of rent. Two major questions are raised by this. First, why did tenants react so immediately and dramatically to these circumstances, particularly given—as Donnelly has pointed out—that they had not done so during an equally severe economic crisis in the early 1860s?[38] Secondly, why, given the traditions of landlordism and the practice of it in England in this very period, did not landlords respond to the economic recession by offering reductions of rent to their tenants?

Donnelly's explanation of the tenant reaction is that the recession of 1877–9 had followed upon a long period of steadily increasing prosperity during which tenant farmers and their families had come to expect to sustain a higher standard of living, whereas in the early 1860s they had barely pulled themselves out of the economic trough in which the Great Famine had left them. 'Progress and prosperity', Donnelly writes, 'had given the rural community much more to defend against mutilation or erosion', and the land war was thus 'a product not merely of agricultural crisis, but also of a revolution of rising expectations'.[39] Samuel Clark does not find this an adequate basis of interpretation,[40] although the emphasis he places on the role of credit in the farming economy[41] does provide a specific example of the working of the 'rising expectations' theory. A farmer's inability to meet his debts to shopkeepers and traders,

and the possible consequent withdrawal of further credit, represented a very immediate measure of the inadequacy of present
income to meet the commitments of an earlier time. Moreover,
the decline in income set in stark relief for the tenant the fact
that, of the two major demands on his resources, the maintenance of his credit position by the payment of his debts to
shopkeepers was more comfortable for him, economically,
socially and politically, than the payment of his rent to the
landlord. This preference was no doubt assisted by the perception
of tenants that landlords had resorted to all possible strategems to
cheat the tenant of the benefits meant to accrue to him from the
1870 Land Act. It is not difficult, therefore, to see a range of
reasons, purely at the level of immediate economic and practical
assessment, for the tenants resorting to so determined a stand
against the payment of the full rents being demanded by the
landlords.

These being the circumstances, had reductions in rent appropriate to the fall in income been granted expeditiously by the
landlords, the crisis might have been averted. There were expectations that this would be done, and some landlords did in fact
agree to reductions in rent. There were many precedents from
the past, and from wider British experience, for this to happen.
Within the principles of a market economy it made sense. The
major determinant of a market rent was, in theory, the prevailing
price levels for the produce of the land, and so it seemed consistent with economic principles for a reduction in rents to occur in
the circumstances which had now arisen in Ireland. There is no
doubt that landlords were both angered and deeply aggrieved by
the 1870 Land Act and what it portended in terms of their status
and rights as landlords. But 'bloodymindedness' is not a very
valuable analytical concept for dealing with an action with such
far-reaching implications as this refusal to reduce rents proved to
be. In any case, it is not necessary to rely on so flimsy an explanation. The conclusions which arise from the work of W. E.
Vaughan and Barbara Solow give us a much more solid basis for
understanding what happened. Many of the traditional assumptions about Irish landlords as greedy, voracious, rackrenting
exploiters of their tenantry do not stand up to examination.
Indeed, even those landlords who helped to justify this stereotype,
when they are examined more closely, hardly fit the image, at
least as far as the economic basis of their actions was concerned.

In the quarter of a century which followed the Famine agricultural prosperity in Ireland had risen dramatically, but rents had not. In other words, the major benefits of growth and improvement in the Irish agricultural sector had served to ameliorate the standard of life of the farmers, and thus in economic terms the landlords had been effectively writing themselves out of the farming economy. Always lacking the economic opportunities of their British counterparts, many Irish landlords had enjoyed, even at the best of times, only a precarious economic viability. These years of relative prosperity gave them their chance to re-establish their economic role within Irish society, but this depended in part upon increasing rents in line with improved prosperity. As Vaughan shows, some of them attempted to do so, but the contrast between them and most of their fellows undermined their credibility and by singling them out from the general rank made them more vulnerable to attack, mostly in ways that served to reduce the amount of rent actually collected, but occasionally in more violent forms. Vaughan shows that there were within the culture of Irish landlord–tenant relationships a variety of pressures and incentives for landlords not to attempt to increase rents, although he argues that they could have shown more initiative than they did in establishing more flexible mechanisms of rent-fixing.[42] But the general picture, which is confirmed both by Solow's examination of the economic data generally and by Vaughan's intensive and penetrating analysis of a sample of fifty-six estates, is one where the tenants and not the landlords were the major beneficiaries of economic prosperity.[43] The reason landlords did not voluntarily reduce rents when recession set in was that, quite apart from their sense of the injustice of having to do so, in many cases the consequences might well have been extreme embarrassment in terms of their current income, upon which many Irish landlords were highly dependent.[44]

Why, then, had landlords missed this opportunity? Vaughan places great emphasis on their impotence to do anything about this situation; he acquits them of the charge of greed and rapacity, only to condemn them for their negligence.[45] Solow sees them as the victims of a political strategy on the part both of their tenants and of politicians by which they lost the capacity to control their own affairs. There is truth in both conclusions; but Vaughan in tending to disparage their competence and Solow in presenting them as victims both give inadequate attention to the very context of their relationship to the land which so weakened their position. The Irish landlords, especially after the advent of *laissez-faire* ideology (with its more interventionist expectations of landlords) and the devastation of the Great Famine, had found themselves increasingly caught between the defensiveness forced on them by their alien origins, both ethnically and in the very concept of land tenure implicit in their existence, and the new pressures on them, of economic ideology and an English and imperial value system, to use their land in the most economically productive way, irrespective of indigenous custom and expectations. In economic terms, it was clearly a mistake to have forfeited so large a part of the benefits of prosperity in the decades preceding 1877—but what were their alternatives? That is a question which cannot be asked without first attempting to look again at the issue from the tenant point of view.

The demand for a 'fair rent' lay at the bottom of almost all aspects of the land tenure system as far as tenants were concerned. It is this question which gives us the key to the tenant perspective. It was the total failure of the 1870 act to recognise its importance which doomed that legislation to ineffectiveness. Put in its most basic form, the case regarding rent in Ireland, as far as the tenant farmers were concerned, was this: the only fair rent would be no rent, for there was no acceptance of the legitimacy of the institution of landlordism nor recognition of the landlords' right to extract an income from land which they had acquired by confiscation. Indeed, the very process by which more liberal administrations had removed the disabilities against Catholics itself served to undermine retrospectively the very basis upon which much of that confiscation had been justified. That connection had been noted at the end of the eighteenth century by Lord Clare, who—in defending continued restrictions against Catholics—referred to the historical process by which property in Ireland had been granted by successive monarchs to English colonists:

Confiscation is their common title; and from their first settlement they had been hemmed in on every side by the old inhabitants of the island, brooding over their discontents in sullen indignation.[46]

By the 1870s the truth embodied in this eighteenth-century view was as valid as it had ever been, but the moral framework and the political efficacy by which it could be justified were totally redundant and utterly repugnant to the spirit of the age. This gave a sharpened edge to tenant views about rent, made potentially vulnerable its very existence, and, at the level of theory at least, could be used to justify the most aggressive view of its inequity.

To present the question from the tenants' point of view in so blunt, and indeed so theoretical, a form is, however, to underestimate their recognition of the realities of the world in which they lived, and to ignore their only too evident willingness to accommodate their demands to what they thought achievable within the confines of the system which had evolved. In an earlier period, not yet subject to the pressures of the new, more assertive landlord philosophy, tenants appear to have accommodated themselves to coexistence with a landlord type characterised by acceptance of custom, toleration of tenant beliefs and attitudes, and generally non-interventionist in estate management. This pattern of landlordism did not, of course, conform to the prevailing English model, and with more pressure on the landlord to change his ways the tenants became more assertive of their own rights. But even then the ubiquitous concept of tenant right to which they attached their hopes was not one which could be said to dispute the right of the landlord to a continuing role; indeed, leading advocates like Sharman Crawford had partly in mind the need to strengthen the landlord's position by removing a major cause of social and economic discord. Even the more far-reaching reform demanded by Conner in the 1830s and 1840s was set in the context of an assumption of the landlord's continuing right to rent and social role. So why, at the end of the 1870s, did the tenant population organise itself with such effect to undermine fundamentally the landlord's continued role within Irish society?

Substantial reductions of rent as the agricultural recession set in after 1877 might well have won some recognition from the tenantry, but their refusal to continue to pay the same level of rent as had prevailed in better times was the product of a complex series of factors. Inability to pay was by no means the only element, and indeed this factor varied considerably between categories of farmers. In the case of smaller farmers in the more impoverished areas of Ireland, the gains of earlier prosperity were relatively slight, and the capacity to turn them to capital account very limited, and were therefore of little relevance in cushioning the impact of the recession. For many of them it would have been impossible to continue to meet their normal level of commitment. For more prosperous farmers there had indeed been a cumulative benefit from the years of prosperity, and they had become more substantial farmers with a social position and role above that of their earlier years or of their parents before them. But it is absurd to suppose that for these farmers calculation as to any equity in gains and losses relative to those of their landlords would have played much part in the assessment of their situation. For them their relative elevation in the world was something which had been hard-won and which was to be defended at all costs. There was a specific Irish context within which this can be set. The Famine had left a particular legacy. The enlargement of farms which had occurred as a consequence both of loss of population and of post-Famine evictions had begun to create more of a culture of economic advancement among Irish farmers. The Famine had also created a potent sense of insecurity on the land, which was bound to ensure that any sign of economic reversal would provoke a fierce response. In addition, there was the continued excessive demand for land in Ireland, which meant that many were willing to pay an uneconomically high rent for land, thereby putting potential pressure on occupying farmers in terms of what others might be prepared to pay in order to dislodge them; this gave too great an economic incentive to landlords to accept new tenants, and this in turn created an accompanying readiness among farmers to resort to combination against intruders.

There was also a wider and a less specifically Irish context to the determination of the farmers to hold on to the gains they had made. The *laissez-faire*-driven transformation of agriculture, which was having such an effect throughout the British Isles, created an expectation among farmers that they would begin to operate as capitalists, gradually building up their capital resources and ensuring that agriculture became an efficient industry within a wider capitalist economy. This had significant implications for the financial mode of thinking of farmers; and just as their English counterparts expected and received a reduction of rents in line with falling prices, so the economic sense of Irish farmers was offended by the failure to make the same concession for them. But being a capitalist farmer also carried with it social implications. Writers on agrarian society in England in the second half of the nineteenth century stressed the upward mobility of farmers *vis-à-vis* their landlords, evidenced in the changing patterns of education for their children, the altering lifestyles and pastimes of their wives and daughters, and the character and style of their housing. Part at least of the explanation of the mobilisation of Irish farmers in 1879—and this in particular helps to explain the participation of wealthier farmers—was a determination not to allow the landlords to use the recession as an opportunity to cut back the social pretensions of a class beginning to challenge the landlords' own ascendancy in Irish society. That many of these farmers were also carving out an identity as a distinctive new Catholic elite must have further intensified their determination to preserve and consolidate the advances they had made, rather than allow their gains to be lost back to the largely Protestant landlords. In part these factors conform to Donnelly's emphasis on a 'revolution of rising expectations', but they also point to a wider conflict of economic and social interest between farmers and landlords beyond the purely Irish context.

If this rivalry of landlord and tenant for economic and social status had its basis in the expectations and class structures of a modern capitalist economy, it was in Ireland powerfully reinforced and given distinctive form by circumstances peculiar to that country. Samuel Clark's use of the concept of 'the challenging collectivity' helps to give a focus to these circumstances. Clark argues that the Land League differed from any of its predecessors in Ireland in that it drew its major support from the poorer western areas rather than from the more prosperous farming areas of Leinster, and that its emergence involved more than just a demand for particular reforms, but in fact constituted a challenge to the existing power structures of the society.[47] The major contribution of Clark's work, however, is to show the form and manner by which the majority population reasserted its power to the effective exclusion of those in whom power had in the past been formally vested, principally the landlord class. The mechanisms used by the Land League, the boycott, intimidation and other forms of collective action, enabled that majority to draw a sharp line between what might be termed the 'legitimate' society and those who fell outside it. A crucial role in that process was played by townsmen, especially shopkeepers, publicans and others upon whom the farmers depended in varying degrees economically and socially, and the Catholic clergy, whose participation gave an important sanction and cohesion to the 'collectivity'. The economic relationships of the farming community powerfully reinforced this formation. The nexus between farmers and the shopkeepers and suppliers in the towns was one in which economic interdependence existed within a context of a wider cultural affinity. On the other hand, the rent nexus increasingly represented the sole element of the connection between landlord and tenant, and that was largely a one-way relationship. In return for rent the tenant got the use of land to which he considered—and was increasingly reinforced in this view by a wider collective consciousness—he had a traditional right independently of the landlord. The other theoretical benefits of landlordism had always been weak in its Irish manifestation, for reasons not entirely due to the landlords' own inclinations or actions. What residue still remained of recognition of the landlord's paternalist function was dealt a death-blow by the refusal willingly to grant reductions in rent in accord with the fall of incomes after 1877. The combination against payment of rent was an obvious and appropriate response, and one which enabled the tenant to sustain the culturally and economically more relevant relationship with other sections of the community.

This collectivity represented in the mobilisation of the countryside through the Land League had a significance far beyond its role in relation to the land question. Through this experience, the integral link forged in the late 1860s between nationalism and land became a fusion in which separation of the two issues became in practice impossible. The effectiveness of the Land League in organising the countryside in terms of a collective opposition to the payment of rent, unless with a reduction, and the prevention of new tenants occupying farms on which evictions occurred had the effect of creating a *de facto* statement of nationalist solidarity against the institutions of British rule in Ireland. Not only did this phenomenon create a rural solidarity of the tenant farmers themselves, but it consolidated the links between them and the rest of a social order which could now begin to be described as 'nationalist Ireland'.

Rural Fenians and Fenian sympathisers, who had always found their principal constituency among the tenant farmers, now found that the menu of action offered by the Land League was a welcome break to the long fast from political action imposed upon them since the cloak-and-dagger diet of the early Fenian movement. The flirtation with violence involved in some of the peripheral actions associated with the League and the more direct confrontation with the forces of law and order through the open theatre provided by the League's mainstream demonstrations all contributed to a sense of participation, albeit to a degree vicariously, in a form of warfare against British rule itself.

The advent of the Land League raised serious apprehensions in the minds of many Catholic clergy, and more particularly members of the church's hierarchy. The spectre of revolution, so large a factor for the church in its wider European context over the preceding century, haunted the relationship of the church in Ireland to nationalism. The agitational method of politics which sustained the whole concept of the Land League, the necessary element of confrontation which lay at the heart of withholding of rent, and the narrowness of the line between the League and resort to violence alarmed churchmen, who saw it as a potential threat to law and order and to the social structure in general. The task the leaders and organisers of the League set themselves was to reassure the clergy as to the limits of the League's actions and of their commitment in general to legal, open and constitutional political action. In this task they were greatly assisted by the enthusiasm with which many Fenians abandoned their overt appeal to revolutionary violence and flocked to the new movement, for this led churchmen to perceive the danger that these more extreme elements might gain more influence if the clergy were not there as a countervailing force. One of the most compelling arguments for the involvement of the clergy in the Land League, and a means of neutralising the church's opposition, was the capacity of the priests to encourage restraint and ensure that moderate counsels prevailed within its organisation. The more evident it became that Fenians were entering the organisation, the more vital from the church's point of view that the clergy should also be involved. Once the clergy were involved in significant numbers, the more difficult it became for the government and the police to secure support for their measures against the

League. Once this had happened, the agitation represented an almost total unity of the community, making it a powerful statement of nationality and facilitating its extension more widely across Ireland in those terms. The involvement of the clergy was the seal on its legitimacy and the sanction for its further expansion.

The consequences of this for the landlord class were far-reaching indeed. Within their own conception of social structure they were the pinnacle of a social pyramid in which a degree of cohesion and interdependence had always been their goal. Inhibited from the start by their status as inheritors of the land confiscations of an earlier century, they had been bedevilled by changing circumstances in which pressures largely imposed from without had exacerbated the difficulties which arose out of the specifically Irish environment. The economic demands imposed by a British state which had committed itself to *laissez-faire* and a landlord counterpart in that country which had used the industrial and economic transformation of their society enormously to increase their economic power had made life increasingly more difficult for Irish landlords, for whom social conciliation, perhaps even more than economic efficiency, remained a precondition for their continued operation. The Famine, the responsibility for which was by some attached to them, further destroyed their standing, they themselves contributing to this by their resort to extensive evictions in its aftermath. These factors all played a part in their failure to capitalise on the prosperity of the post-Famine decades, and the natural defensiveness of their position in Irish society was further aggravated by the encroachment upon their rights of a British parliament grappling with the unwelcome problems thrust upon it by Irish land tenure, these readily blamed upon the inadequacies of Irish landlords. Now, unable to lower rents to meet a major economic downturn, they found themselves face to face with a combination which finally spelt out their effective marginalisation within the society in which their whole social, economic and political role existed. They now had to recognise writ large the reality portended by the disestablishment of the Church of Ireland in 1869, and foreshadowed even earlier, during the 1829 House of Lords debates on Catholic Emancipation, in Lord John George Beresford's prophecy that in granting Emancipation parliament would 'transfer from

Protestants to Roman Catholics the ascendancy of Ireland'.[48] Effectively the socially cohesive pyramid which had been the landlords' own model of society had now come into existence, but in a form self-contained within Catholic Ireland, and with the landlords themselves excluded from it; new elites consisting of the urban professional and business bourgeosie had replaced them at the top. And all this had been given sanction by a church and clergy to which they did not belong. Land may have been the issue around which this mobilisation cohered, but at stake was the much larger question of nationality and the relationship of the landlord class to it.

Not only did this mobilisation drive a cleavage between the landlords and the rest of Irish rural society, but it also transcended the differences and conflicts of interest between other rural classes. One of the most significant of these conflicts was that between the demand of small farmers for the break-up and redistribution of grazing lands to tenant farmers and the important social, economic and political role increasingly attaching to the large graziers themselves. As David Seth Jones has pointed out, 'investment in grazing land became one of the main channels of upward mobility in Irish society',[49] and the graziers saw themselves as a new elite within rural society. Often themselves shopkeepers and town businessmen, these graziers were dependent on the landlords for their land but also sought to avoid ostracism from the community with which they most naturally identified. Thus, while the Land League condemned grazing as a misuse of land rightfully belonging to the tillage farmers, many graziers came to play an active role in its leadership and helped to establish and give credibility to the new 'collectivity' from which the landlords were being excluded; a particularly significant example of this phenomenon was John J. Louden of Louisburgh, County Mayo.[50] The larger nationalist character which the movement was acquiring diminished the contradiction between their involvement and the declared opposition of the League to large-scale grazing, and the coexistence of groups with rival economic interests further consolidated the League as a national rather than merely agrarian body.

This is not to say that in the longer term conflicts of interest within the majority 'collectivity' were unimportant. Indeed, central to Paul Bew's analysis is the view that the Land League, while unquestionably creating an unprecedented unity of purpose against the landlords, involved significant conflicts between the major classes involved in the mobilisation: the rural bourgeoisie, the middle and poor peasantry, and the agricultural proletariat. The strategy of 'rent at the point of a bayonet', which characterised the reality of the Land League 'no rent' campaigns, was the crucial instrument which brought this conflict to the fore. It was a conflict which influenced the final outcome of the Land League campaign,[51] but it also helped to shape longer-term legacies of the land question into the politics of twentieth-century Ireland.

The mobilisation of the Irish countryside through the Land League cannot, however, be isolated from what was happening in Irish politics at a national level. Dr Vaughan, in questioning as explanations of the land war of 1879–81 theories put forward by Donnelly and Clark, asserts that 'The one incontestable fact that emerges is that 1879 was the only year of serious agricultural depresssion that found a united and powerful political leadership, ready to exploit agrarian discontent.'[52] This leadership represented distinct and powerful elements of Irish political life which had come together as a potential alliance— and had done so, as Vaughan stresses, before the onset of the worst of the agricultural depression in the winter of 1879.[53] These leaders were thus well placed to channel the economic discontents into a political strategy which transformed agitation which might otherwise have been both transient and spasmodic into an unprecedented demonstration of Irish disaffection. What turned the agitation of 1879–81 into the 'Land League Revolution' was this strongly based political leadership and direction. In effect this represented a drawing together of the three distinct forces of land agitation, Fenianism and parliamentary nationalism. It involved the development of a subtle but effective co-operation between three critically placed figures, Charles Stewart Parnell, parliamentarian, Michael Davitt, ex-Fenian prisoner and land reformer, and John Devoy, leader of Clan na Gael, the American Fenian organisation. The story of these developments, the 'New Departure' in Irish politics, has been unravelled and told in the work of T. W. Moody, first in his 1949 essay 'The New Departure in Irish Politics' and then in his comprehensive analysis in *Davitt and Irish Revolution*. Moody describes and analyses three 'New Departures', the first dating from 1873 and involving the support given by the Fenians to Butt's Home Rule movement, the second in 1878 involving Devoy's commitment to Parnell's strategy of parliamentary action, and the third in 1879 arising from Davitt's formation of the Land League, 'a scheme for a popular front on the land question under Parnell's leadership, which grassroots Fenians in Ireland and Clan na Gael were expected to support unconditionally'.[54] Cumulatively these developments represented the coming together of forces in Irish politics and society between which, in the past, co-operation had been extremely difficult, if not impossible. Out of this was formed, from 1879, a political movement based on a mobilisation around the land issue, but in a form which constituted a formidable national combination against British control in Ireland. While new in its political form and organisational structure, it was, however, something which had been prefigured in Butt's drawing together of Fenian support and ideas with a parliamentary Home Rule movement, sustained by an ideology which Butt had partly drawn out of his distinctive analysis of the land question.

Margaret O'Callaghan has emphasised the limitations of causal explanations of the Land League. Out of a diversity of factors there emerged a political and social reality of enormous transforming importance:

> It was the nationalisation of the issues of Mayo through the organisation of the Irish National Land League, which was controlled nationally by the Irish Parliamentary Party, that rendered the movement politically potent.... Structuring the underlying diversity of aims and intent stood a central formal organisation and a touring circus of stable performers—parliamentarians, paid League officials, urban journalists, providing a directional impetus to what would otherwise have been another chapter in an old story.... And why the Land War started does not seem to be the interesting question.[55]

In this view she gives priority, as does Dr Vaughan, to the political circumstances, but it is an interpretation characterised by a recognition of a complexity which must of necessity defy attempts at narrow classifications. The great value in the burgeoning mass of writings on the Land League is not that any of them gives an adequate explanation of *why* it occurred, but that collectively they create a much fuller and rounded picture of the phenomenon which came into existence. Indeed, it is greatly to the credit of the historians involved in this scholarly explosion that rarely do they suggest any exclusivity to their own analyses, and that the cumulative effect of their work is inclusive and accommodating. As a result, it is now possible to set the land war into a broader and longer context, its complexity and nuances more open to observation. Dr O'Callaghan's work makes its own very significant contribution to the literature of the Land League in integrating that organisation—and indeed the whole issue of land—into the detailed political and administrative governance of Ireland, demonstrating the extent to which the linking of land and nationalism was a composite achievement of land agitators, nationalist politicians and British government.

The major immediate legislative consequence of this new political phenomenon was the Irish Land Act of 1881, which gave at last to the Irish tenant farmers the 'three Fs' which they had long claimed as their right. The task of doing this, as well as of endeavouring to govern an Ireland dominated by the agitation of the Land League, fell to Gladstone, returned to office in April 1880 as the result of a general election. His initial step was to appoint a royal commission to inquire into the working of the 1870 Land Act. Headed by the Earl of Bessborough, an Irish landlord distinguished as a cricketer, author and amateur actor, and comprising an able and broadly based membership, this commission set forth in its report an analysis of the issues at stake in Irish land tenure which was lucid, comprehensive and penetrating. Basing their views firmly upon an historical perspective, the commissioners explained the problems of Irish land in terms of the misapplication of English land law:

> That law may have been beneficial in its operation in a country where it was merely the embodiment of existing relations . . . but when transplanted into a country where the relations between landlord and tenant were of a different character . . . not only did it fail to change those relations into the likeness of English traditions, but also, by its attitude of continual antagonism to the prevailing sentiment, it became detestable to tenants, and helped to bring the Courts that administered it, and the Government that enforced it, into

undeserved odium. In the result, a conflict of rights, legal and traditional, has existed in Ireland for centuries.[56]

In recommending the granting of the 'three Fs', the commissioners claimed:

> The principle which we adopt as a guide is that partially embodied in the Land Act [i.e. of 1870], of giving legal recognition to the existing state of things. It appears to us that the condition under which land has been held by yearly tenants in Ireland has been such, that the occupiers have, as a general rule, acquired rights to continuous occupancy which, in the interest of the community, it is desirable legally to recognize. . . . The legal effect of these changes may be described as amounting to the enlargement of the tenancy from year to year into a new kind of statutory tenure, defeasible only upon decree of the Land Court, for the breach of certain well ascertained conditions, and held subject to the payment of a rent, the amount of which should in the last resort be fixed, neither by the landlord nor by the tenant, but by constituted authority.[57]

There was nothing new in this. In both analysis and remedy, the Bessborough Commission saw the land tenure question in much the form in which William Conner had promulgated his doctrine of 'a valuation and a perpetuity' in the 1830s and 1840s. In legislating in these terms in 1881, parliament had fully endorsed the traditional perception of the relationship of landlord and tenant as the tenants had envisaged it, and had satisfied the aspiration of Gladstone, unfulfilled in the 1870 act, for the restitution of traditional rights. Parliament, the state and, indeed, those representing the tenant farmers had now escaped from the *cul-de-sac* of 'Ulster custom' into which they had been led, originally by Sharman Crawford and his supporters. A well-intentioned effort to make the pursuit of land reform more palatable to British taste had served to misrepresent in a fundamental way the real nature of the Irish land problem. None of this, however, should diminish the major implications for *British* conceptions inherent in so massive a departure from their accustomed ways; as Florence Arnold-Forster, adopted daughter and confidante of Gladstone's Chief Secretary, W. E. Forster, put it,

'One feels as though one were assisting not so much at a reform as a revolution.'[58]

In grappling with the problem of Irish land tenure, the act of 1881, like that of 1870, had come too late to satisfy the heightened expectations of Irish public opinion. The machinery it created for determining a fair rent was elaborate, based upon a system of land courts or tribunals which heard disputes between landlords and tenants and fixed what it determined to be appropriate rents. The tenant was then guaranteed fixity of tenure so long as that rent was paid. The right to sell his interest in the land, largely conceded in the 1870 act, was now unambiguously granted. The act also improved the conditions for a tenant purchasing from the landlord, increasing the proportion of the purchase price advanced to the tenant. The act had thus, as the Bessborough Commission recommended, granted the 'three Fs' which had long been the tenant demand, but the wider context in which this happened had now significantly changed.

'Dual ownership', which was in reality what the 'three Fs' represented and which soon became the way in which the system set up by the 1881 act was described, was predicated on an assumption of a shared responsibility between landlord and tenant and of a co-operative approach to both agricultural and social questions. This was indeed what most land reformers, from Conner and Sharman Crawford to Butt, had hoped to achieve. The circumstances through which the 1881 act came about, however, irretrievably destroyed that possibility. The Land League, as will be seen more fully in the next chapter, represented much more than a demand for reform of the land tenure laws; it involved a mass repudiation of the concept of society upon which the continued role of landlordism depended. While that ideal had always been more fragile in its Irish than in its English form, it had been possible to believe that a compromise between landlords and tenants over the distribution of rights of property might provide a stable basis for the survival of landlordism in Ireland. After the Land League that was no longer a credible belief. Thus Gladstone's commitment to the 1881 act as a reform compatible with the traditional concept of landlordism was comprehensible in the context which preceded the events of the late 1870s, but by 1881 its effect was to provide a machinery for, and to accelerate, the process by which the whole apparatus and philosophy underpinning that concept was dismembered in the sweep of an aggressive, highly organised and increasingly credible democratic alternative. What had been meant to be a procedure through which fairness to both sides could be achieved became in practice a weapon by which a new power established in mass organisation could be used in the pursuit of larger and more far-reaching political and social objectives. Nowhere is this reality more clearly demonstrated than in the rapidity with which Conservative policy-makers and many Irish landlords themselves began to look with new interest at the pos-sibilities of the transfer of sole ownership to the tenants through schemes of land purchase.

Barbara Solow and W. E. Vaughan make very strongly the point that the economic problems of Irish agriculture in the nineteenth century were not the product, as they were so often perceived to be, of the law of land tenure. Indeed, it can be argued that the form of agriculture which was protected by the reforms which the tenants finally secured locked Ireland into an agrarian structure of small farms which was not in the country's long-term interests. However, there is another sense in which the issue of land tenure had far-reaching effects, not least in economic terms. The belief of the tenant farmers in their pro-prietory rights in the land was longstanding, deeply held and ultimately vindicated in the 1881 Land Act. Had those rights not been stirred up by the more determined assertion of their non-existence, largely under the influence of more capitalist ideas of the landlord's economic function, then the uneasy but generally not intolerable relationship of landlord and tenant might have evolved into a distinctively Irish form, allowing the landlords to sustain and develop a role for themselves in a co-operative rela-tionship with their tenants. Alternatively, an earlier recognition of a need for a change in the law to accommodate it to the realities of practice might likewise have enabled the evolution of a positive relationship between landlords and tenants, in which economic and management decisions about the use of land could have been made in a less adversarial context and based on acknowledgment of interest on both sides.

The failure to resolve the conflict over land tenure law and its consequent aggravation and intensification over four decades had a number of major effects. First, the line of cleavage in social and cultural terms—marked both by the legacy of conquest and religious difference—between landlord and tenant became ever more clearly defined. Secondly, the vaguer sense that the tenant had of his customary rights, and to which he had accommodated some grudging acceptance of the landlord's existence, became clarified to a point where there seemed logically little place for the landlord. Thirdly, the doubt as to the nature of the proprietorship in the land meant that neither landlords nor tenants could perform as good capitalists in developing the potential of their land. Fourthly, the failure to resolve the conflict kept landlords on the defensive as to their place in Irish society, thereby making it more difficult for them to manage their estates and in particular to ensure that the level of rent being charged was appropriate. Fifthly, once the principle of independent determination of rents was established under the 1881 act, the pattern of conflict had become so well established that social order, rather than economic considerations, tended inordinately to influence the process. Sixthly—and perhaps most importantly—the refusal to grant the tenant farmers recognition of what they claimed, and with it a clearer responsibility for their farms, protracted their failure to address the real agricultural problems they faced, enabling them to shelter behind a sense of grievance, legitimately based, which served as an explanation of their difficulties. The long dispute over land tenure had helped to stereotype Irish agriculture in a traditional form and had made it far more difficult for anyone, government, landlords or tenants, to face questions about its structure. Decisions which landlords could not make, because of tenant resistance, might have been made by tenant farmers confident in their possession of their farms. In this sense there were significant economic consequences from the conflict over land tenure.

Instead of marking the final resolution of the land question which it might at an earlier time have been, the Land Act of 1881 set down the terms for a new phase of conflict between landlord and tenant. It had this effect partly because the slippery slope on which landlordism had been placed economically and the status which had come to be accorded to land agitation ensured that the process of rent determination would mirror more the capacity of the tenants to disrupt than the need of the landlords for financial security. It was also a product of the development of policy within the Land League itself, by which the tenants now for the first time openly stated their ultimate goal as a peasant proprietorship. Implicit in many earlier expressions of their aspirations, this was now for the first time defined in practical and explicit terms as involving the abolition of the very institution of landlordism. But perhaps most importantly of all, the continuation of conflict was assured by the interconnection which had been created between the issue of land and the issue of nationality, by the value that had been established for land agitation as an instrument of nationalist strategy, and by the fact that the landlords had allowed themselves to become a characterisation of British rule, thereby helping to ensure that their own fate was intertwined with that of the system of government. Land had become a metaphor for nationalism, and neither tenant nor landlord, nationalist nor unionist, could any longer draw a clear line between the two.

4

The Land as Metaphor

The Land League was dissolved by Parnell in 1882, having largely served the twofold purpose important to the consolidation of his authority and power as the 'uncrowned king' of nationalist Ireland. In the first place, it had identified him with the issue central to the social and economic aspirations of the most significant segment of nationalist society, which was also that part of the population most clearly on the ascendant in terms of their status and influence within society in general. This had been a major factor in Parnell's rapid rise to ascendancy in Irish politics, and in particular had enabled him more fully than could have been done through any other issue to construct out of his background as landlord and Protestant a politically positive projection. Secondly, his identification with the Land League had established for him a reputation by association with radical and extra-parliamentary politics which equipped him extremely well in his dealings with two fundamentally opposed elements, the more advanced nationalists on the one hand and the British government and parliament on the other. He had effectively demonstrated his ability to transcend the normal parameters of constitutional politics, thus conveying a sense of formidable power, attractive to those more extreme elements whom he needed to neutralise, and politically intimidating to those, like governments, whom he needed to make more amenable to negotiation.

The Land League, however, had created a political and social formation with implications far beyond the use which it might be to Parnell's more immediate political interests. Through its role in the mobilisation of Catholic and nationalist Ireland around the complex political structures which came into existence as a result of the 'New Departure', the Land League had constituted a model for political action which shaped the development of Irish politics, especially in relation to the twin issues of land and nationality, for the next quarter of a century. Moreover, it was a model in which those two issues became increasingly intertwined in courses of action based on a consciousness which involved little distinction between them. To a degree the land question during this period loses its identity as a separate issue, becoming a metaphor for the larger issue of nationality. This was in part a consequence of the growing confidence of the tenant farmers, for whom advances in their tenure conditions, culminating in the 1881 Land Act, had engendered expectations of eventual control of their land and with it a new status for themselves socially which could only be fully realised through an acknowledgment of their distinctive nationality—a symbolic reversal of the past demeaning subjection of their Irish and Catholic identity. Home Rule was sometimes seen as a means to the eventual rectification of the land tenure question, but it was more the prize which would confirm the meaning of a control over the land already largely secured. The nature of this fusion of the two issues can best be understood by a closer analysis of the character of the Land League and of subsequent organisations constructed around the issue of land tenure.

The term 'Irish land war' is often used to refer to the conflict which occurred through the Land League mobilisation during the years from 1879 to 1882, but it is better applied to the whole of the period from the beginning of that organisation in 1879 until the Wyndham Land Act of 1903. If that time-scale is adopted, there are three separate phases which can be discerned as integral to that conflict, each embodying its own distinct organisational form. The first of these is that of the Land League, from its inception in 1879 until its dissolution by Parnell in 1882 and replacement by the very different Irish National League; included in that phase is the Ladies' Land League, which made its own distinctive contribution to the conflict of these years. The second phase is that of the Plan of Campaign, from 1886 until the split in the Irish Parliamentary Party in 1890, during which the political vacuum created by the failure of Gladstone's first Home Rule bill was increasingly filled by a return to conflict over land. The third and final phase of the land war is that of the United Irish League, founded in 1898 and culminating in the 1903 Land Act, although—unlike the Land League—the name of this agitation lived on in what became the organisational structure for a solely parliamentary strategy after that date. These three agitations need each to be understood in three ways: their overt purposes; their organisational methods; and what they represented in terms of the changing consciousness of those caught up in them. In analysing the purposes of the agitations, it is necessary to distinguish between the policy objectives explicitly espoused and the roles which these organisations can be seen in retrospect to have performed. The latter can best be discerned from looking at the methods of the organisation and changing consciousness in the community, but the overt policy objectives provide a useful initial framework of understanding.

The Land League, as has been seen, arose most immediately from a setback in economic circumstances and the refusal of landlords to abate rents in line with the fall in agricultural prices; the League's primary objective, therefore, might be defined as the securing of such reductions. At this level it had significant successes. The meeting at Irishtown on 20 April 1879 which effectively launched the new organisation resulted in an immediate reduction of rent by 25 per cent on the estate in relation to which the demonstration had been arranged.[1] From then until the 1881 Land Act came into effect, this pattern of conflict secured for many tenants similar reductions in rent, and these were often further cut by the working of the new legislation.[2] In this sense the League enjoyed considerable immediate success. But its purposes were also defined from the outset in more general ways, and in particular with a new use of the phrase 'the land for the people' as the goal to which Irish farmers should be striving. The connotations of this phrase remained relatively broad, accommodating on the one hand the fulfilment of the 'three Fs' aspiration left incomplete by the 1870 act, but also pointing towards the goal of peasant proprietorship. At the Irishtown meeting John O'Connor Power was quite explicit about this ultimate objective:

> Now, if you ask me to state in a brief sentence what is the Irish land question, I say it is the restoration of the land of Ireland to the people of Ireland. And if you ask me for a solution of

the land question in accordance with philosophy, experience, and common-sense, I shall be equally brief and explicit. Abolish landlordism, and make the man who occupies and cultivates the soil the owner of the soil.[3]

This appears to be the first time that the demand for peasant proprietorship had been made within a popular movement in Ireland, bringing back into the debate at that level the ideas which had been current before the Great Famine. One of those who had been involved in the framing of resolutions for a similar Land League meeting in July 1879 captured in his comments the extent to which that was now being seen as a 'modern', not just an Irish, objective:

I drew up the resolutions on that occasion; but I was loath to be the first to propound publicly the doctrine of 'a peasant proprietary' for Ireland. I was asked however this question— 'did I wish to be less zealous for the good of Ireland ... than an Englishman—namely John S. Mill?' I answered 'Certainly not'—'But he advocates that doctrine: English statesmen admit that he is right'. And I knew that the nations of Europe from their peasant homes proclaim the truth, that a peasant proprietary is vastly superior to the Feudal system of landed rights, which has directed land tenure in England & in Ireland too, (speaking generally) since the coming of the Norman nobles to these countries.[4]

There had indeed been earlier advocates in Ireland of peasant proprietary, but not in the mainstream of political action. Thomas Neilson Underwood, a Presbyterian from Strabane and a supporter of the Tenant League in the 1850s, put forward a plan for owner occupancy in 1857; he had been influenced by the ideas of English freehold land societies.[5] Even earlier, in 1848, a comprehensive proposal for peasant proprietorship in Ireland had been published by W. T. Thornton.[6]

As the connection between the Land League on the one hand and Parnell and the Home Rule movement on the other became stronger the inclusion of self-government as part of the League's programme also occurred, often as an extension of the general slogan of 'the land for the people'. Thus the wider political objective was grafted onto the agrarian one, helping to fuse the two in a single consciousness. But in terms of the League's narrower objective, the act of 1881 seemed to constitute a satisfactory conclusion; it was no doubt this that helped Parnell, who carefully distanced himself from excessive satisfaction with that act, to consider that the League had done its work and that it could be dissolved. In taking this view he showed perhaps too little appreciation of the continued value of such a popular organisation for the nationalist purpose which was his own priority; for him the land grievance was indeed what Florence Arnold-Forster called it, his 'magic wand', but her prediction that his followers, rather than he, would be the ones who abandoned it once reform had been carried by parliament was wide of the mark.[7]

This is not to say that his critics were necessarily right in their view of the course he took through and after the Kilmainham 'Treaty'. The crisis of confidence associated with these events, and involving in particular the differences of perspective personified in Charles Stewart Parnell, Michael Davitt and Anna Parnell, must be examined by reference to objectives which differed significantly from one to another. The most trenchant and sustained criticism of the course taken, not only by Parnell but also by the other Land League leaders, including Davitt, was that mounted by Anna Parnell in the manuscript she completed in 1907, *The Tale of a Great Sham*.[8] The Ladies' Land League, forced to take responsibility at short notice for the conduct of a campaign which had been set in its course by a male leadership now mostly in prison, understandably was highly critical of a strategy, characterised as 'rent at the point of the bayonet', which had the effect of subsidising the landlords from the funds of the Land League. How this had come about, however, needs careful analysis.

For Davitt the Land League represented an empowerment of the people most oppressed by the existing social and political order, and no matter what part it played in the advance of the nationalist cause, its existence was also to be defended in the long term as a social mobilisation with the potential eventually to change and reform the social order. For him the rent strike represented an assertion of power, but one which had to be handled with great caution, for its success depended on the participation of a cross-section of farmers, many of whom could not risk the loss of their farms. It was for this reason that farmers were encouraged to withhold their rents, but then to pay them just short of eviction. This was indeed a sham, but it was the price of a show of solidarity upon which much might in future be built. For Anna Parnell, on the other hand, real and immediate sympathy for the farmers locked in this conflict with their landlords cloaked what was more fundamentally a priority for the cause of nationalism. There were two logical responses to the realisation of the 'sham', one being to call off the whole rent-strike strategy, the other to try to force farmers to take it seriously, even at the risk of losing their farms. The fact that Anna Parnell chose the latter suggests that confrontation with government, leading—whether consciously or not—to a semi-revolutionary outcome, was her path. However, this preferred course of hers would unquestionably have had as its consequence the break-up of the campaign, in the form of a split between more prosperous farmers, unwilling to forfeit their land, and the smaller farmers. Perception of this may have caused Davitt to equivocate over a full-scale rent strike, whereas Anna Parnell—seeing through the contradiction and the equivocation—lacked an appreciation of their causes.

For Parnell himself there were no contradictions, for the purposes of the Land League were essentially transient. A rent strike could be mounted and called off, rent could be withheld and paid at the point of the bayonet, because the need of the moment was to drive home to the British government the fragile balance between order and disorder in Ireland, and the role in that balance of the new polity being constructed around his party, with the intimate connection which it enjoyed with discontent in the country. The Kilmainham 'Treaty' represented his judgment that new terms of discourse between the two countries, as personified in himself and Gladstone, had been set in a way which fulfilled the substance of what the Land League, in his view, had been meant to achieve. He could not be expected to share the hopes of Davitt for a social transformation to which he was opposed, or that of his sister, whose political strategy for nationalism was diametrically opposed to his own. Where his judgment may be impugned is in his assumption, characteristic of his style, that the army could be disbanded now that the battle was over, without regard to the outcome of the war. The Kilmainham 'Treaty' made most sense in a context in which Home Rule was achieved on the first run; it did not allow for having to re-create from scratch a renewed assault on the bastions of British power—and that, after 1886, was what his nationalist strategy would require. When his colleagues attempted to rebuild in that later context what he had eliminated with his suppression of the Land League, he was to be singularly lacking in appreciation of its political necessity.

The contribution of the Ladies' Land League was immensely important to the impact of the Land League agitation, taking up the cudgels at a critical time in terms of ensuring that, with the male leaders in prison, unrest in Ireland would increase rather than diminish. That they were women was also crucial in establishing a broader credibility for the sense of the agitation as a mass mobilisation of the whole community, in which values of fundamental importance to the community's perception of itself were involved. In fact peasant women had already been active in the forefront of agitation, although with little wider acknowledgment of their role,[9] but the Ladies' Land League, with its middle-class and aristocratic involvement, gave an important aura to the whole agitation, even though it so significantly breached Victorian moral and religious, especially Catholic, precepts as to the place of women. That the women's organisation became so critical of their male counterparts, and that the grounds of their complaints in practical terms could be so well sustained, also played its part in providing a precedent for both autonomous and unconventional female involvement subsequently in Irish politics. But on the issue of the land, what the Ladies' Land League showed was the danger of pushing the question of land from a generalised issue of ownership and control to one of social protest on behalf of the economically most deprived section of farmers, for this was to break the solidarity on which the whole mobilisation was founded. It was this which played its part in holding Davitt back from openly venting his anger at Parnell's suppression of the League, an anger felt on behalf of the women as well, for Davitt took the view that 'Parnell never made a greater mistake or a more mischievous blunder than in suppressing the Ladies in the manner he did.'[10] It was, however, Anna Parnell who pressed the issue to the brink, thereby revealing inadvertently the dangers of a strategy which alienated the less deprived farmers. Out of this tension can be observed the extent to which the land agitation had come to serve national purposes in a context in which reform and expectation of a continuing reform momentum had substantively alle-viated the more material grievances of farmers in relation to land tenure conditions.

It was again economic recession which served as the trigger to the next phase of agrarian agitation, the Plan of Campaign. Here, though, a very different sequence occurred from that in the 1870s. A new fall in agricultural prices began to impinge on Irish tenant farmers as early as May 1885, and landlords and nationalist leaders were well aware of the worsening situation through the rest of 1885.[11] This was, however, the period in which the focus of nationalist energies was the pursuit of the Home Rule issue and the need to maximise the possibility of positive response from either of the major British parties. It is revealing, therefore, that the concerns and agitation of the tenants were largely suppressed during this period; as Laurence M. Geary writes:

> The refusal of the National League to recognise and, more importantly, to give financial assistance to striking tenants, precipitated the collapse of the majority of combinations on Irish estates, as Parnell had, no doubt, intended. He was at the apogee of his power and he dictated the policy of the National League through his control of the parliamentary party. In his quest for Home Rule, Parnell, quite simply, emas-culated the agrarian agitation in Ireland.[12]

It was only after the collapse of Gladstone's attempt at Home Rule and the return of a Tory government, now unequivocally (in the new terminology) 'Unionist', that the Plan of Campaign was launched to give support and direction to agrarian discon-tent. It occurred still without the endorsement or approval of Parnell, whose sense of nationalist strategy continued to be one based on parliamentary pressures, but the involvement of his colleagues in it was manifestly more than a commitment to agrarian reform alone. As with the Land League, the objectives of the Plan of Campaign were both of an immediate agrarian kind and of a more far-reaching nature.

Under the Plan of Campaign, tenants were to combine on an estate to offer their landlords what the tenants considered, in the deteriorating economic situation, a fair rent; if the proffered amount was refused, it was to be handed over to Plan of

Campaign trustees until such time as the landlord agreed to an acceptable reduction. The objective was thus, at this level at least, about securing rent reductions in line with diminishing returns for agricultural products. And at this level the Plan of Campaign was notably successful. This was in part because of a deliberate strategy of targeting landlords who were more financially vulnerable, thus forcing upon them the difficult choice between a continuing but reduced income on the one hand and no income at all and immediate bankruptcy on the other. The conflict was the more intense as rents under dispute were now 'judicial' ones, those settled as a fair rent by the tribunals set up under the 1881 act, and landlords felt doubly imposed upon in being expected to lower them. Conversely, as William Walsh, the Catholic Archbishop of Dublin, was so cogently to argue in an interview in the *Pall Mall Gazette* in December 1886, the relationship between landlord and tenant in Ireland was no longer a matter of simple contract. Effectively—as Tory leaders were among the readiest to admit—there was now a dual ownership in the land, and the financial nexus between the partners was determined on the basis of an assessment of a 'fair rent' based on factors such as price levels at the time of fixing. Should the factors on which that rent had been determined alter—as a result, for example of depressed market prices—the tenant had a right to insist on its review, not as a contracting party who could go elsewhere if no longer content with his contract, but as a part-owner who could hardly be expected to forgo his right of property in order to redress an inequity in the partnership.[13] The 1881 act had to that extent substantially recognised the claim of the tenants to an equity in the land, and made the issue of their right unilaterally to adjust their rent—what they were essentially doing through the Plan of Campaign—a more complex moral and legal question than it would have been previously.

Rent reduction was, however, only one of the objectives of the Plan of Campaign. The involvement of so many of Parnell's closest associates was testimony to the importance attached to the Plan by nationalists, despite the reluctance of their leader. Nor can this just be explained, as it sometimes is, by reference to the more agrarian inclinations of some nationalists. Active participants in the Plan of Campaign from among nationalist politicians included John Dillon, William O'Brien, Timothy

Harrington, Thomas Sexton, T. D. Sullivan, and John and
William Redmond.[14] While the first three of these might be
generally identified as being especially associated with the cause
of the tenant farmers, this cannot be particularly said of the
others. On the other hand, among those who, like Parnell, stood
aloof from the Plan were Timothy Healy and Joseph Biggar,
primarily associated with the political side of the movement, but
also Michael Davitt,[15] founder of the Land League and pre-
eminently of the agrarian wing. A closer look at the two leaders
most in control of the Plan, O'Brien and Dillon, who also
emerge in the longer term as the most dominant of Parnell's
successors, demonstrates the inadequacy of characterising individual roles in terms of the priority given to agrarian or political
objectives.

John Dillon came of a highly political family, the son of the
Young Irelander, John Blake Dillon. He was qualified as a
surgeon and entered parliament in 1880 as a strong supporter
of Parnell. William O'Brien, on the other hand, had origins
which were less suggestive of political involvement. It was
proximity to the Fenian disturbances in County Cork in the
1860s which in his youth raised his political consciousness, and it
was his professional work as a journalist which led him to
acquire a knowledge of the conditions, and a commitment to
the cause, of the tenant farmers.[16] But, like Dillon, he entered
nationalist politics under the auspices of Parnell, who appointed
him editor of his newspaper, *United Ireland*, in 1881; he was first
elected to parliament in 1883. For both Dillon and O'Brien,
involvement in the land issue, genuinely seen as a major
grievance of Irish life, was part of a broader commitment which
can best be defined as nationalist. While Parnell was in
command both men tended to be more identified with agrarian
agitation, but this reflected, at least in part, the higher priority
they gave to extra-parliamentary action in the countryside than
did their leader. Later, after Parnell's death, when Dillon effectively had primary responsibility for the conduct of the
parliamentary party, it was O'Brien who tended to be characterised as pre-eminently an agrarian leader; again this
divergence came from differing views of the requirements of the
nationalist movement at that time. Thus the commitment to the
Plan of Campaign of both Dillon and O'Brien can best be seen
as a statement of their belief that agrarian agitation was an

essential component of an effective nationalist strategy, rather than as an indication that they gave priority to the interests of the tenant farmers. More generally, it can be asserted, the distinctive commitments made by members of Parnell's movement reflect the extent to which the two issues of nationality and land had become two sides of a single coin, and the relative involvement of individuals in different facets of the movement should be seen as indicating differences of emphasis in the pursuit of a largely unified and coherent objective.

This view of the Plan of Campaign, as a reactivation of land agitation to meet the necessities of the nationalist movement, also better explains why such a low priority was given to the specifically tenant farmer interest when renewed hardship first struck during 1885 but when the competing demands of the Home Rule cause dictated a suppression of agitation. Michael Davitt was alienated from this phase of the land war precisely because of its lack of priority for the agrarian and social concerns close to his heart; in correspondence with Dillon in July and August of 1887 he made clear his objections to the use of money raised in America for evicted tenants to assist those participating in the Plan of Campaign.[17] Parnell's aloofness from the Plan, given this primarily nationalist function, therefore raises questions about how he saw it. As shrewd as he generally was in his political judgments, he appears in this period not to have appreciated the danger of a vacuum being formed in Irish popular politics while the official focus of his party was upon the politically important, but for Irish opinion relatively remote, 'Union of Hearts' with British Liberal thought. Those of his lieutenants who lived closer to the sources of nationalist inspiration than did Parnell himself sensed the dangers of this situation and the importance of a sustained campaign around the issue of land and against the dual elements so largely responsible for the frustration of Home Rule, the landlords and the Conservative Party. Like Parnell, the nationalist leaders involved in the Plan remained aware of the need to avoid antagonising British Liberals, but they also saw the Plan of Campaign as essential to retaining both the allegiance and the enthusiasm of their supporters in the country. To have said that the ghosts of Fenianism still haunted the Irish countryside would have seemed to these politicians very much an understatement of the real and tangible presence of alternatives to their own constitutional strategies.

More than had been the case with the Land League, the Plan of Campaign involved an explicit linking of the immediate economic and agrarian imperative of reduced rent to wider nationalist objectives. In this it reflected the advancing tenure and social status of the tenant farmers and their greater willingness to confront the landlords in a way that was clearly designed to put pressure on them to abandon their role as owners. The alternative of peasant proprietorship, already receiving some endorsement as a final objective by the Tory government itself, made tenants readier to use their new status under the 1881 legislation to tell landlords that they could get out altogether if they disliked their situation. This gave an edge to the agitational pattern of the Plan of Campaign which reinforced the more radical agrarian objective while also highlighting the conjunction of the agrarian enemy, landlordism, with the destroyers of Gladstone's Home Rule initiative, Unionists—in Ireland entities which were largely coterminous. In addition, of course, it echoed exactly the tribal atavism which had always lain not far below the surface in the relationship of landlord and tenant in Ireland. The shift of strategy of the Salisbury administration, implicit in the change of Chief Secretary in March 1887 from Sir Michael Hicks Beach to Arthur Balfour, further strengthened this dimension of the conflict. In abandoning the more subtle positioning of the government on a number of issues, as Hicks Beach had attempted, and instead turning the fight against the Plan of Campaign into the sole fulcrum upon which the government's strategy in Ireland turned,[18] the government played directly into the hands of those wishing to submerge specific agrarian issues within a wider nationalist strategy. The government's actions were no doubt good for its standing among its own supporters—gratifying the desire articulated by Salisbury himself that the Irish should 'take a licking'[19] before getting the benefits of reform—but fatal to any hope of driving a wedge between different interests in Catholic and nationalist Ireland. The hegemony of nationalist Ireland was thus firmly reinstated and the fissiparous tendencies inherent in the failure of the 1886 Home Rule initiative stemmed. The damage which this might have done to the Unionist government's longer-term handling of Irish matters was minimised by the political split in 1890 over Parnell's leadership, spelling out as it did the final destruction of both the Plan of Campaign and the political and financial capacity to protect those who had put their tenancies at risk as part of that agitation.

The responses of the Salisbury government, characteristically crude as they were, had been prefigured, albeit in more subtle tones, in the Liberal reactions to the Land League in the years 1880–82. In his increasingly obsessive determination to 'enforce the law', the Chief Secretary, W. E. Forster, had then effectively predetermined the maximum confrontation between the government and the Land League, in many areas extensively supported by the people, thus forcing the conclusion which the Nationalists wanted, namely that the government had lost the capacity to govern. This accelerated what would no doubt have happened in any case, the necessity for Gladstone to reach a political settlement with Parnell, at the expense not only of Forster's strategy but also of his political career. As had been the case with Forster, so with Balfour—the sacrifice of political understanding and management to the imperative of a single idea, the enforcement of law in its narrowest sense, served the cause of nationalism to perfection. In this sense, as Dr O'Callaghan has perceptively expressed it, the achievement of the Land League was a product not only of nationalist propaganda but also 'of an intimate and symbiotic connection between the nature of nationalist manipulation and British government policy'.[20] Whether this course was knowingly embarked upon as a deliberate strategy to smear the constitutional nationalist movement with the odour of criminality,[21] or as a tribal, atavistic response of British imperialists and nationalists, or as a consequence of Arthur Balfour's too-clever-by-half approach to political problems remains arguable, but its consequences for Britain, as well as for Ireland, were far-reaching and damaging, contributing to the crisis of nationhood and empire which its proponents were so passionately committed to averting.

In 1898, as on the two previous occasions, economic recession again provided the occasion for the launching of a new agitation. By this time, however, the ostensible objectives of agitation had fundamentally changed. The two central agrarian issues were the question of how to secure for the tenants the ownership of their farms and the need for some restitution to the 'wounded soldiers of the land war', the evicted tenants—the most directly affected victims of the collapse of the Plan of Campaign in 1890–91. The first of these was, of course, not new.

As has been seen, the establishment of peasant proprietorship had been an aspiration which had underpinned and explained attitudes to land tenure in Ireland throughout the nineteenth century. While it had been the 'long shot' objective of the Land League, in the Plan of Campaign it had been seen as an achievable consequence of putting economically more vulnerable landlords under acute financial pressure. But by 1898 it had become the first and most immediate objective of the new United Irish League. This was largely because of the direction of government policy since 1885, and the success of that policy in accustoming both tenants and landlords to the idea of purchase. How that policy came about, and the attempts at its application, needs explanation in order to understand the context within which the third phase of the land war, that conducted by the United Irish League, occurred.

Even before Gladstone had put through the 1881 Land Act some Conservative leaders were concerned that they should have, as Sir Stafford Northcote explained to Edward Gibson (later Lord Ashbourne), 'some plan of our own, which we could bring forward if occasion served; and to which, at all events, our arguments against the Government's plan should be made to conform'.[22] His own suggestions were ones which, with the retrospect of later years, would seem better to have served the interests of the Conservative Party, and of the relations between the two countries, had they been implemented more systematically and with a greater sense of urgency. Stressing the necessity of security for the investment of capital in Irish agriculture, Northcote adopted a pragmatic attitude to the question of peasant proprietorship, suggesting that it might be more appropriate in some cases than in others—'we must give free play to both systems, and let the people try what they can make of each'—but that they 'ought to afford all possible means for the fair trial of the experiment'. He argued for following the lines of the 'Bright clauses' in the 1870 act, but removing some of the existing restrictions, in order to facilitate the purchase by tenants of their land. In stating the need to resist confiscation of landlords' property, he revealingly left out initially the qualifying phrase 'without compensation'. He elaborated on his point of view, however, by suggesting that compulsory powers of purchase might even be used to acquire land for resale to its occupying tenants, covering himself with the proviso that 'If the terms offered were fair, there would probably be no necessity for compulsion.' He was disinclined to emigration as a policy and generally not favourable to free sale and fixity of tenure, although he had some sympathy with the idea of a tribunal to determine a fair rent.[23] What he advocated was a balanced and efficient shift towards at least a partial peasant proprietary, and Gibson—who was close to Irish landlord opinion—had no hesitation in stating that such an outcome 'is now much favoured by Irish landlords'.[24]

In his reply to Northcote, Gibson had predicted—wrongly as it transpired—that the Liberal legislation about to be introduced would have as a major feature the creation of such a peasant proprietary, probably along the lines proposed by G. J. Shaw Lefevre.[25] While the main thrust of Gladstone's policy in the past had been towards tenant protection measures, two Liberal measures—the Irish Church Act of 1869 and the Irish Land Act of 1870—had established the principle of purchase, although with limited practical effect. When it came, the 1881 act slightly extended the provisions for purchase, but to a much lesser extent than Gibson had apparently anticipated. It was only with the 1886 land bill, introduced in conjunction with the Home Rule bill, that Gladstone appeared momentarily to embrace the principle of comprehensive government-assisted purchase, and the fate of that bill exemplifies the political difficulty which the Liberals faced in pursuing this course. While many Liberals and radicals, such as John Bright, had long been committed to the principle of a peasant proprietary in Ireland, proposals which sought to facilitate this by the use of government credit could very easily come to be seen as a subsidy by British taxpayers to Irish landlords; and given the well-established British Liberal view of the responsibility of Irish landlords for the agrarian plight of their country, this was understandably difficult for them to swallow. When this was combined with a measure for Home Rule in Ireland, it assumed an even more threatening character, for it left the security for the return of interest payments and, eventually, capital with an Irish government. It was the outcry against such a land purchase scheme from the Liberal Party's own supporters in England and Scotland which led to the almost immediate dropping of the 1886 land bill from the legislative programme, for its unpopularity had threatened to diminish support for the principle of

Home Rule itself; indeed, in the judgment of Graham Goodlad, even though the land purchase bill had been buried well before the general election of July 1886, 'it helped to bring disaster to the cause of Home Rule from beyond the grave'.[26] Given this, Gladstone's final contribution to the Irish land question was to be the creation of the novel concept of 'dual ownership' of land, very possibly where he preferred to leave it anyway; Allen Warren has demonstrated the extent of Gladstone's commitment to the 1881 settlement and the underlying depth of his hostility to land purchase.[27] On the other hand, the distaste of the Tories for Gladstone's measures, and particularly the innovation of dual ownership, helped to drive them towards a solution which posed less problems for them than it did for the Liberal Party; by April 1882 Lord Salisbury had himself declared his public support for peasant proprietorship.[28]

The ideas mapped out in the correspondence between Northcote and Gibson on the eve of the 1881 Land Act defined the direction that Conservative policy on the Irish land question assumed for the future; indeed, it was Gibson, as Lord Ashbourne and Lord Chancellor of Ireland, who steered through the initial Conservative legislation on these lines in 1885. What has come to be known as the Ashbourne Act provided the first satisfactory scheme to facilitate purchase by tenants of their farms, and it was followed by a succession of similar acts under the Chief Secretaryship of Arthur Balfour, culminating in a measure brought in by Gerald Balfour in 1896. These later measures were all less effective than Ashbourne's, but collectively they established the pattern of Conservative policy. While the decision to give priority to repression of the Plan of Campaign rather than to conciliation and reform kept alive land agitation, the cumulative effects of purchase under these acts steadily confirmed it as the way forward in the minds both of landlords and tenants. Notable examples of successful purchase schemes accustomed landlords and tenants to the idea, and the Congested Districts Board, established by Arthur Balfour in 1891, undertook a small number of schemes which set a model for purchase of grasslands and very poor estates, where redistribution of holdings could do something to address underlying problems of agrarian viability. Thus, as the most immediate objective of the United Irish League—the achievement of the final transfer of landownership from landlords to tenants—was in line with the government's own aspirations, this new agitation occurred within a distinctly different context from that of the Land League and the Plan of Campaign. Why, then, did this movement assume such large dimensions, creating a new rural conflict as bitter as in the previous agitations, more protracted than they had been, and provoking a government largely in agreement with its overt objective to revive coercion on so extensive a scale?

The focus of the new organisation's campaign was on the means by which the objective of a peasant proprietary was to be achieved. While landlords, tenants and government were now all in favour of comprehensive purchase, there was not agreement on how it should be achieved. Landlords recognised that to be successful any scheme had to keep purchase instalments for tenants at or below what they paid in rent, or they would not see a benefit in purchase; one landlord had written in 1890 about the bill then under consideration that unless it were altered to keep tenants' instalments low enough, 'it is useless for the Government to take all the trouble that carrying it through the House of Commons will entail, for it will not be taken advantage of by the tenants'.[29] The landlords themselves, needless to say, were not in the business of showing charity to the tenants who had made life so difficult for them in the past, and were making their own calculations as to the real value of their interest in the land and their future financial status. If the government was to play a role, it had to strike a deal which gave the incentive to both sides to come to an agreement, while not allowing too comfortable an arrangement between them at the expense of the British exchequer. The United Irish League had its own solution to the impasse created by this, the one envisaged as a possibility by Sir Stafford Northcote as early as 1880 but now rejected out of hand by both the government and the landlords. Compulsory purchase of estates by the government, at an official valuation, was in the League's view the expeditious way of achieving the objective on which all the parties agreed.

This view was given greater credibility as a result of the mounting from 1900 onwards of a parallel campaign by Ulster Presbyterian tenant farmers, led by the Liberal Unionist MP, T. W. Russell, also in support of compulsory purchase.[30] There the grievances of tenants at some of the consequences of land reform legislation had stirred up fresh hostility on the land issue, particularly insofar as rulings of the Land Courts had in some respects undermined what had been seen to be attributes of Ulster custom as previously practised. This had been aggravated by increasing perception of landlord and Conservative indifference to the plight of Ulster tenant farmers, in terms not of decreased prosperity but of diminishing benefits from their traditionally advantageous arrangements.[31] This campaign, led by one who had been a member of the Unionist government, was a very significant challenge to the credibility of an administration which had made a commitment in principle to land purchase as the solution of the Irish land question but had not been effective in carrying it into practice. It helped immensely to give ideological credence to the new agitation in the rest of the country.

Compulsory purchase became the catchcry of the new United Irish League, which brought into play the range of agitational tactics which had evolved through the past experience of the Land League and the Plan of Campaign. The plight of selected evicted tenants, as well as the onset of bad seasons and poor crops, was used by the League to stir up sentiment in the country; indeed, this new agitation dated back to 1895, with the beginnings of what became a steadily increasing pattern in the west of anti-landgrabber and anti-grazier action. The United Irish League succeeded in giving direction and purpose to this agitation and instituting anew the patterns of boycotting and intimidation which had been central to the success of previous agitations.[32] The new body was to entrench itself very quickly in the Irish political system, expanding rapidly from its origins in the west to the rest of the country. As such it consolidated and built on the experience of its two predecessor organisations.

The founder of the United Irish League was William O'Brien, one of the major figures in the Plan of Campaign. During that previous agitation he had established considerable notoriety for himself through repeated imprisonments, which he had used to great effect to conjure up in the public consciousness a sense of theatrical jousting between himself and the government; perhaps one of the most famous of these episodes resulted from his refusal to wear prison clothes and the subsequent smuggling into his prison cell of a tweed suit. It was the ability to transform into political organisation this sense of gladiatorial combat with the government which marked his management of the United

Irish League. Of equal importance was O'Brien's capacity to draw in supporters of the Parnellite faction from whom he and his colleagues had been alienated since the split over Parnell's continued leadership following the O'Shea divorce case. His own disinclination to break with Parnell had been well known, and this made many of Parnell's followers readier to rally to him than they would have done to any other anti-Parnellite. In this connection, his friendship and co-operation with the Parnellite Timothy Harrington played an important part in establishing the new League's viability, for Harrington did much to prepare the context within which a united popular organisation could emerge—even in the face of opposition from the official Parnellite leader, John Redmond.

After that of O'Brien, perhaps the most significant individual contribution in the crucial first two years of the new League was that of Michael Davitt, the founder in 1879 of the Land League. Davitt embarked on this reconstruction of what had already been achieved once before with extraordinary zest and enthusiasm, making available to O'Brien and the new body his knowledge of the people, especially in the west, who were crucial to its success, his memory of the methods by which organisational objectives had been achieved, and his exceptional talent in stirring again the commitment of the people who had followed him and worked for him in the previous mobilisation. This impressive and experienced leadership, quickly drawing on the support of other nationalists, both those with established records and many younger men newly emerging into active political life, was able largely to replicate the patterns of political action which had characterised the Land League.

The ready adoption of the methods of the past by those involved in the new League was in part the atavistic response of a people who well understood the roles they had already learnt to play in previous struggles; and the responses of landlord and, more especially, Tory leaders to this new agitation bore a similar instinctive mark, a determination to beat the 'troublesome blighters' or, in Salisbury's phrase, to make them 'take a licking'. There was a wider framework within which this return to tribalism was being expressed. Attitudes to empire and national power were changing in the last two decades of the nineteenth century. Even within the Liberal Party Gladstonian anti-imperialism was giving way to the new attitudes of those like

Lord Rosebery who imagined that the democracy of Britain could be won over by the polemics of jingoism. Within the Conservative Party—and not least within the new alliance formed out of Joseph Chamberlain's defection from Liberalism—there was a growing commitment to a strong and sustainable empire, an attitude both stimulated by and in turn further provoking the pretensions of other powerful nations to challenge the British imperial monopoly. This new obsession with both the power and the vulnerability of Britain unquestionably contributed to the abrasiveness with which Salisbury's government confronted signs of political restiveness in Ireland; indeed, much of the tone of that government's approach to Ireland had been set by Salisbury's own preoccupation with the nineteenth-century equivalent of the 'domino theory', as exemplified in his article 'Disintegration'.[33] The belief that any sign of weakness in response to Irish agitation would set a precedent for other parts of the Empire motivated a show of force in Ireland, which in turn helped to make the fear a self-fulfilling prophecy. It would certainly have been more rational to have accelerated the purchase policy to which the party was already committed than to suspend it in order to put on a demonstration of the superior power of empire.

The determination of the United Irish League to rise to the challenge of renewed coercion was also influenced by more than the wish to secure comprehensive land purchase. The development of that organisation coincided in time almost exactly with the course of the Boer War, and there was a powerful identification across a wide spectrum of Irish opinion with the Boers. Indeed, abhorrence of British actions in South Africa was one of the many factors which facilitated the rapid extension of the League from its origins in the economically deprived west to the rest of the country. The revelation of a more ugly face to imperialism served to reverse the more benign feelings towards Britain which had emerged in the context of Gladstonian Liberalism, and thus contributed to the willingness of many Irish people to lend wholehearted support to another phase of agitation. The government measures designed to repress this agitation fuelled the belief that, when it came to the point, the Irish land movement would be treated much as were other expressions of autonomy within the Empire. Thus, as with the Land League and the Plan of Campaign, the United Irish League came to express a sentiment which went far beyond the issue of the land on which it had been ostensibly based. The government would have better fulfilled its own purposes had it responded more speedily with the measures necessary to complete purchase, rather than let that issue provide a legitimate basis for continuing and growing agitation over the five years from 1898 to 1902, when the government eventually, as will be seen, was rescued by others from its own tardiness.

The nationalist political dimension to the United Irish League was more specifically exemplified in the reasons given by its founder for its establishment. At the time of the formation of the new organisation Irish nationalism was rent by the divisions which had emerged from the fall of Parnell in 1890–91, and—partly as a consequence of this political disaster—the whole edifice of constitutional nationalism which had emerged from the 'New Departures' of the late 1870s was at risk. The trauma associated with the fall of Parnell had driven many younger nationalists away from the whole idea of parliamentary action as then envisaged, and a consequence had been the strengthening of organisations which were attempting to create a new, more separatist nationalism, in some cases rebuilding the structures and purposes of the old Fenianism. The approaching centenary of the 1798 rebellion threatened to give a further fillip to these tendencies. The emergence of the United Irish League reversed, at least for a time, that drift, and William O'Brien later explained the purposes which drove its formation:

> The approach of the centenary of the insurrection of 1798, with its inspiring memories of the United Irishmen, furnished not only the idea but the happy title for a new organization which, drawing an irresistible strength and reality from the conditions in the west, would also throw open to the free air of a new national spirit those caverns and tabernacles of faction in which good men of all political persuasions had been suffocating for the previous eight years.[34]

The United Irish League was thus intended as a specifically political answer to the problems posed by the breakdown of nationalist organisation and unity, and in this sense there was less subterfuge about its underlying nationalist function than in either of the preceding agitations.

By the time the United Irish League had been formed in 1898 the lines on which the issue of agricultural land tenure in Ireland was to be resolved had largely been set, although there still remained much in detail to be achieved before that solution could be said to be fully implemented. That issue, however, had by now largely been lost within a much wider context. The interplay of land and nationality which had been a characteristic of Irish politics at least since the Independent Irish Party of the 1850s had now become a fusion of the two issues to a point where, in the world of practical politics, they were largely inseparable. As has been seen, this outcome had been steadily established not only through the conscious development of an interconnection by Irish leaders, especially Butt and Parnell, but also by the forms in which British governments, especially that of Lord Salisbury, had responded to the more specific demands for land reform. More important than these factors, however, had been the activation within the lives of ordinary people throughout Ireland of a political culture and related institutional structures within which land as a metaphor for nationality had become part of an instinctive understanding at a popular level. While many opponents of nationalism hoped—and many nationalists feared—that the disruption of the nationalist movement in the 1890s, and the emergence of a Conservative Party in Britain more subtle in its conduct of Irish affairs, portended a more ready acquiescence of Ireland into an increasingly anglicised culture and a framework of imperialism from which there were potential benefits for Irish people, it can be argued that a template had already been welded which probably predetermined otherwise. It is in a close examination of the cumulative experience of land agitation between 1879 and 1902 that such a view must be justified.

5

Land Agitation and a Proto-State

Each of the three agitations which collectively comprised the land war transcended in its purposes the issue out of which it took its rise, and was in the longer term equally important to the emergence of a nationalist consciousness as to the achievement of land reform. The impact of these agitations on the conscious-ness of the people involved in them can better be assessed by analysing them in terms of three attributes common to them all, and by relating these attributes to an emerging nationalist paradigm. If one looks beyond the immediate agrarian objective of each agitation, it is possible to characterise these common elements as: passive resistance as a means of consolidating community identification; an undermining of the credibility of British government actions and institutions in Ireland; and the creation of *de facto* Irish institutional structures, providing the basis effectively for an alternative system of government. This analysis is particularly informative in relation to the United Irish League, but a comparison of the three agitations suggests both many similarities and a significant cumulative effect in terms of instinctive community reactions. The strongest focus in what follows will be on the United Irish League, not only because it has been less written about than the others, but by reason of its importance as the most developed of the three agitations and the one which embodied the accumulation of experience from the other two.

In all three agitations the objective was to maintain the basic elements of an open, constitutional movement, adhering to the law and avoiding violence. This was not always easy to achieve, given the impact of agitation on the temper of the countryside and the cover it sometimes gave to individual acts of violence unrelated to the agitation. The rapid development of the Land League meant, moreover, that courses of action had not always been systematically mapped out by the leadership and were thus not able to be restrained within these central principles. The disillusionment of Anna Parnell with the strategy of the Land League demonstrated some of the problems involved in holding together, through a sense of common strategy, the more radical elements with the formal leadership of the movement. What was needed in these campaigns were methods strong enough to be noticed by government and aggressive enough to attract the enthusiasm and commitment of more advanced nationalists, who supplied so important a component of the muscle of the agitation and yet had to be persuaded of the superiority of non-violent means. This required a developed and active strategy based on a principle of passive resistance, and the agitations successively built this up through evolving practices, experiments and the lessons learnt of mistakes. By 1898 the management of the United Irish League was much more effective, and a more systematic and more widely understood strategy of passive resistance was able to operate.

As the principal architect of the Land League, Michael Davitt brought with him experience which no doubt played its own part as a model for elements of the Land League's strategy. One of the major influences on the development of Irish agrarian agitation was the experience of British trade unionism, and it was no coincidence that so much of Davitt's background had been formed within the environment of industrial, working-class England. Many of the elements of passive resistance which were developed within the three land agitations were partly derived from, and in turn reinforced and validated by, trade union practice. The parallel was an ingenious one, and peculiarly well suited to circumstances in Ireland, even though the relationship of landlord and tenant was rather different from that of employer and employee. The basic tactics of the Land League, linked to an explicit statement of the parallel with trade unionism, were outlined in August 1880 by Patrick Egan, the treasurer of the organisation:

> We, therefore, reiterate our call to the country to press forward with the organisation of the National Land League,

to refuse to pay all unjust rent, to take no farm from which a tenant has been evicted, to buy no cattle, crops, or other property seized for rent, and to form generally an industrial union against landlord monopoly.[1]

By the time of the United Irish League this parallel had become more explicit and central in the legitimation of the agitation. Boycotting of landgrabbers—those who took farms from which previous occupants had been evicted—was by 1899 being explicitly equated with the appeal 'trades unions make every week against blackleg labour'.[2] William O'Brien said he preferred to call such boycotting by 'its legal name of picketting'[3] and advocated that the basis of the fight with the government should be 'a policy of universal Trades-Union boycotting of landlords, landgrabbers and graziers'.[4] In the earlier agitations the use of the term 'rent strike' reflected a similar influence, although by the time of the United Irish League this particular tactic was avoided, the legacy of its ill-fated past being still present in the large number of evicted farmers from earlier agitations who had not yet been reinstated. But defence of intimidation and boycotting by reference to trade union practice provided a neat moral and quasi-legal justification for what was a central mechanism of passive resistance, comforting for participants in Ireland and providing an effective line of communication to many would-be sympathisers in Britain. It was such boycotting and intimidation which became the basis of the major demonstrations and protests around which each of the three agitations was shaped.

The most substantial advantage of a 'passive resistance' strategy is the dilemma in which it places government, for it creates a challenge to authority which can be confronted only by methods which often serve to facilitate the agitation. The forcible breaking up of non-violent public meetings by the police had the effect of increasing participation in the meetings and more general involvement in the agitation. The imprisonment of leaders likewise strengthened the very activities the government was endeavouring to prevent. Nor could the government, apparently, even win by more subtle approaches. By the time of the United Irish League they had learnt not to arrest more prominent leaders, but to 'pick off' lesser agitators; this led to extensive 'courting of arrest' by the leaders, thus demonstrating publicly the government's political cowardice in not acting against them. In other words, the issues on which agitation was focused and the degree of alienation from government in Ireland were such that any common action that was organised, non-violent and articulating the 'collectivity' of the majority population was bound to secure greater cohesion than the forces of government could combat.

This phenomenon has to be understood in terms more extended than late nineteenth-century agitation. One context is that of the residual defence of a 'moral economy' deriving from the instinctive forms of a traditional society. The work of E. P. Thompson on eighteenth and early nineteenth-century England demonstrates that these forces were potent elements of an old society, but—whereas in England they were largely destroyed by the impact of industrialisation, modern political economy and the political repression born of the French Revolution, or else transmuted into new forms like trade unionism—in Ireland a number of factors sustained them and gave them new form. These factors included the continuance of many aspects of a pre-modern rural economy, the continuing—and even accentuated—disjunction between religion and official institutions and ideologies, and—as has been seen—the role of the land issue in constantly re-legitimating the popular tradition. Thus, while Thomas Bartlett identifies 'an end to moral economy' in Ireland in the period of the French Revolution,[5] the land agitations of the late nineteenth century display the survival and re-expression of a still fundamental identification with a tradition of protest based on an alternative moral legitimacy.

In a fictional form, Anthony Trollope—a most perceptive observer of Irish social relationships—captured the essence of a concept of passive resistance endemic to Irish life. His first novel, *The Macdermots of Ballycloran*, was published in 1847; it is an exposition of the injustices inherent in a society in which too great a cleavage existed between an over-powerful ruling elite and the rest of society. The climax of that novel is the execution of Thady Macdermot, the tragic outcome of a manslaughter which could only be deemed murder in a system in which the political need of a vulnerable elite to demonstrate strength of will took precedence over the manifest demands of justice. On the morning of the execution, in a culture and time in which public hangings normally attracted a big crowd, the town of

Carrick-on-Shannon demonstrated its own sense of morality, the mobilisation of public opinion having been already arranged:

> Not one human form appeared before the gaol that morning. Not even a passenger crossed over the bridge from half-past seven till after eight, as from thence one might just catch a glimpse of the front of the prison. At the end of the bridge stood three or four men guarding the street, and cautioning those that came, that they could not pass by; and as their behests were quietly obeyed the police did not interfere with them. Among them were Joe Reynolds and Corney Dolan, and they did not leave their post till they were aware that the body of him to whom they showed this last respect had been removed. The shops were closed during the whole day . . . [6]

In this representation of public opinion we can see many of the elements which provide the basis of later agrarian agitation and explain the ready ability of the mass of the population to identify with its methods.

A strategy of passive resistance, drawing as it did on deeply ingrained habits of behaviour and a sense of moral legitimacy, needs in practice to be reinforced constantly by further evidences of its validity. This the government itself often supplied, either by inability to do otherwise or by misguided interventions. Thus, when from late 1900 onwards the United Irish League intensified its agitation, the new Chief Secretary, George Wyndham, determined—like his Conservative predecessors—that before there could be further reform he 'must enforce the law'.[7] He attempted to do this not through prosecution of individuals for direct breaches of the law—these were hard to find, Lord Salisbury having to admit to the king that 'the evidence of overt acts of illegality was very imperfect'[8]—but by the use of exceptional and draconian measures. These measures involved proclamation of meetings under special crimes acts and the use of a statute of the reign of Edward III which enabled courts, in these circumstances often temporary magistrates set up under the coercion laws, to imprison persons who refused to enter into recognisances to be of good behaviour. By 1902 these measures had been so extensively used that very large areas of Ireland had been brought under the general provisions of such exceptional laws. This helped to validate, both in Ireland and

Britain, the claim of the League to be acting in accord with the law, as normally understood, so further diminishing the government's chances of combating the unrest.

The use of the heavy hand of the law to repress boycotting and intimidation generally set the scene for escalating a situation in which the government appeared increasingly absurd in the eyes of those whom it wished to wean from these methods. One example of a meeting proclaimed by the government as illegal will serve to illustrate the dynamic by which this happened. A meeting was announced to be held at Cushlough, County Mayo, on 20 February 1898 for the formation of a branch of the United Irish League; the police secured a proclamation for its prohibition because they had discovered that it was to be held adjacent to the farm held by Peter Scahill, a land-grabber. The meeting had, in fact, only been announced the evening before, and these last-minute preparations had stimulated additional excitement in the locality. About 150 League members marched past Scahill's house, where they gave derisive cheers, but without attempting to hold a meeting. A force of police, variously estimated at between fifty and two hundred men, followed them, but still no attempt was made to hold a meeting. The police, not able to take any risks, were kept marching back and forth for seven or eight hours along a deserted stretch of road in bitterly cold weather, greatly to the amusement of a local population intent upon subjecting the police to ridicule. The occasion was subsequently depicted in the press—and in a House of Commons debate—as a successful hoax upon the police, the late announcement giving credence to the view that there had been no intention of holding a meeting but only of making the police look ridiculous.[9]

Also in the early months of the United Irish League William O'Brien, still famous in the popular mind for his jousting with government and exploitation of imprisonment during the Plan of Campaign, made most effective use of the government's unwillingness to embark on another such experience. In an angry speech in the House of Commons, the Chief Secretary—at that time Gerald Balfour—had accused O'Brien of using illegal language, thus enabling O'Brien to challenge him to prosecute. When the government explained that they had only newspaper reports, which were inadmissable as evidence in the courts, O'Brien offered to repeat the same language in the presence of police reporters.[10] In accordance with that offer, O'Brien wrote to Assistant Inspector-General Cameron a fortnight later, giving him notice

> that I intend addressing a meeting of the Central Council of the West Mayo United Irish League in Westport on Thursday 24 March, and that I will be happy to give an official reporter every facility for recording my observations on that occasion.[11]

Maximum publicity was given to this letter and to O'Brien's demand that he should be prosecuted; the intention, on O'Brien's part at least, was that prosecution should be averted, and in this he was successful. Records compiled by the police indicate that they were satisfied that O'Brien really did seek prosecution in order that the League might thereby 'get a fillip', but, as was so often the case in these situations, the police were losers whichever horse they backed. In terms of public perception, O'Brien had won the round, the government and police had been made to look ridiculous, and the League's credibility had been greatly strengthened. More importantly, both the effectiveness and the relative impunity of passive resistance as a technique had been further confirmed in the public consciousness.

Later in the same year, when internal divisions momentarily posed a threat to the progress of the new League, momentum was restored when the police proclaimed a meeting planned for 16 October in Ballinrobe, County Mayo. On the day of the meeting two hundred police were in Ballinrobe, and all the roads into the town were blocked by them. William O'Brien and Michael Davitt, who were to speak, were prevented from entering the town by the police, occasioning lively scenes in front of the crowd which soon gathered. While O'Brien kept the police distracted, Davitt slipped away—apparently retreating— and crossed Lough Mask in a boat, thus entering Ballinrobe by water and briefly addressing a crowd of 5,000 people before the police could break up the gathering. O'Brien retreated to nearby Partry, holding a meeting there, which was again suppressed by the police. The effect was that three meetings instead of one were held, and with much more excitement and theatre than the League could have achieved without police involvement.[12] In addition, Davitt—whose active involvement in the

League was vitally important to its future—was greatly encouraged, arriving back at the O'Briens' house delighted at 'his journey across the lake and his sudden apparition in Ballinrobe to the dismay of the baffled peelers'.[13] These activities were crucial to the consolidation and expansion of the organisation in this area.

The principal victims of these sorts of activities were usually the government, the police, landgrabbers and other 'offenders' from within the community. But the concept of passive resistance was a stimulus to other ingenious initiatives, some of which more directly affected the landlords. As L. P. Curtis has demonstrated, the Land League campaign to put a stop to foxhunting during 1881 and 1882 was a most effective form of protest once the organisation had been suppressed and its leaders imprisoned.[14] It also exemplified *par excellence* the technique of passive resistance. Its most distinctive features were the mobilisation of vast numbers of people and the opportunity for reliance on actions entirely and indisputably legal. On the day of the hunt the crowds—men, women and children—combed the territory over which the hunt was to ride and surrounded all the fields. If in the process the protesters caught a fox, that was a bonus; it was, after all, the land rented by the farmers over which the hunt rode. But the consequence of so noisy a scouring of the countryside was that not a single fox would be likely to be about when the hunt set out.

Once again, Anthony Trollope, writing in this instance at the time of the Land League, gives us in fictional terms the essence of this form of action. In his novel *The Land-leaguers* Tom Daly, the master of the Galway hounds, is determined that no Land Leaguer will disrupt the sport of which he is a passionate devotee. He goes on this occasion to the hunt with a pistol in his pocket, expecting that those known to be about to prevent the hunt would attempt physically to restrain him:

> To shoot a man who should lay hold of him or his horse, or endeavour to stop his horse, had seemed to him to be bare justice. But he had resolved that he would first give some spoken warning to the sinner. After that, God help the man; for he would find no help in Black Tom Daly.

The reality he found to be quite different from his expectations, and not at all amenable to his supposed remedy. He was told on arrival that there would be no hunting that day:

> 'Why should they not hunt ... ?', said Mr Daly, who, as he looked around, saw indeed ample cause why there should be no hunting. He had thought as he trotted along the road that some individual Land-leaguer would hold his horse by the rein and cause him to stop him in the performance of his duty; but there were two hundred footmen there roaming at will through the sacred precincts of the gorse, and Daly knew well that no fox could have remained there with such a crowd around him.

Kit Mooney, a baker turned Land Leaguer, taunts Daly, telling him: 'The boys are just taking their pleasure themselves . . . ':

> Begorra, you'll find 'em all out about the counthry, intirely, Mr Daly. They're out to make your honour welcome.... There is not a boy in the barony but what is out to bid yer honour welcome this morning.

The hounds were sent home, Trollope himself making a succinct summary of the effectiveness of this piece of passive resistance:

> It was useless to allow a hound to go into the covert of Moytubber. The crowd around was waiting anxiously to see the attempt made, so that they might enjoy their triumph. To watch Black Tom drawing Moytubber without a fox would be nuts to them; and then to follow the hounds on to the next covert, and to the next, with the same result, would afford them an ample day's amusement.[15]

In this fictional vignette we see nicely displayed a method of political action which neatly showed that authority could be asserted from below, rather than from above.

The experience of Lord Waterford, a landlord generally thought to be well liked by his tenants and also one of the most eminent and respected leaders of the hunt in Ireland,[16] shows that this form of passive—or perhaps not so passive—resistance took similar form in real life, as can be seen in this account of the episode which caused him to call off all hunting in County Waterford:

> On Thursday last . . . after hunting for some time Chapel bells began to ring and horns to blow, and over 200 men surround- ed the wood. Armed with pitchforks, sticks and stones [they] pelted the hounds and all of us. But whenever we went at them [they] ran away like curs, as they are. Several hounds were struck with pitchforks, and though I continued hunting for two hours after they began pelting us, at last I had to give in and left the wood pursued by a mob with stones, who we soon left behind, but all along the road were men and women armed with stones on the banks as we passed. We charged them and knocked them over with our whips whenever they tried to stop us and got through safe. I am told that the whole county came in after we left and that there was a mob of over 1000, which came from all directions.[17]

Maybe the hunt was not essential to the economic and political life of the country, but its importance is captured by Lord Waterford in his plaintive cry that:

> No one who has not had experience of what hunting is for a county can imagine what a fearful thing this is totally irrespec- tive of the sport which is destroyed. It will destroy all social relations and will take thousands and thousands of pounds out of the county besides throwing hundreds of people out of work.[18]

It was certainly a serious enough deprivation for Lord Waterford to take himself and his whole hunting establishment across to England for the duration.[19] It was testimony indeed to how well the Land League had scored its target.

A strategy of setting out to discredit in every possible way the credibility of British government and its agents and institutions in Ireland was the second of the major attributes evident in all three agitations. By the time of the United Irish League this was a most urgent task, for a number of factors had led to an improved status for the government in the eyes of many Irish people. The benign pattern of 'constructive Unionism' in

Ireland in the 1890s,[20] the apparent disintegration of nationalist effort as a result of the Parnell split, a new spirit of positive imperialism abroad in European thought generally, and increasing cultural and material anglicisation occurring in Ireland—all contributed to a lessening of hostility towards British rule. However, the new League was able very effectively to exploit a number of issues, helping to re-create within a relatively short time a situation in which British government and its agents and institutions in Ireland again became the subject of widespread ridicule and contempt.

The effectiveness of 'passive resistance' depends ultimately upon the moral strength of the position which it is being used to defend. It was on the land question itself that the British government made itself most vulnerable between 1898 and 1902 and provided the best opportunity for the new agitation to take the high moral ground. Given that all parties had by now accepted purchase as the solution to the land tenure problem, the government undermined its own credibility by allowing the issue to remain as a justification for protest and agitation. Even the official report of Wyndham's visit in 1901 to Clare Island—purchased through the agency of the Congested Districts Board—was so fulsome in its praise of purchase that it was reproduced in the League's own newspaper.[21] The government's position became even more untenable after T. W. Russell, a minister in the previous Salisbury government, refused office in order to mount a campaign among the Presbyterian tenant farmers of Ulster in support of the United Irish League's campaign for compulsory purchase. This represented a powerful endorsement, although solely on the issue of land, of the agitation in the rest of the country, and it left the government looking both negligent and ridiculous for giving priority to repressing agitation rather than proceeding with reform.

This failure on the part of government created a more favourable environment for the League to discredit its other actions. The use of coercion exposed to attack and ridicule that most sensitive of official institutions, the judicial process. In particular, attacks were mounted against the use of contempt of court and conspiracy charges when no specific breaches of the law could be established. Irish landlords who were also Privy Councillors and who signed proclamations under the Crimes Act had their integrity publicly impugned, in some cases being accused of having 'violated their oaths and prostituted their power as Privy Councillors in order to serve their own selfish class interests as landlords'.[22] The use of jury-packing was vigorously attacked, especially by P. A. McHugh, a member of parliament and a journalist, who was imprisoned for seditious libel in 1901— sentenced, appropriately, by Lord O'Brien, popularly known as 'Peter the Packer'. Defending himself later before a Commons privileges committee, McHugh admitted that his language had been extreme, but explained that he 'would not have used such language if the court was constituted in accordance with the ordinary law'.[23] 'Coercion courts' and all that they represented in terms of the status of Ireland within the larger British polity lent themselves most effectively to the League's goal of undermining the moral standing of British government in Ireland.

If judicial processes were being put to a use in Ireland which would have been totally unacceptable elsewhere in the United Kingdom, the same was also true of the police. In all the agitations every opportunity was taken to make them look ridiculous, ineffective and repressive; their attempts to prevent meetings taking place, as has been seen, greatly facilitated this. Capital was made out of the quasi-military character of the Royal Irish Constabulary, of its excessive cost, and of the practice of charging half the cost of extra police to the local ratepayers of disturbed districts. Police scandals and malpractices were also rigorously pursued, and demands were made for inquiries whenever such abuses were uncovered. These attacks, together with those on the judicial system, were an important part of the process by which the government was put on the defensive in relation to its actions against agrarian agitation.

What came to be known as the Mulrany forgery case served the United Irish League extremely well in its early development in 1898 and 1899. Sergeant James Sullivan of the Mulrany constabulary had been indited by John McHale, the president of the League, for the forgery of his signature to a letter instigating a conspiracy to commit an outrage. The discovery of this case had been greeted by William O'Brien in May 1898 as being 'as awkward for the police as the Pigott letters were for *The Times*'.[24] The ruling of the Westport bench of magistrates—a body well known for its hostility to nationalist agitators—that there was no case against Sullivan was overruled by the grand jury of the county of Mayo, which ordered true bills to be brought against

him on the three accounts of forgery, criminal libel and solicit-
ing persons to commit an outrage.[25] As a consequence of this
ruling, Sullivan was suspended from duty and the government
took over the prosecution from McHale,[26] but before this
happened O'Brien had already launched an appeal to raise
funds for the case against Sullivan, and this appeal was carefully
exploited as a means of drawing attention to the activities of the
League and the actions of the police against it. Newspapers such
as the *Cork Examiner* gave extensive coverage to the Sullivan case.
The Inspector-General of the RIC believed that the case was 'the
most useful weapon which Mr O'Brien has yet discovered', and
he conceded that 'the allegation, with such evidence as has been
made public, had been worked with exceptional skill by Mr
O'Brien in his Mayo campaign'.[27] The Sullivan case, prolonged
in the courts for many months and finally dismissed because of
the failure of a jury to reach agreement, proved an excellent
leitmotif to the steady expansion of the League's influence
throughout the country. It received widespread publicity when
Lord Coleridge, shocked at the way the matter had been dealt
with, raised it in debate in the House of Lords on 12 June 1899;[28]
on 22 June 1899 Davitt was responsible for its discussion in the
Commons.[29] But the real significance of the Sullivan forgery case
was that it provided a highly personalised focus for the conflict
between popular organisation and those who collaborated with
an alien government.

In the case of the United Irish League, it was the war in South
Africa which gave the best opportunity of all to expose what was
seen as the underlying moral flaws of British power, whether
elsewhere in the Empire or in Ireland. The Boer War created
among Irish nationalists a sense of exhilaration at what was the
first major setback for a very long time to the apparently impreg-
nable advance of British imperialism. This played a significant
part in checking the tendency to anglicisation in Ireland and
was, of course, especially significant in assisting the development
of a new nationalism around Arthur Griffith, Maud Gonne and
others in the Transvaal Committee—eventually to lead to the
political formation which became Sinn Féin. More immediately
significant was the hope raised among a much larger body of
nationalists that this shaking of British confidence might create
an environment in which they had a better chance of advancing
their cause, and this greatly assisted the United Irish League. In

March 1902 the cabinet advised the king that he should postpone his proposed visit to Ireland until after the war had ended,[30] thus marking another step in a diminishing status in Ireland for the institutions of British rule.

The story of Irish nationalism in the nineteenth century is in part the history of an aspiration to fill the void left in Irish life by the abolition of a separate Irish parliament at the time of the Union in 1801. That aspiration was the source of a rich theoretical tradition based, either explicitly or implicitly, on an assumption that the Act of Union had been invalid and on the desire to re-establish a moral and legitimate basis for a reassertion of a separate Irish political identity. It underlay O'Connell's concept of a Council of Three Hundred, advocated in 1843.[31] It was a theory which found its earliest developed expression in Charles Gavan Duffy's concept of 'an Authority', 'entitled to speak for the nation'. Duffy envisaged that, by seizing 'upon all the institutions which still remain to the country' and 'by employing the moral weight belonging to official position to give force and authority to the demand of the nation', the Irish people could give their claim to national independence both a focus and a legitimacy:

> When the representatives in Parliament had made the cause of Ireland plain to all men, and when the organization at home had been so successful as to raise these representatives to the undeniable position of the spokesmen of a nation, it would be their right and duty (as it is demonstrably within their power) to stop the entire business of Parliament till the constitution of Ireland was restored.[32]

Under Parnell, the parliamentary tactics described by Duffy were being put to the test, and the beginnings of Duffy's ideas for the creation of a basis of authority in Irish institutions and organisation had been laid through the model of land agitation begun with the Land League. 'League courts', as an alternative to official ones, emerged within the Land League, and this was another development in line with this strategy; similar courts also operated in the United Irish League. This concept of *de facto* government was subsequently to play a major role in the wresting of independence from Britain during the Anglo-Irish conflict of 1917–21, and the agrarian agitations of the late nineteenth century provide a crucial stage in the translation of the theory derived from Gavan Duffy and others into a practical political strategy understood and activated by the mass of the people, at least within crucial regions of the country.[33] Even those fiercely opposed, as W. E. Forster was, to such movements recognised this aspect of the conflict, as in his reference to 'the authority of the Queen's government, as distinguished from the govt of the Land League with its unwritten law'.[34]

The theory of alternative or *de facto* government was present in all three of the agitations under discussion, but became central to the strategy of the United Irish League, and the guiding principle by which that organisation determined its policy towards institutional structures. This can be seen in the development of three closely interrelated institutional concepts: the League itself as constituting an authority representative of the nation; the Irish Parliamentary Party as the embryo of a *de facto* national parliament; and local government as a statutory means of legitimating the popular will.

The organisational expression of the popular mobilisation of the people, in this case the United Irish League, came to be seen as incorporating the authority vested in all representative institutions in the country. This was the product of the application of a democratic principle to the theory of Duffy's 'Authority' and of the coalescence of the political role of the Land League with the electoral function of Parnell's National League. The democratic and representative structure of this new organisation was such as to substantiate the claim made of its first convention that it 'represented the Irish nation more fully than any Assemblage of Irishmen since the Union'.[35] John Redmond described its second convention as 'a parliament of the Irish people',[36] and this terminology—reflecting so well the basic concept of the organisation—continued in use, with subsequent conventions being referred to as 'the National Parliament of the Irish People'.[37]

Early in the history of the United Irish League this view of the authority of its organisation became evident in the development of the concept of 'League courts'. This was implicit in O'Brien's suggestion that, at the meetings of the League executive, anyone with a grievance should be 'invited to come and lay the facts before this tribunal of the delegates of the people'.[38] Glenisland in the Castlebar district provides an example of a branch which had been used in this way in Land League times. During October 1898 this branch summoned before it a number of people charged with breaches of the League 'laws'.[39] John Dooker of Glashnee, for example, had been called before the branch because his son was working for a grazier, P. Fahy. When Dooker refused to attend, an intimation was given to Mrs Dooker that she would be deprived of religious ministrations by the clergy unless her son left Fahy's employment; this threat was effective in leading her to withdraw her son from his job with Fahy.[40] 'League courts', either by the exercise of actual jurisdiction or by the cloak of legality they lent to intimidation, were to become a major feature of the later development of the United Irish League. More than 120 'cases', including some for 'contempt of court', were brought before branches of the United Irish League in the twelve months between October 1899 and October 1900.[41] What appeared to many observers as a lawless exercise of intimidation and blackmail was to those involved an application of the only type of control over their own society which the constitutional realities of their country allowed them.

The quasi-governmental role of the League was similarly revealed in the distribution by the United Irish League of relief funds to those suffering from economic distress in the west of Ireland. When in June 1898 Patrick Ford of the New York *Irish World* decided to distribute money from his newspaper's relief fund for the people affected by distress in the west of Ireland, he sent it to O'Brien.[42] Further money he sent to Davitt, which found its way back to O'Brien.[43] In all, between June and October, £500 was sent to O'Brien and Davitt by Ford for the relief of distress;[44] this money was distributed through the League, thereby enhancing its reputation in a role which would normally have belonged either to government or to public charities. O'Brien was quick to seize upon the significance of these funds as a means whereby his organisation was fulfilling responsibilities in Ireland which had been neglected by the British government. He contrasted relief distributed by the League, as an instrument of the Irish people, to the 'degradation of begging from an anti-Irish parliament' and from a charitable but alien public.[45] By making available such relief from Irish resources, the League was reducing the sense of dependence upon the British government and thereby helping to re-create the strength of national feeling and self-reliance which had been lacking since the fall of Parnell. The American provenance of much of this money further reinforced the dimension of autonomy.

The second of the concepts which underpinned the theory of alternative government, which informed much of the strategy of the land agitations, was that of the Irish Parliamentary Party as the national expression of elective representation. The party began to be seen differently in relation to the national organisation, symbolised in its abstention from the opening of parliament in December 1900 in order for its members to attend the national convention of the League being held in Dublin. There were also increasing expectations—not in the longer term fulfilled—that the organisation would exercise greater control of the party. Simultaneously with these changing attitudes about the role of the Irish Parliamentary Party, a new concept was being developed around Arthur Griffith's 'Hungarian parallel', whereby the parliamentary party would play a vital role in legitimating a national council in Dublin. This concept derived directly from Gavan Duffy's 'Authority', and nothing in it was incompatible with the direction in which the United Irish League was moving. Even the later doctrinaire attachment of Sinn Féin to abstention from parliament was not yet present in Griffith's ideas, and so there was still an opportunity for accommodation between his theory and the League's practices. In this concept great potential was present for broadening the base of the new nationalist organisation and accommodating a wider range of support.

In its early development, the leaders of the United Irish League had seen the parliamentary party at Westminster as evolving a new sense of purpose by integrating its strategies with the purposes of the League in Ireland. The fact that the main anti-Parnellite party was led by John Dillon, who was so closely associated with William O'Brien, augured well for such a relationship. But in practice it did not work that way. Dillon had become staunchly committed to assiduous attendance upon his parliamentary duties in a way which gave priority to issues as they arose at Westminster, whereas O'Brien wished the tumult of agitation and repression in Ireland to become the touchstone of relevance for the parliamentary party. In this sense the United Irish League was from the beginning predicated upon an assumption that political initiative would pass to it, and that the parliamentary party would be shaped by popular agitation and in turn become part of the means of legitimating a source of authority firmly based in Ireland. When the parliamentarians failed to co-operate in this strategy, the League changed its tactic and by the middle of 1899 had adopted a policy of a 'clean sweep' of the existing parliamentary representation, aimed at replacing it with a party largely consisting of new men drawn from the active ranks of League agitators and more amenable to its discipline and purposes. This policy was aborted by the premature reunion of the parliamentary factions in January 1900,[46] but the aspiration which had lain behind it demonstrated a clear view of a role for the parliamentary party as part of a wider movement which embodied the concept of alternative government.

The third of these concepts was that of local government bodies, sustaining national policy and strategy and giving legitimacy to them through their statutory authority. The basis for this strategy had been set during the time of the Land League, with the wresting of control of poor law boards of guardians from the landed elite.[47] Using, although in a more measured way, the power which the Land League had learnt it could wield, the United Irish League had added to that power a legitimacy derived through the elected representatives of the people and the authority conferred by statute on county, borough and district councils throughout Ireland, by now very largely amenable to the influence of the new League as a consequence of the Local Government (Ireland) Act of 1898. This proved the most substantial basis for the development of the League's strategy of using Irish institutions to give authority and legitimacy to its objectives and strategies. Despite problems with the Local Government Act, councils found ways of effectively 'affiliating' with the League and officially endorsing and validating its policies and actions. There was also conflict between some county councils and the high sheriffs and the government over the use for political purposes of courthouses which had come under the physical control of county councils, thus creating dramatic conflicts between rival legitimacies. Significantly, many councils attempted to fly what were described as Irish flags from courthouses, much to the chagrin of unionists,[48] but thereby demonstrating the nationalist thrust with which these institutions were being managed.

During the United Irish League period this role for local government was pursued quite explicitly in the public statements of its leaders. William O'Brien had from the beginning welcomed with enthusiasm the innovation of democratic control of local government in Ireland. He believed that if every county in Ireland had an organisation comparable with that of the United Irish League in Mayo, then '30 of the County Councils would be simply 30 Irish Parliaments.'[49] The energies of the League were applied to achieving such a result, the significance of which in terms of popular self-government were fully apparent to O'Brien, who pointed out to a correspondent that one of the motives for re-establishing popular organisation in Ireland was that the Local Government Act, 'for the first time since the Norman invasion, places vast departments of local government in the hands of the native race, with the certainty that the powers at present given can be made the means of winning still wider ones'.[50] The introduction of democratically elected local councils in Ireland brought control of local government into the hands of nationalists, but it also enormously strengthened the claim of the League to constitute an alternative government. It is significant, for example, that one of its leaders in County Tipperary should have conceived the idea that urban and district councils should form themselves into actual branches of the League.[51] In fact councils controlled by the League applied themselves wherever possible to asserting their own authority as national representatives of the Irish people and to increasing the links between councils and the organisation. This was later to lead to considerable conflict with the Local Government Board and with the government, but by establishing such a system of local government the British government had itself provided its opponents with a powerful alternative authority much more in accord with the will of the people than government from Westminster could ever be. County councils increasingly gave official expression to sentiments against land-lordism, in favour of national independence, in support of the Boer cause in South Africa, and along other lines hostile to British rule in general and to Tory government in particular. In this way the League used its dominance of local councils as a vindication of its claim to be the national authority to which the Irish people owed allegiance.

This analysis of developments in the agitations which

comprised the land war demonstrates the extent to which agrarian purposes became largely indistinguishable from nationalist ones, submerged together within actions and practices which were the accumulation of experiences constituting in reality a statement of nationality. Perhaps nowhere is that so evident as in the way that reluctant elements within the community were drawn inexorably into these agitations despite initial disinclination to become involved. In isolating those who violated the community's land code, a distinction was drawn along a line which demarcated those who wished to be of the 'collective' and those who did not. At its beginning, while the focus was more directly upon the land issue out of which it arose, each agitation most resembled an economic or trade union combination. But as the organisation expanded, its function became a different one, namely the statement of a wider social unity, a means of defining a community identity, an expression of a sense of national distinctiveness. The land question acted as a catalyst to the expression of sentiments and emotions of a more complex kind. This was a process which excluded as well as included, although virtually no category of person was excluded as of necessity. There were two factors which normally determined the side of the line on which individuals were most likely to stand: their relationship to the land, and their religious affiliation. But not even these were immutable in their effect, as the case of Parnell himself shows, although they were normally crucial. For those whose underlying identity was unambiguous, this kind of agitation acted as a powerful magnet in drawing even the most reluctant into cooperation.

Actions specifically related to land agitation gave rise to a type of public activity which assumed a national character. In particular, the increasing involvement of the police helped to bring to the surface a latent national feeling which gave added impetus to the movement. Most notably, once the conflict between tenants on the one hand and landlords, landgrabbers and graziers on the other had been transformed into a struggle between the people and the government, more extreme nationalists, especially the Fenians, were unable any longer to hold back. In the Land League, Davitt had played a key role in securing Fenian support,[52] and his active involvement in organising the United Irish League enabled him to reactivate those old connections. In the Land League, many Fenians joined in order to advance their own particular aspirations and to some extent used the League as a cover for more characteristic activities, including building up their arms arsenal.[53] Donald Jordan suggests that Davitt was himself implicated in this, and he explains the apparent contradiction in terms of the need to balance both constitutional and revolutionary positions in order to secure 'the impetus needed to expand the land movement during the winter of great distress'.[54] In the United Irish League, the existing model provided by the Land League enabled Fenians to accept more readily in its own terms the new agitation, and they provided an important element of hard work and commitment of a more organisational kind; perhaps advancing years for many of them assisted this change of approach. James Daly of Castlebar, an active if ultimately disenchanted Land Leaguer,[55] was not a Fenian, but he shared with them a deep distrust of national politicians and had in 1898 attached himself to the movement for commemorating the centenary of the 1798 rebellion and was attempting to remain aloof from the United Irish League. He could not, however, remain indifferent to a new agrarian agitation, for—like many other nationalists in the west of Ireland—he could not afford to be identified too completely with political action which was disembodied from the realities of rural society. Once he had failed in his attempts to manipulate the new organisation so that he could retain his autonomy from it, he seized the first available opportunity to support it unconditionally.[56] Daly's position was reflected among large sections of the politically more advanced nationalists of the west. Demonstrations, clashes with the police, intimidatory processions and deputations and boycotting all had an immediate and dramatic impact with which the more romantic celebration of battles long ago or receptions for Irish-American tourists associated with the 1798 centenary could not compete.

While for the Catholic clergy both the issues of land and nationality were ones with which there were varying degrees of identification, both ecclesiastical discipline and more general apprehension about agitational forms of politics ensured that many of the clergy, especially those more senior and from more socially elite backgrounds, initially opposed any resurgent agrarian agitation. Again taking the United Irish League as an example, the great bulk of the clergy in west Mayo were initially hostile to its establishment and growth.[57] As the League extended its influence in the community, however, the clergy faced the dilemma that their failure to participate in the agitation undermined their status and authority with their congregations. Moreover, once the League had established its viability, many of the priests recognised that it was only by giving their support and participating in the League's affairs that they could have a moderating influence on its actions. The increasing involvement of Fenians highlighted this pressure, and consequently a steady accretion of clerical support for the agitation occurred. Likewise, the attitude of the church's hierarchy changed as the agitation became more successful. Archbishop McEvilly of Tuam had been opposed to agrarian agitation and had discouraged his clergy from involving themselves in the United Irish League. By September 1898, however, he had begun writing to clergy opposed to the League directing them to withdraw their opposition, on the grounds that the organisation had been so warmly taken up by the people that clerical opposition would lead to friction between priests and people.[58] This followed very closely the pattern of the Land League, when a previous Archbishop of Tuam, the famous MacHale, had opposed the early meetings of the League, but the clergy had soon identified themselves with it, first attempting to secure support for more Catholic issues but, when refused, unconditionally.[59]

In a series of volumes on the Catholic church in Ireland, Emmet Larkin has developed the hypothesis that what came into existence with Parnell's rise to supremacy was a *de facto* Irish state; he writes that 'In making the Irish State real between 1878 and 1886, Parnell had architected a concordat between the Irish Church and the Irish Party.'[60] While his concentration on the high politics of the Irish church, the Vatican, and British and Irish political leadership does not provide an adequate basis for establishing this theory, it is unquestionably borne out by the study of agrarian agitation, which shows not so much that a 'concordat' was established at the top of the ecclesiastical and political hierarchies, but that a very real *de facto* state existed in the consciousness of the population, exemplified in its most developed form in the agrarian agitations of the late nineteenth century. Indeed, as the example of Archbishop McEvilly demonstrates, senior ecclesiastics were drawn by the force of popular opinion to lend the church's authority to the reality of what was happening in the country. What had been created out of these agitations was a structure of alternative government legitimated in a most significant way by the countenance of the church, an endorsement initiated at the level at which it had most impact, that of the parishes. In a sense, the issue of land was purely incidental, the occasion from which this essentially nationalist edifice arose.

Graziers, an expanding category of landholders in Ireland in the second half of the nineteenth century, stood in a unique position in relation to the traditional divide between landlord and tenant. Taking advantage of the increasingly profitable trade in livestock in the period following the Great Famine, they took up large areas of grassland, often on eleven-month tenancies, thus removing it from the available market in land for tillage farming. Only those with capital could take advantage of these opportunities, for the grazing lands had to be stocked. Many of the graziers were, therefore, also town tradespeople. Occupying land on a large scale, enjoying relative affluence and able to elevate their own and their family's social status, they became more and more closely identified with the landlords, for whom they were an economic boon on account of their willingness to pay high rents with minimal security. In many cases they were coming to assume the status of a new rural elite, but they were doing so at the cost of the enmity of the tenant farmers, whom they were undercutting in the market for land. In each of the great land agitations they were the object of hostility, and yet paradoxically they were often supporters and even leaders of these organisations.[61] Why did they occupy so ambivalent a position?

Graziers were an overlapping category with those engaged in business and trade in the towns, and their role in relationship to agrarian agitation needs to be understood partly in that context. A significant component of the local leadership of agrarian agitations consisted of traders and other business leaders in the towns—publicans, shopkeepers, dealers in agricultural supplies, newspaper proprietors—and there have been various theories as to what it was that attached these interests to the cause of the tenant farmers. One theory is that agrarian agitation was used by traders against their competitors, and that involvement in agitation enabled a shopkeeper to win customers on the basis of his political alignment; given that farmers were invariably and inevitably in debt to their suppliers, this enabled townspeople to exploit the farmers' issues for their own economic and political advantage. In this view, the connection between traders and farmers within the agitation was a matter of 'debt bondage'; it was more a question 'of predators and prey than of townsmen and countrymen'.[62] Another analysis doubts so rigid an economic nexus and sees instead an important social and political role attaching to the town tradespeople which naturally led them to be mediators for the farmers. Their establishments—pubs, shops and so forth—were meeting-places for a large cross-section of the population, and they themselves were more mobile than the farmers within the larger national society. They also had the time and the facilities for the work of politics. The tradespeople were, therefore, a natural link between local farmer aspirations and political and national leadership; 'the world of the shop and the world of the farm intersected'.[63] Yet another view sees clear regional distinctions as important in determining these relationships. Donald Jordan bases his analysis of County Mayo politics on a distinction between a 'core' region comprising the more prosperous parts of the county, where graziers, traders and 'strong farmers' were dominant, and a dependent 'periphery' of impoverished tenant farmers.[64]

Perhaps the most significant social and economic division bridged by the agrarian agitations of the late nineteenth century was within the tenant farmer category itself. As has been seen, the difference in position and outlook between the prosperous tenant farmers of the eastern side of the country and the impoverished tenants of the poor western side was enormous. And yet ultimately the major agrarian agitations came to encompass both. While in the Plan of Campaign the primary focus on rent reductions created a different frame of reference, both the other agitations arose immediately out of the economic distress of the poorer tenants in the west. In both cases the agitation addressed not only the issue of tenure, but questions of economic viability in the poorer regions. In both the Land League and the United Irish League it was this arousing of the commitment of the impoverished tenant farmers around the issue of redistribution of land as well as tenure reform which provided the basis for what turned out to be a national movement with rather different priorities. In this process the 'strong' farmers, both in the areas in which the agitation originated and elsewhere in the country, took up the land reform component of the initial agitation, exploited the social and humanitarian issues on which the agitation had established a wider sympathy, and diverted the agitation into new channels with new directions. These directions were ones in which the twin issues of land and nationality most strongly reinforced each other. It was among the more prosperous farmers that the desire to own their land arose as much from social as economic aspirations, and the desire for Home Rule was an extension of the wider cultural demand by a new, relatively wealthy, largely Catholic elite to displace the old Protestant ascendancy in land and government. Recognition of the legitimacy of this emergent class, linked as it often was socially and politically with the new Catholic middle-class elite in the cities, lay at the heart of the convergence of the land reform movement and the nationalist movement. The graziers, as well as many of the rural town tradespeople, were part of this wider thrust for national social and political supremacy. The smaller farmers in the west—like what remained of the agricultural labourer class[65]—were drawn inexorably into this national consensus, in which a continuum of cultural factors and a wider sense of identity served to subordinate the economic issues which had defined the original agitation. As Paul Bew has shown, this suppression of the aspirations of the poorer farmers remains a common feature of Irish agrarian politics from the Land League through to the 1940s.[66]

Whatever view is taken of what held these diverse classes and interests together within the agitations which comprised the Irish land war, there are four things which stand out preeminently. First, the various agrarian organisations formed in the last quarter of the nineteenth century encompassed within them tenant farmers, both poor and 'strong', merchants and other tradepeople, agricultural labourers, and even the graziers against whom these bodies were in part formed. Secondly, there were clearly economic interests and interdependencies which consolidated these alliances. Thirdly, all these disparate classes were held together in common identification with what might broadly be called a Catholic cultural and religious community. Fourthly, it can be fairly firmly generalised that the landed

Protestant ascendancy were demarcated outside this alliance, and that the collective force brought together was partly intended to marginalise—and ultimately to exclude—this category, economically, culturally and politically. There was, in other words, a close coincidence of economic, political and cultural affinity within these agitations, and this can best be understood in nationalist terms. The persistence of the grievance over land tenure had served to give organisational strength and ideological direction to a phenomenon which had its roots in a pervasive and—by the second half of the nine-teenth century—largely intractable alienation from the system of political and economic management under which Ireland was governed. Many of the apparent contradictions that have been observed in the role of various classes in agrarian agitation can perhaps be accommodated within the single observation that the landlords had become—or, as Dr Vaughan would put it, had made themselves—expendable. Insofar as one of the triggers of agitation was the demand for rent reductions, it might be argued that farmers (both rich and poor) and shopkeepers, debtors and creditors, priests and parishioners, and even graziers, could all gain from a redistribution of the economic cake in which the landlords' share was reduced. In an economic recession, in particular, the landlord became a rival creditor to other interests more integrally connected in social and cultural terms. As Professor Clark has shown, after the Famine it is the division between landlords and others which becomes the major cleavage in Irish rural society, and once this happened, 'class divisions within the Irish agrarian population were not obstacles to collective mobilisation, but instead were the very basis on which agrarian collective action was built'.[67] It is a cleavage in which economics is powerfully reinforced by ethnic, religious and cultural identities.

Indeed, combining the character and practices of these agita-tions with the breadth of this alliance of diverse economic groupings, a *de facto* Irish state can be identified as already in operation over a wide cross-section of the society. Through all the diverse historiographical journeyings of recent scholarship, the most persuasive conclusion is that the crucial element in late nineteenth-century agitation was that of political leadership. As Dr Vaughan concludes in relation to the agrarian explosion of the 1870s, 'The one incontestable fact that emerges is that 1879 was the only year of serious agricultural depression that found a united and powerful political leadership ready to exploit agrarian discontent.'[68] It was the exigencies of the national political situation after the defeat of Home Rule in 1886 that drove a cohort of Parnell's most talented colleagues back to the agrarian dynamics of the Plan of Campaign. In 1898 it was William O'Brien, with the help again of a small knot of national political leaders, who transformed spasmodic agrarian outrage into a coherent organisation, with the overt and calculated intention of turning it to the service of the national cause. The *de facto* state existed in large part because, whatever the particular aspirations of classes and groups within the society, there was a common point of reference to which ultimately they all owed their allegiance, and that was provided by political leadership, whether in the symbolised form of the 'uncrowned king' or in a more general commitment to a cause which after 1879 came to be embodied in a cadre of leaders. Agrarian grievances were the fabric out of which skilled political leaders crafted an entity in which diversity of interest was consolidated into strong institutional form. But so intertwined by now was the question of nationality with that of land that settlement of the latter—already by the end of the century near to achievement—would inevitably raise major and far-reaching questions about the shape and direction of the former.

6

'Chancing an Arm'

Exhibited in St Patrick's Cathedral, Dublin, is a door through which a rectangular hole is cut. This hole, in what was once the door of the cathedral's chapter house, was that 'pierced at a trice' in 1492 by the Deputy Lieutenant of Ireland, the Earl of Kildare in order to reassure the Earl of Ormond, who had locked himself in the chapter house against the angry citizens of Dublin who supported the Geraldine interest, that he intended him no harm and 'to the end both the Erles should have shaken hands, and bee reconciled':

> But Ormond surmising that this drift was entended for some further treacherie, that if he woulde stretch out his hand, it had been percase chopt off, refused that proffer, until Kildare strecht in his hand to him, and then the dore was opened, they both embraced, the storme appeased, and all their quarrels for that present, rather discontinued than ended.[1]

The sting in the tail of Stanihurst's account of the reconciliation of the two earls is a precaution against any too sweeping deduction from this momentary lull in the long conflict between the FitzGeralds and the Butlers, but the story has a romantic appeal for those in Ireland who hope for national reconciliation—to which aspiration, indeed, this display and its inscription in St Patrick's attests. The real moral of the story, however, is the role of mutual interest, rather than idealism, in bringing about such reconciliation.

In September 1902 Captain John Shawe-Taylor, the son of a County Galway landlord, called for a conference between the

representatives of Irish landlords and tenants to settle the long
dispute over land tenure. He was neither a leader nor an official
representative of any party or class, but—as one of the official
leaders of landlordism, Lord Barrymore, described him—'a
wholly irresponsible gentleman'.[2] His gesture, therefore, carried
none of the weight of that of the Earl of Kildare towards his
adversary. It was, nonetheless, given a retrospective authority
through endorsement by fellow-landlords against the wishes of
their official leaders and by the eventual success of his efforts.
His action was, in fact, to mark the beginning of the final phase
in the abolition of Irish landlordism, and was thus momentous
in its significance. This initiative, grounded like that of the Earl
of Kildare in self-interest, bore some of the same gallantry of
style. Moreover, it was an appeal, not only for a solution to a particular economic and social problem, but to a sense of common
nationality rare at this time in the attitude of Irish landlords
towards their nationalist compatriots. Shawe-Taylor, chancing
not only his arm, thrust his whole person into the Capel Street
offices of the United Irish League and the *Irish People*, and put
his case in these terms:

> We don't see one another; we don't understand one another;
> we abuse and curse one another; and while we thus divert
> ourselves Ireland goes down.[3]

His commitment, persistence and very considerable political
acumen paid off, and his gesture led not only to the final
transfer of landownership in Ireland from the landlords to the
tenants, but also provided a basis for a reorientation in Irish
politics.

Unlike the Earl of Kildare's, Shawe-Taylor's antagonist was
not besieged in any chapter house. In fact, given the effects of
twenty years of agitation and tenant right legislation, it could be
said that the tables were turned the other way. Desirous of an
escape from a vicious circle in which they were caught between
mounting debt and diminishing control over their principal
resource, most landlords were readily attracted to Shawe-
Taylor's overture. At stake they saw not only their economic
interests, but their future influence and identity within their
country. Likewise for tenant farmers and nationalists, the
moment was a critical one. Now that a continuing capacity for

agitation had been demonstrated through four years of sustained action by the United Irish League, a tangible basis existed for negotiation. To refuse the proffered hand would be to put at risk both moral and tactical advantage, delay for the tenant farmers the realisation of their major goal, and possibly undermine the organisational basis on which nationalism largely depended. Moreover, a number of nationalist leaders were aware of the difficulties of sustaining traditional agitation, and they recognised that the moment was opportune, and perhaps unique, for suing for peace with the landlords. To this conjunction between the interests of landlords and tenants must be added the failure of the strategy pursued by the Chief Secretary, George Wyndham. Having used coercion over the preceding two years as a sop to the extreme wing of unionism, and to buy time to devise a new land bill, he now faced the collapse of his plans. His proposed bill had been dropped, and as a consequence he had been forced to intensify coercion, no longer to secure time but as a mask to cover his policy bankruptcy. The last hope of his Chief Secretaryship lay in the prospect of an agreed solution between the Irish parties to the dispute, and his growing perspicacity as to the limits of English wisdom in solving Irish problems disposed him towards generosity in facilitating such an agreement.

Despite initial negative reactions, Shawe-Taylor secured the conference for which he had called. The nationalist decision to co-operate was attributed by William O'Brien to Wyndham's remark in a published letter that 'Any conference is a step in the right direction':

Here was a declaration which lifted Captain Shawe-Taylor's proposal from the insignificance of an irresponsible newspaper squib to the proportions of a national event of the first magnitude.[4]

The official leaders of the landlords, however, still refused to countenance the conference, and the individual landlords named by Shawe-Taylor as representatives declined to participate. However, Shawe-Taylor persisted and was eventually to secure wider landlord support for a conference. Often depicted as an innocent catalyst of these events, Shawe-Taylor was privately backed by Wyndham, and both landlord and nationalist leaders were aware of this. A letter from Shawe-Taylor to O'Brien, written after Wyndham's declaration of support but before the nationalist leaders had publicly agreed to participate, made two significant revelations. First, it revealed that Wyndham's letter had been written at Shawe-Taylor's instigation. Hearing that the Chief Secretary was to stay with Lord Barrymore, Shawe-Taylor had sought an interview to stress the importance of Barrymore's support for the conference. Barrymore was not persuaded, but Wyndham's declaration in favour of a conference was the result of the interview. The second, and more important, aspect of Shawe-Taylor's letter was the revelation made to O'Brien of views expressed by Wyndham, who had told Shawe-Taylor that:

(1) Now was the time for a Conference before Parliament met, as it would strengthen his hands in squeezing the Treasury.
(2) That he believed Parliament would do a big thing now if they saw any prospect of an agreement.
(3) That British credit was unlimited.
(4) That the nearer we [landlords and tenants] were to one another, the more he could do.[5]

Presumably similar information had become available to Lord Castletown, who announced in the press that he was 'informed on fairly good authority that both sides in Great Britain are prepared to help a settlement of the land question'.[6] The acceptance by nationalist leaders of the suggestion of a conference with landlords was based on a recognition that, as a result of the agitation of the preceding years, the government and the landlords were both in a mood which could easily be exploited in the interests of a settlement.

The means by which the Land Conference was brought about and the spirit and methods which guided its course are themselves informative, both in relation to the individuals involved and to the basis on which agreement was reached. Once the initial public manoeuvres—in which John Shawe-Taylor and William O'Brien played the principal parts—were over, the crucial roles behind the scenes were played by a triumvirate consisting of Lord Mayo, Timothy Harrington and Lord Dunraven. In particular, Lord Mayo was associated with a sustained attack on the bastions of landlord leadership. At the Landowners' Convention—the official organisation of landlordism—held on 10 October 1902 the idea of a conference was rejected, an action condemned by Lord Mayo and others on the grounds that the representatives to that meeting had been selected from the counties before the conference idea had been publicly mooted.[7] He then joined with a small group of other landlords, including Shawe-Taylor, to form a Provisional Committee to test the sentiment of landlords more generally.[8] Once the plebiscite organised by the Provisional Committee had shown a substantial majority of respondents in favour of a conference, the committee reconstituted itself as the Land Conference Committee and proceeded with the detailed work towards the convening of a conference.[9]

In taking this course, Lord Mayo had set himself hard against the wishes of the Landowners' Convention committee, of which he was himself a member. Their objections to his actions were characterised in a long response from their secretary, G. de L. Willis. Petulant and aggressive in tone and defensive in substance, this reply exemplifies the extent of the divide which was emerging in Irish landlordism. Willis reiterated that the Convention was opposed to any conference which was not preceded by the exclusion of compulsory purchase as an option—a condition which would have ruled out any prospect of tenant participation. He attacked 'the disruptive action of your lordship's committee', which was deemed both to have created the impression that the landlords were divided and to have, in some mysterious way, betrayed the interests of smaller landlords, whom the Landowners' Convention, it was claimed, had always attached the greatest importance to defending. The letter attacked the credibility of the poll taken by the committee, on the basis that the 1,128 landlords who voted in favour of holding a conference, while being a two-thirds majority of respondents, were a minority of the total 13,000 Irish landlords. Finally, in a comment on the fact that Lord Mayo had conceded the right of the Irish Parliamentary Party to nominate the tenant representatives to the conference, Willis conveyed the view of his committee that it was

unfortunate that a body so generally and deservedly discredited as the Irish Parliamentary Party, representing the United

Irish League, should be to any extent reinstated in public opinion by an invitation from a body of Irish noblemen and gentlemen to nominate representatives to a joint Conference.[10]

This letter the committee of the Landowners' Convention then sent to the press for publication, thus prompting from The O'Conor Don—a member of the Convention committee absent from the meeting which had approved the views expressed but himself also opposed to the conference proposal—to dissociate himself from the letter and to comment that by it the Convention committee had themselves 'retarded if they have not destroyed that unity of action to which they themselves attach so much importance'.[11]

While attacking the arrogance of the committee of the Landowners' Convention, Lord Mayo had gently nursed the susceptibilities of his fellow-landlords. Not wanting to take their views for granted, his committee had followed up the plebiscite on the principle of a conference with a voting paper enabling landlords to express their own views as to who their four representatives should be. This ballot paper was sent not only to those landlords who had voted 'yes' in the plebiscite, but also to those who had failed to respond. The paper gave ten names from which the landlords could choose, and provided four spaces for other names if they were preferred.[12] It was on this basis that the four landlord nominees for the conference, Lords Dunraven and Mayo, Colonel Nugent Everard and Colonel Hutcheson Poë, were chosen, except that the last-named was substituted as a representative specifically of northern landlords when Thomas Sinclair declined to accept his election.[13] This consideration for the views of ordinary landlords had been reinforced by other developments. The publication of the names of landlords who had voted 'yes' in the plebiscite must have reassured many landlords of the respectability and political sophistication of the proponents of a conference. The publication by the Landowners' Convention of Willis's letter of 28 November had given Lord Mayo the opportunity of publicly responding, enabling him to disregard all the points made in the letter except the accusation that a conference would put at risk the interests of smaller landowners:

We repudiate this statement in the strongest terms, being convinced that the policy we further is essential for the salvation of the smaller landowners, while it may be a matter of comparative unimportance to the wealthier landowners, whose incomes are not entirely derived from landed property in Ireland.[14]

The Land Conference Committee was quick to publicise information which helped to establish support for the conference idea, including the unanimous vote of Queen's County Council in favour of a land conference and, perhaps of special significance, the 'Extract from a Newspaper that the Tenants' Organisation would put no obstacle in the way of Hunting in Ireland pending the coming Conference'.[15] The committee, which had as a small working group undertaken the detailed process of bringing about landlord support for a conference, was now enlarged in its membership to help give a sense of widening support for its efforts.[16] All this added up to a shrewd political campaign to make landlords more amenable to the proposed conference, and in this Lord Mayo unquestionably played the key role.

The most venomous part of the Landowners' Convention's attack on Lord Mayo had been due to his support of the right of the Irish Parliamentary Party to nominate the tenant representatives to a conference; but in this there had been a carefully developed strategy in which the Irish Nationalist MP and current Lord Mayor of Dublin, Timothy Harrington, had played a crucial role. At a speech at a Bankers' Institute function on 17 November attended by Harrington, Lord Mayo had made the 'observation that the tenants were entitled to the same freedom in electing their representatives as the landlords'.[17] In an atmosphere in which some landlords had been attempting to reassert semi-feudal attitudes by claiming the right to dictate how tenants representatives should be chosen, Harrington was quick to recognise that Lord Mayo's tune was a different one. He took the initiative in writing to him to say so, and to put his own views about the responsibilities of the parliamentary party and other matters associated with a land conference. While recognising that Harrington had been expressing personal views, Lord Mayo quickly took up this opening to secure reassurance on the one point about tenant representation on which landlords did have a legitimate concern if selection was to be in the hands of the Nationalist Party:

I am asked by the Provisional Committee which was brought together for the purpose of ascertaining the feelings of the Irish Landlords on the subject of a Conference, to state that they take it for granted that the Irish Parliamentary Party, in nominating the Tenants' representatives, will make due provision for the adequate representation of the Northern Constituencies.
Can you satisfy me on this point?[18]

Being equally careful in his choice of words, Harrington replied that he had not the opportunity of consulting his colleagues, 'but, you may fully rely upon my assurance that the Irish representatives will take very good care in any delegation they form to have the views of Ulster fully represented'.[19] This reply was annotated by Mayo: 'I think this will do but after Wed. Nov. 19 we shall know for certain as he will see his colleagues.'[20] In this subtle exchange the beginning had been created of a trust which was to persist through the conference proceedings and which indicated the extent to which key individuals were bridging the great tribal chasm which others were so crudely seeking to preserve. It also demonstrated how large mountains could be diminished into molehills through resort by individuals to quiet and unconventional modes of communication. In the end the Irish Parliamentary Party simply endorsed the tenant team nominated by Shawe-Taylor in his original call for a conference back in September, thus neatly sidestepping any formal choice of a Unionist by the Nationalist Party, but leaving in place T. W. Russell, the leader of the predominantly Presbyterian and Unionist Ulster tenant farmers—the other three being William O'Brien, John Redmond and Harrington himself.

Once the political preparation of the landlord class for a conference receded and the negotiations themselves commenced, the role of Harrington, still largely covert, continued to be of major importance, while that of Mayo gave way to the more public function of Dunraven. Once again, historic class and ethnic divisions quickly dissolved in a close working relationship. The correspondence between Harrington and Dunraven during the course of the conference makes apparent the basis of the axis between the two men. Dunraven's especial talent was for taking the technical questions raised in relation to land purchase and expressing them in language which took cognisance of the complex political environment into which the conference's report would be thrust. Harrington likewise had a deep understanding of the relevant technical issues, a similar sensitivity to the importance of language, but also something which Dunraven valued greatly—the skills and understanding of a talented practitioner of the law. As Dunraven put it, in proposing that he and Harrington be deputed to settle some of the verbal intricacies of the conference's draft report:

> I suggest you and I [*sic*] because you will understand well the legal meaning of words and as the chairman is always held more responsible than any other member for the phraseology employed I should like to go over the whole thing carefully with you. The draft as finally agreed upon by us could be submitted to the whole conference if desirable.[21]

But the relationship between these two men was also critical in a more directly political sense. Dunraven felt at ease in raising with Harrington problems which arose in dealings with other members of the conference. Ironically, most of these were in relation to T. W. Russell, the northern Unionist whom the landlords had been so concerned to secure on the tenant team, but who found it harder than did his Nationalist counterparts to grasp the full implications of the decision not to resort to compulsory purchase.[22] More generally, however, Dunraven as chairman found it possible to work through Harrington in order to communicate ideas to tenant representatives which might have been misunderstood if they had come directly from him.

Harrington's relationship with both Mayo and Dunraven was in part the product of the individual qualities of the three men, reflected especially in the directness and courtesy which characterised the conduct of all three, but in which awareness of the historic and tribal triggers for misunderstanding was always sharply evident. Nowhere was this more manifest than in the delicate way in which Dunraven worked out with Harrington the language to be used in relation to reinstatement of evicted tenants so as to avoid the deep pitfalls that existed on each side in relation to this emotive and explosive issue.[23] As well as personal qualities, however, Harrington's holding of the office of Lord Mayor of Dublin appears to have facilitated the processes of communication. It meant that he encountered men like Mayo and Dunraven in the course of his ordinary duties and in ways which did not cause eyebrows to be raised, and it also made such men feel able to take the initiative in approaching him privately without arousing suspicion, whether on their own side or on Harrington's. Without doubt, the particular circumstances in which Harrington was able to cultivate the lines of communication thus opened up to him helped to smooth the potentially turbulent process by which the divide between landlord and tenant was being bridged.

The report of the Land Conference, agreed unanimously, was signed in Dublin on 3 January 1903. It formed the basis of a new land bill, presented to parliament in March, approved by a national convention of the United Irish League in April, and passed into law in August. This achievement had been made possible by the expectation of a substantial government subsidy to bridge the gap between the price at which tenants would be willing to buy their farms and the amount which would provide the necessary incentive for landlords to sell; it was this which enabled the tenant representatives to drop their demand for powers of compulsory purchase, which had before the conference constituted the main obstacle to agreement between the two sides. The conference had accepted that conditions of sale should be made as favourable to the landlords as was consistent with the interests of the tenants in the hope that this would discourage a mass exodus of landlords from Ireland. For Irish people more generally, the very considerable exchequer contribution was seen to provide some compensation for the over-taxation of Ireland which it was generally believed had occurred during the nineteenth century; British politicians were able to defend the expenditure in terms of savings which would accrue from agrarian peace in Ireland. It was essential, therefore, that the scheme should be seen in England to be based on a substantive agreement in Ireland between landlords and tenants. As Wyndham made absolutely clear, it was only on the basis of such a consensus that he could persuade the government and parliament to agree to 'the *big* thing' which he personally, after years of exploring alternatives, knew to be necessary.

The Wyndham Act, as it has generally been known, provided

for advances by the Land Commission for the purchase by tenants of their holdings in those cases where the whole of a landlord's estate was made available for sale. The 1881 act had provided for judicially determined rents to be revised after fifteen years from the first such fixing of rents, and the 1903 act provided for a differential in the amount of the purchaser's annuity according to whether the rents applying on the estate had been fixed before 1896 (first-term judicial rents) or after the land act of that year (second-term). In the case of tenants in the former category, the annuity was to be not less than 10 per cent and not more than 30 per cent below the existing rent; in the case of the latter category, the annuity would be not less than 20 per cent and not more than 40 per cent below the existing rent. These were the 'zones' within which, if vendor and purchaser agreed, the sale would be automatically approved by the Land Commission; a sale falling outside these parameters would require the commissioners to be satisfied as to the security for the advance and the equitableness of the price. Thus there were incentives for each side to avoid excessive bargaining, and the assurance of automatic approval meant that an agreement once struck could be acted upon immediately. This was one of the most attractive attributes of this legislation, simplifying the complexities of potentially frustrating and embittering negotiation and obviating delay in bringing about the transfer of ownership. It did, however, engender a fierce controversy on both sides during the progress of the legislation, some nationalists resenting that prices could not be forced down further, and some landlords that they could not be pushed upwards.

Two provisions of the act were especially attractive to the landlords. Section 27 provided that the payments to the vendor were to be in cash, as distinct from earlier legislation which provided for payment in land stock, the value of which fluctuated with the market, and had recently done so in a downward direction on account of the Boer War. Perhaps most appealing, and providing the mechanism which bridged the gap between what tenants were prepared to pay and landlords to accept, was the payment to a landlord who sold his estate of a 'bonus' of 12 per cent of the total purchase price, provided from a land purchase aid fund, the money for which came from a Treasury allocation of up to £12 million. The act also dealt with the problem of debt-encumbered estates, allowing a special procedure for ensuring equity to the debtors while not on that account denying to the tenants the benefits of purchase under the new arrangements. There were also special arrangements for 'congested estates', defined in section 6 of the act as 'an estate not less than half of the area of which consists of holdings not exceeding five pounds in rateable value, or of mountain or bog land, or not less than a quarter of the area of which is held in rundale or intermixed plots'. Whereas in other cases the commissioners had to be assured that they could carry out the purchase of an estate and its resale without financial loss, in the case of a 'congested' estate the condition of resale without loss could be relaxed to the extent determined by the Lord Lieutenant.

In these provisions concerning congested estates, as in other aspects of the act, can be seen an intent not only to address problems of agricultural viability in large areas of the Irish countryside, but also to carry out some elements of rationalisation which had attended the work of enclosure commissioners in England in the late eighteenth and early nineteenth centuries but which had never occurred in Ireland. Thus the Land Commission was given powers for the improvement of estates, including: possible redistribution of farms and redefining of their boundaries; the settlement of sporting rights by agreement, either attaching to the vendor or purchaser, or, in the absence of agreement, remaining with the Land Commission; the vesting of mineral rights in the Land Commission, for eventual disposal as parliament should determine; the transfer of the ownership of ancient monuments or other areas of special historical interest from the owners of the land to the Commissioners of Public Works; the extinction, either with or without compensation as the value in each case determined, of intervening rights attaching to middlemen, so as to secure eventual ownership to the occupying tenant, the intent being to abolish sub-tenancies and remove inefficient sub-divisions; and reinstatement, in the course of redrawing of farm boundaries, of 'a person who, within twenty-five years before the passing of this Act, was the tenant of a holding to which the Land Law Acts apply, and who is not at the date of the purchase the tenant or proprietor of that holding' (section 2)—intended, although without great effect, to enable restitution to those evicted during the land war. Thus this legislation, although primarily remembered for what it achieved most thoroughly, namely the transfer of ownership from landlords to tenant farmers, was also an important element in the modernisation of an agricultural system which had fallen behind developments occurring elsewhere.

The Wyndham Act, in all its aspects, must not be seen as an isolated piece of legislation. It represented both the completion and the cumulative outcome of a whole series of legislative actions dating back to at least 1870. It addressed not only the major grievance and tension-point of Irish agrarian life, but also set out to codify and reform many lesser aspects of agricultural society. It built upon legislative precedent established in the Incumbered Estates Act of 1849 and the Landed Estates Court (Ireland) Act of 1858 to remove the last of that distinctively Irish phenomenon of insolvent landlordism, while also complementing and making use of the valuable 1891 innovation of the Congested Districts Board to redress the other perennial problem of Irish agriculture, lack of employment and the impoverishment of farmers on pockets of land too small or physically unsuitable for viable agriculture. Building upon the logic, especially for Conservatives, of Gladstone's 1870 and 1881 acts, the 1903 act found practical and easily understood solutions to the inadequacies of the plethora of Conservative land acts passed since the Ashbourne Act of 1885. Its unique genesis as a piece of legislation, the outcome of a representative conference of Irishmen from opposed sides of the agrarian equation, seems to symbolise what was the completion of a long, untidy and largely bitter transformation from a colonised to a self-managing polity, from a pre-modern to a capitalist agricultural system, and from a conflict to a consensus form of dispute resolution. In that sense it marked as much a potential precedent for the future as a completion of a past process.

The Land Act of 1903 was of a scale to match the needs of the situation it was designed to meet. Most importantly, it was based upon an appreciation of the sensitive financial considerations which each side would take into account in any proposal for sale and purchase. In particular, the imperative for tenants of comparability between rent presently paid and purchase annuities was recognised, as well as the need to relate this calculation to whether the rents were first- or second-term rents with respect to the working of the 1881 act. Simplicity of procedure and administration was also achieved. Undue complexity had been largely responsible for the ineffectiveness of Arthur Balfour's Land Purchase Act of 1891, and this experience had forewarned George Wyndham of the dangers of being too clever by half, as Balfour had been inclined to be, in formulating elaborate provisions to meet every possible nuance of land occupancy and many of the variations of political preference. It was for this reason that Balfour had made so much less of an impression on the progress of purchase than had Lord Ashbourne; as L. P. Curtis has commented, 'The tenants . . . preferred the Ashbourne Act simply because they could understand it.'[24] Ashbourne had, of course, been an Irishman, and the achievement of the legislation of 1903 through a conference of the opposing Irish sides maximised the chance of the outcome being—in the jargon of a later age—'user-friendly'.

Other problems in previous purchase provisions were remedied in the 1903 act. Especially important was the system of zones, which enabled approval of a sale to be accelerated if the agreed price fell between predetermined minimum and maximum figures. For the tenants the main advantages were simplicity of procedure and an assurance that annuities would be less than rent payments. While the tenants were, paradoxically, probably less eager for the transfer of ownership than were the by now embattled landlords, there was a genuine eagerness for ownership, and sufficient observation of the working of purchase since 1885 to allay the apprehensions that more wary tenants might have of such a change to their accustomed arrangements. Whatever the benefits of the Wyndham Act, however, different tenants were affected in different ways. There were three elements to the grievances over land still existing at the time of the legislation. The first of these was that of ownership or possession, the redressing of the major historic grievance at the heart of the Irish land question. This the Wyndham Act addressed very substantially, providing the mechanism and apparently the resources for the total transfer of title of all the tenanted agricultural land of Ireland from landlord to tenant. There were, in fact, to be problems in fulfilling the promise of the act, but at the time it represented an apparently comprehensive measure to settle finally this major question of ownership, which—as has been seen—lay so much at the heart of the whole history of the Irish land question. The second element was redistribution of land and resettlement of farmers, in order to resolve the problem of the congested districts, where agricultural population far outstripped the resources of inferior quality land. Here the original issues, form and location of both the Land League and the United Irish League had greatly encouraged the aspirations and expectations of farmers on the edge of survival, who mistakenly saw the purpose of these agitations as primarily directed to alleviating their own hardship and vulnerability. For them the Land Act of 1903, despite a recognition of their problem, offered little more than a general hope for the future. The third element was the plight of the evicted tenants, those who had lost their farms through their wholehearted commitment to the agitational strategies of their nationalist leaders. Generally described as the 'wounded soldiers of the land war', they perhaps equated them-selves more to prisoners of war, and when the 1903 act did little to reinstate them on their farms, they must have found odd a truce which did not secure 'release' for those 'imprisoned' during the 'warfare'.

Even in relation to the matter which the Wyndham Act dealt with most fully, the transfer of ownership, there remained scope for difference of opinion among farmers. There was the question of price, for instance. While the benefits of ownership were attractive to the tenants, there was also recognition that new responsibilities also attached to proprietorship. Apprehensions could therefore arise in relation to whether the purchase annuity, and the number of years for which it had to be paid, would impose too heavy a burden. And what if agricul-tural prices fell? The consequences of defaulting on purchase payments could be far more serious than a failure to pay rents, and a concerted combination for rent reduction would no longer be an option. On top of that was the matter of the alter-native method of acquiring ownership, the one that nationalist and tenant leaders had made into the major demand of the United Irish League. The tenant movement, both among the Presbyterian farmers of Ulster and in the rest of the country, had set its heart on compulsory purchase, with its potential to keep down the price to the tenant. In addition to any economic advantage, the very notion of compulsion also gave emotional satisfaction, given the long history of opposed legitimacies.

There was, therefore, much material upon which tenant discontent could be built, despite the satisfaction of their leading representatives with the basic provisions of the Wyndham Act.

In fact, among the leadership of the nationalist movement, criticism of the recommendations of the Land Conference and the provisions of the legislation, as they emerged, was not long in expressing itself. In particular, it came from a section of the leadership, comprising especially John Dillon, Michael Davitt, Thomas Sexton and, through the control of the latter, the principal nationalist newspaper, the *Freeman's Journal*. Discontent was evident very shortly after the recommendations of the Land Conference became known, although, significantly, critics of the proposed legislation were reluctant to take any action which might jeopardise the land bill, as they recognised how eagerly the tenant farmers looked forward to ownership. John Dillon had little to say publicly during the period in which the bill was being discussed, partly because he was absent from the country for much of that time, but he admitted privately that only loyalty to the party prevented him from opposing it.[25] Davitt expressed his objections more publicly, but withdrew a resolution he planned to put before the national convention in April, apparently after a widespread belief had developed that it was designed to wreck the bill rather than improve it; Thomas Condon, a Nationalist MP, said of Davitt's resolution that it 'bears on its face the willing-to-wound-but-afraid-to-strike principle'.[26] The *Freeman's Journal* maintained a low-key criticism of the proposals, while again being careful not to jeopardise the bill's chances by undermining the Chief Secretary's claim that it enjoyed general support in Ireland.

The grounds of this criticism of the Land Conference, its recommendations and the proposed legislation varied. For Dillon, the settlement of the land question was potentially threatening to the nationalist cause, insofar as it undermined the use of agrarian agitation as a weapon to be wielded in pursuit of Home Rule.[27] For Davitt, socialism and a belief in land nationalisation had always mitigated his commitment to peasant proprietorship; this perspective made him naturally distrustful of a settlement which appeared to be generous to the landlords, potentially at the expense of tenants whose aspirations for ownership might make them over-ready to settle with their former oppressors. In the case of Sexton, the combined force of a pessimistic outlook on all matters political, a solitary and gloomy temperament and a renowned dexterity with figures made it almost impossible for him to desist from using his control of the most important nationalist newspaper to explore and expound the arithmetically worst-case scenarios for hypothetical tenant purchasers. Denis Kelly, the Bishop of Ross, was later penitent over his own role in criticising the Land Act, and confessed that he had allowed his 'love of figures' to betray him 'into neglecting to take many matters into account that are not to be found in the Arithmetic';[28] this, minus the element of repentance, perfectly represents Sexton's approach. For these critics, there was another element to their discontent. Their careers had been built upon a clear recognition of an enemy, and that enemy was landlordism. Rather than base their actions on the future needs of their cause, as in the context of rapidly changing circumstances they ought to have done, they fell back upon the habits of the past and recoiled from what Davitt described as 'coquetting with the Landlord party'.[29]

For those who by this time were far more directly responsible for the conduct of the nationalist movement and the agrarian cause there was no hesitation in embracing the outcome of the Land Conference. William O'Brien, the founder of the United Irish League and largely the architect of the post-Parnell reconstruction of the nationalist movement, and John Redmond, the chairman of the reunited Irish Parliamentary Party, had both been tenant representatives at the Land Conference, and both were enthusiastic supporters of its achievements and of the legislation being prepared by George Wyndham. This is unsurprising, as the settlement made a great deal of sense in the longer-term, although differing, strategies of both men. But acceptance of it was also a course to which there was no political alternative. Even though the Wyndham Act did not solve every problem that arose from the long struggle over land occupancy in Ireland, it did address in a most substantial way the central and major issue, that of ownership and control, which affected the majority of tenant farmers, including those who constituted the most prosperous—and therefore economically most crucial—part of the Irish agricultural community. Moreover, in what it did the act also succeeded in addressing what was symbolically at the heart of the long dispute over land tenure, namely the question of who were the rightful possessors of the soil. It represented, also, such a substantial achievement that it made easier the next steps towards resolving those problems not directly tackled by it. No responsible political leaders could have rejected this opportunity, and indeed degrees of responsibility were crucial in determining attitudes to the legislation. While men like Davitt, Dillon and Sexton had played significant roles in the nationalist past, by 1903 none of them occupied positions of primary political responsibility and their responses to the land bill were intrinsically oppositional and took inadequate cognisance of the realities which the leaders of the movement had to accommodate. That is why their criticisms were so muted while there was still a risk that they could be held accountable for the failure of the bill; once it had passed into law, that was to change.

For O'Brien, in particular, there was a further factor which must have shaped his responses to the land bill, as well as to the Land Conference which had preceded it. No one had made quite the same commitment as he had done to the revival and sustaining of agrarian agitation since the fall of Parnell. The effect of his work in establishing the United Irish League had made possible the reunion of the Irish Nationalist Party at Westminster, but in the aftermath of that event he had sought to keep an active agitation operating in the Irish countryside, both for the purposes of securing a final settlement of the land question and for laying a new basis for a longer-term nationalist strategy. By the middle of 1902 he had achieved much success in evolving the kind of passive resistance agitation which he believed necessary to achieve these goals. But in doing this he began to encounter increasing obstacles from among his colleagues.

One of the most substantial disappointments to O'Brien in building up the United Irish League from its beginnings in 1898 had been the lack of substantive support from John Dillon, to whom O'Brien had looked for future leadership of the nationalist movement. In the early days of the organisation Dillon had consistently neglected to participate in its activities and had failed to appreciate the potential of the new agitation to revive the fortunes and energies of the parliamentary movement. He became a late convert to the League when he saw it as a means of expressing his own disenchantment with the choice of John Redmond as chairman of the reunited party, but then again failed to support its initiatives in the aftermath of reunion. In particular, in 1901 he refused to co-operate with the initiative of a 'Settlement of Connaught Committee', which had been devised by O'Brien in order to give a higher public and parliamentary profile to the issue of congestion in the west, in the hope of securing for that issue the attention which the question of purchase had already achieved.

O'Brien also experienced increasing problems as a result of the failure on the part of many of his colleagues to understand the strategy which underlay his campaign in Ireland. Thus, during his absence in Australia and Egypt in early 1902, agitation on the de Freyne estate had been escalated into a 'no rent' strike, a weapon which had been hitherto carefully avoided in the United Irish League. Neither Dillon nor Redmond appeared even to understand how far this was removed from O'Brien's intentions; they did nothing to prevent it and made remarks which could be interpreted as approving it. Even O'Brien's own newspaper, removed from his normal surveillance, endorsed the actions on the de Freyne estate.[30] This misunderstanding made the League more vulnerable to prosecution, potentially incurred financial costs for the organisation, and put ammunition in the hands of the government. Following support by the national directory of the League for an intensification of agitation, O'Brien and Redmond went together to address a meeting at Limerick early in July, their purpose being to explain the character of the agitation and to correct misapprehensions such as had fuelled the de Freyne affair. Again, confusion was evident. Redmond's speech was couched in such generalities that it could have served as an encouragement for hot-headed and violent actions, and O'Brien had to spell out in detail the objects of the agitation and the limits beyond which it was not to be taken, specifically ruling out 'no rent' strikes, violence and other undesirable actions.

Following this Limerick meeting, O'Brien received a letter from T. P. O'Connor representing the views of colleagues, including both Dillon and Redmond, and indicating disenchantment with O'Brien's stirring up of agitation in Ireland:

You think Ireland is too quiet; here we have the impression that Ireland is utterly disturbed.[31]

It was this letter which finally made O'Brien realise that continued agitation along traditional lines was now unsustainable. This shortly preceded Shawe-Taylor's initiative on the Land Conference. O'Brien's responses to that, and to the land bill and its implications, must be seen, at least partly, in the context of this realisation.

For Redmond and O'Brien there were broader political implications of the Wyndham Land Act with which the nationalist movement had to reckon. The agreement necessary for the bill to proceed had been achieved through a conference with landlord representatives, and the progress of the bill itself had depended on continuing co-operation. The terms of the legislation did, however, provide for negotiation between landlord and tenant which, within defined limits, would determine the eventual price. This was bound to be a sensitive business, as both O'Brien and Redmond were well aware. The tenants had to be protected and assisted to get their farms at the best possible price, but on the other hand the processes had to accommodate the fact that—unlike situations in the past—the landlords were now themselves willing and ready participants. What was required was a continued and steady endorsement of the process, including the landlords' role in it, but also strong support by the United Irish League for the tenants in negotiating prices. From the experience involved in all this there emerged a recognition of how much had been changed for the nationalist movement as a result of the new relationship with the landlords.

How was this to be dealt with? Land had become a surrogate for nationalism for so long, and the methods, the organisation and the ideology of nationalism had been constructed—at least since the 1870s and arguably earlier—in terms of the land issue. It is true that aspects of the land question remained unresolved by the 1903 act, but the substantive issue of the ownership of the bulk of the land of Ireland was well on its way to resolution, and this had been achieved with the co-operation of those who historically had personified the enemy against which nationalism had constructed itself. What were the implications of this most significant development to the way in which nationalism was to develop thereafter? Within nationalism the view of the landlord as enemy had coexisted, even during the height of the land war, with a quite different tradition. The Fenians, depending on the grievances of the tenant farmers for many of their political gains, had nonetheless been aware of the potential importance of the landlord class to the cause of nationalism. Some of them, including John O'Leary, had opposed Parnell's endorsement of the land war because they saw it as anti-national in its necessary alienation of the landlords. Parnell himself had emphasised the need to resolve the land question as a priority in order that the landlord class could come to see its interests as lying in self-government; some of his responses to land agitation, such as his dissolution of the Land League in 1882 and his opposition to the Plan of Campaign, perhaps arose in part from his ambivalence about the role of the landlords in Irish life. Redmond himself, as leader of the Parnellite faction in the 1890s, had taken up this aspect of Parnell's outlook and based the political strategy of his faction on the concept of conciliation with the landlord class. The success of the United Irish League, and the failure of Redmond to remain independent of it, reflected the bad political judgment on which this course of action had been based. Not only had such a posture served to alienate much of his own support in the countryside, caught up as it still was with the conflict over land tenure, but it was also unsound in terms of the continuing impact that the land issue was bound to have on any attempt at co-operation. One of those most fiercely critical of Redmond's premature adoption of a conciliation policy had been William O'Brien, but much of his writing had already contained within it a strong appeal to the Irish landlords to identify more directly with the fortunes and hopes of their own country. Indeed, he had made a very specific tribute to their importance in a paper published in 1887.[32] His opposition to attempts at political co-operation with the landlord class in the 1890s was based upon the fact that the issue of land tenure still awaited a final solution, and until then it would vitiate any attempt at working together.

Faced with the reality of what had been achieved in 1903 O'Brien and Redmond had little hesitation in seeing that the time had come to extricate the nationalist movement from its identification with the land issue and open up the prospect of a new orientation for their movement. They responded to the passing of the Wyndham Land Act by preparing a new official policy for the Nationalist Party and its organisational wing, the United Irish League. This new policy embodied the procedure to be adopted in the negotiations between tenants and their landlords, but it also set forward as the future object of the nationalist movement the conciliation of different classes in Ireland. A series of resolutions setting forth this new departure was put before a meeting of the national directory of the United Irish League on 8 September 1903 and approved. These resolutions were formulated by O'Brien, but Redmond made perfectly clear that they 'fully embodied [his] views of the necessities of the moment'.[33] The new policy was based upon the belief, as expressed by O'Brien, that as a result of the Land Act 'The class war between the Irish majority and the Irish minority . . . was at a stroke deprived of the only material pretext for its continuance'.[34] The opportunity now existed, it was decided, to apply the method of the Land Conference—'conference plus business'—to other matters which could best be resolved by discussion, negotiation and agreement among differing interests. The evicted tenants question, the problem of agrarian congestion, the university question and the reform of Irish administration were examples of issues seen as amenable to this approach. Experience of co-operation in these areas could ultimately lead unionists and nationalists to consideration, in an atmosphere of greater toleration, of the more vexed question of self-government.

That this was more than a mere pipe-dream was verified by the significant changes that were evident within the ranks of the landlord class. The success of the plebiscite organised by Lord Mayo, Shawe-Taylor and others against the wish of the official leaders of landlordism had demonstrated a significant split within ascendancy opinion between those wishing to continue the hereditary conflict and those wanting to abandon their traditional economic role and secure a new basis of consensus with the majority of the population. In addition to the role of such landlords in the process of securing the new land act, it was also evident that they intended to pursue a conciliatory approach on these other issues. Under the continued leadership of Lord Dunraven, the chairman of the Land Conference, these more moderate landlords formed an Irish Reform Association with the express object of pursuing change in the context of co-operation, where possible, with the nationalist movement. In this respect the Land Act of 1903 had broken potentially the political mould within which Irish politics had been shaped for generations, and the new initiatives steered through by Redmond and O'Brien appeared justified both in terms of these new opportunities and ideologically in relation to the longer-term necessities of the nationalist cause. The new moves, however, involved no dismemberment of nationalist organisation and solidarity, but rather a use of those structures to take advantage of opportunities which co-operation with the moderate landlords could open up. It was, in a sense, a concept of limited 'power-sharing', creating a common ground upon which a degree of consensus might be formed, and thereby breaking the destructive and ultimately futile polarisation which had been the product jointly of the 1886 Home Rule crisis and of the land war.

The espousal of a policy of conciliation out of the circumstances which had brought about the Land Act served further to inflame the antagonism of those nationalists who were in any case disenchanted with the new land legislation and the way in which it had been achieved. A concerted campaign was begun against the new conciliation policy, despite its endorsement by the national directory of the United Irish League. Fearing the truth of Davitt's view that, as a result of being 'poisoned by O'Brien with a big dose of Dunravenism', the constitutional nationalist movement—'that which has struggled through the treacheries and tensions of the past twenty-five years'—was now dead,[35] Dillon—aided and abetted throughout by the *Freeman's Journal*—made a vigorous attempt to rescue the movement from the trap into which he believed it had fallen. Even before the adoption of the new policy by the national directory he had declared publicly that he had 'no faith in the doctrine of conciliation', that he believed that landlords had only behaved as they had for fear of losing more off their rents as a result of agitation, and that the only course for the nationalist movement was a return to the methods of the past: 'Having won so much by agitation . . . we ought to press on with increased vigour until we obtain all that the country desired.'[36] Taking up what was manifestly the weakest point of the Land Act, he declared that if it did 'not produce substantial results in a year or two in the way of resettlement of the West of Ireland, then I say the Bill is a failure, and we must raise the banner again in the West'.[37] Much of this was remarkable enough given Dillon's record of sustained resistance to agitation, culminating in his endorsement of T. P. O'Connor's letter of disapproval to O'Brien a year earlier, but it was also staggeringly devoid of any sense of political reality. The Land Act, and the circumstances in which it had been achieved, clearly made a considerable difference to the nationalist movement, and it could not simply be ignored. Even were the overture from moderate landlords to be brusquely rejected—and there were serious political implications in that—the effect of the new legislation, regardless of whether it did anything for the western problem, would be to convert the bulk of the tenant farmers into proprietors. How could the party expect these farmers, the backbone of its support and of the social structure of rural Ireland, to continue as participants in an agitation now devoid of relevance for them?

The flag of rebellion which Dillon had raised against the policy of conciliation, however, was certain to attract some support. The habits of enmity had been strongly entrenched in the land war, and the very fact that land had become a metaphor for nationalism meant that the task of disentanglement of the two issues was bound to be a difficult and protracted one. This difficulty was epitomised in the response of one of O'Brien's strongest supporters in the past, the Sligo MP and newspaperman P. A. McHugh. He acknowledged the dilemma for the movement, admitting that 'The strength of O'Brien's position seems ... to lie in the absence of an alternative policy' and even conceding that 'After all the new policy may be the right one.' However, in the last analysis McHugh could not follow:

> The right about is too abrupt for me. I cannot play up to the new note, and I am not prepared to protest.[38]

These were the sentiments which enabled Dillon to draw to him the sympathy of many nationalists around the country, although the unwillingness to protest—a legacy of a decade of dissension and factionalism—was his biggest obstacle, and one which served even to inhibit his own criticisms. His task was made harder because of the widespread recognition of, and support for, O'Brien's leadership and policy. Many saw Dillon's criticisms as motivated by resentment at his own marginalisation, and as threatening another split in the party.

O'Brien received strong endorsement and support from many of those who had been involved in the land agitation. On the other hand, Dillon enjoyed the support of one enormously significant component of the nationalist movement. The United Irish League in Belfast, organised under the effective and astute leadership of Joseph Devlin, had no interest in a policy of conciliation towards the landlords. For Belfast Catholics, the purpose of a nationalist movement was not to bridge the chasm between the majority and minority, but rather to wield the baton of majoritarian politics in the interests of redressing their minority status within Belfast. Dillon found that he could rely absolutely on the support of Devlin and of the northern nationalists in his attempt to divert the movement from the course which had been endorsed by the Dublin directory.

What finally delivered success into Dillon's hand was a failure of nerve on the part of O'Brien himself. Frustrated by the systematic campaign of a leading colleague who had been notably unsupportive in difficult times, by the negative role of the principal nationalist newspaper, and by the unwillingness of Redmond as leader to assert more forcefully the policy of the organisation, O'Brien thought that his own resignation might force upon the public consciousness the necessity of discipline and coherence. Accordingly, without warning, on 4 November 1903 O'Brien announced his resignation from the national directory of the organisation he had founded, his intention to resign his seat in parliament, and the closure of his newspaper, the *Irish People*. What he hoped would be the effect of this was that either Redmond would impose discipline or that there would be an attempt, bound to be unsuccessful, to develop an alternative policy. In fact the outcome was very different. With O'Brien gone, Redmond had no alternative but to secure agreement with Dillon, which he easily did—not on the basis of any change in policy, but on the condition that the conciliation policy should be left on the books but ignored. O'Brien had, through an untimely resignation, handed the effective leadership of the movement over to Dillon and ensured the destruction of the conciliation initiative. He had also failed to recognise that by his resignation he had turned the widespread commitment to unity, which had been working against Dillon's campaign of dissent, against himself.

Paul Bew, in his *Conflict and Conciliation in Ireland*, has developed an analysis of agrarian and nationalist developments over this period which is postulated on a distinction between 'radical agrarians'—a category to which Dillon and Davitt belong—and 'conciliationists' or 'Parnellites', such as Redmond and O'Brien, the latter a convert to this philosophy in 1903. This is a defective framework of analysis insofar as it does not allow for the degree to which the two issues of land and nationality had become synonymous over the years since 1879 and therefore also fails adequately to accommodate the role of the 1903 act as a solvent of that fusion. Redmond had, indeed, been an advocate of conciliation and compromise during the 1890s, but his actions then had been based more on tactical considerations affecting the parliamentary role of his minority party than on an analysis of political realities in Ireland. With the events of 1903, however, there had been a substantive change in the underlying situation of the nationalist movement. Before 1903 conciliation with the minority had been for nationalists an aspiration for the future—one which 'radical agrarians', in Bew's terminology, did not share—but after 1903 it was a reality with which nationalism had to reckon. Its failure to accommodate this change left the Irish parliamentary movement locked into patterns of the past which could only lead to increasing fragmentation of energies and an inability to discover that elusive consensus upon which nationalist success would ultimately depend. The 'New Departure' of the 1870s had brought together forces which had in the past remained separate; after 1903 it was the cleavage between the minority, and especially the former landlords, and the rest of the community which would stand as a major obstacle to the effectiveness of nationalism. For the first time the broader nationalism to which Parnell, among others, had aspired was a possibility in the real world of politics and not just in theory—and this was because it was now for the first time possible to remove the land tenure issue from the centre of Irish politics. However, with the reversion under Dillon to redundant political strategies, the parliamentary nationalist movement missed the chance to realise this new potential.

Bew's distinction between 'radical agrarians' and 'conciliationists' needs careful qualification. In particular, the implicit notion of William O'Brien shifting from one side to the other does not adequately define the basis of his beliefs. In his account of the early months of the United Irish League, Bew follows in the tracks of those who have characterised that organisation as initially directed to an agrarian purpose, land redistribution in the west, and then changing its purpose to a national political one.[39] In fact O'Brien was unambiguously clear from the beginning that the purposes of the new body were nationalist and political.[40] This does not, of course, mean that he was not deeply committed to the interests of the poor western landholders, but rather that he saw the strength of nationalism deriving from the grievances and aspirations of all sections of the population. Indeed, the resolution of the major question of ownership dealt with in the 1903 act made it easier for the issue of poverty and over-population to be addressed in its own terms. But the reform of Irish grievances, as far as O'Brien was concerned, was merely one issue on the road to national autonomy. As Parnell had stressed, while asserting the centrality of his party's nationalist purpose, 'if by the way we tried to obtain other concessions it was because we were anxious to do good to the humbler classes of our countrymen as we went along'.[41]

There is also a problem with characterising Dillon as a 'radical agrarian'. From his own account, his objections to the Land Act arose more from his apprehension that the removal of grievance might weaken the enthusiasm for nationalism than from weakness in the legislation itself, although he also drew attention to deficiencies in it, often the same ones acknowledged by colleagues who supported the act. His advocacy of the need for resettlement in the west and for renewed agrarian agitation, given his failure in these areas in the years before 1903, tends to confirm that he measured the importance of these issues in relation to the needs of the Home Rule cause. In this sense Dillon's perspective was little different from that of O'Brien, but their conclusions as to strategy were totally at variance. Davitt was more convincingly a 'radical agrarian', for his socialist ideology meant that he consistently gave priority to the needs of those with least control over their economic conditions. But in both his and Dillon's case the reactions to the 1903 act are better understood in terms of their acclimatisation to the liberal and radical side in British politics. The wider political formation with which Irish Nationalist MPs became associated after 1886 had imbued many of them with an interpretation of the political world that drew them ever closer to the coalition of anti-landed, anti-Anglican, anti-establishment and anti-imperialist interests gathered together under the umbrella of the British

Liberal Party. For Davitt, the closer linkage between the labour movement in Britain and the Liberals was a further factor in consolidating these allegiances, although in fairness to Davitt it should be pointed out that his opposition to the system of purchase of which the 1903 act was the ultimate exemplification had been made clear publicly as early as 1884.[42] In the ferocity of their opposition to the Conservative-enacted Land Act and to the idea of conciliation, Dillon and Davitt were demonstrating the extent to which the basis of their outlook had shifted from nationalism to class, from a priority for Irish autonomy to a multi-British alliance against privilege and the old elites. They had, in a sense, retraced the journey of Daniel O'Connell from Repeal to the Whig alliance, linking the future of their cause inextricably to a British party. As with O'Connell, the consequence of this was to be the undermining of the Irish political basis of their movement.

It has been said of Lord Salisbury that 'In purchase, he believed, lay the means of dissolving the ties that bound the agrarian and political agitations together.'[43] The truth of this went deeper, perhaps, than Salisbury recognised. In its simple sense, this was the threat that so shaped Dillon's attitudes to any ameliorative legislation for Ireland. But there was another sense in which this captured one of the great challenges to the Irish nationalist movement, one which had been recognised throughout its recent history. While the grievance over land tenure was both an imperative socially which nationalists could not ignore and an opportunity politically which enabled their movement to achieve an unparalleled dominance, the link between the two issues was also bound ultimately to be an albatross around the neck of a movement which needed to establish a national consensus in order to justify its demand for self-government. The breakthrough which occurred with the Land Conference and the consequent Land Act provided the moment at which the nationalist movement needed to adjust its course; in other words, Lord Salisbury's conjecture, if confirmed, might well have been beneficial to nationalism, rather than—as he assumed—detrimental. It was a tribute to the prescience of William O'Brien that he saw so quickly the fundamental change which had been brought about, and a mark of the sophistication of the bulk of the nationalist movement that he should have so readily gained approval and endorsement for the new direction.

It was not so much to his credit as a tactical politician that he did not foresee the need for more careful working of the ground for the new policy among the rank and file. It was this failure, together with his inability to see that the obsession with unity would turn opinion against him once he resigned in protest, that doomed his initiative to an early death.

The land issue could not continue to provide the basis for a nationalist movement; the ties that bound the agrarian and political agitations had indeed been severed. With its reversion to the polemic of continued land agitation, the nationalist leadership doomed the party to a narrowing of its basis of support in Ireland and a shift away from the nationalist ideology which supposedly underlay its central purpose; it became a party of class and sectional interests. The land question, historically so important in shaping Irish nationalism, was now to haunt the future of that movement beyond its own demise as a unifying issue. The failure of the Nationalist Party to shake off the legacy of the land at this crucial moment in its history was to have, in particular, three major consequences.

The first of these was a more fundamental permeation of nationalism with Catholic sectarianism. The land agitations of the late nineteenth century had, of course, deeply sectarian implications, for the basic demographic fact of Protestant/landlord and Catholic/tenant alignment could not be gainsaid. But the perpetuation of anti-landlord sentiment in the context of the abolition of landlordism as an economic system could only, given again the ethnic and religious demography of Ireland, assume the character of a sectarian vendetta. This dimension was greatly enlarged by the circumstances in which the parliamentary movement was wrenched away from the conciliation policy. In developing the United Irish League as a nationalist organisation in Belfast, Joseph Devlin had found that the weapons of sectarianism could not be ignored. Indeed, his first ventures into politics in the late 1890s had seen the defeat of his nationalist efforts by the overt sectarianism of the Catholic bishop, Henry Henry, through his Catholic Association. By 1903, however, Devlin had finally secured the victory of the United Irish League in Belfast, but had done so to a great extent on the back of the very sectarianism upon which Bishop Henry's earlier support had been based. In particular, the Ancient Order of Hibernians, to which only Catholics belonged and which was committed to the advancement of the individual interests of co-religionists, began to play an important part in linking sectarian sentiment in the country to the structures of the Home Rule movement. Devlin played a crucial role in supporting and sustaining Dillon in his campaign against the conciliation policy, and once O'Brien's influence had been removed from the movement it was Devlin who was able to instil an alternative sense of purpose; but he came into the leadership of the movement as a Trojan horse for Catholic sectarianism.[44] George Boyce has said of Devlin that he probably 'did not pause to consider the implications of what he was doing',[45] but the impact on the character of the Home Rule movement was far-reaching. Moreover, this effect was reinforced by the new opportunities for sectarian patronage created by the nationalist control of much of Irish local government and the return to office of a Liberal government pledged to governing Ireland according to 'Irish ideas'—often, in practice, meaning as advised by the parliamentary leadership of the Irish Party.

The second legacy of the nationalist movement's failure to extricate itself from its identification with land agitation was more overtly related to the issue of land occupancy. Once the party had committed itself, as Dillon led it to do, to a continuation of land agitation, there was only one ground upon which such activity could be re-established, and that was in relation to the problem of congestion in the more impoverished western regions. This had indeed been the substantive ground upon which the critics of the Wyndham Act had concentrated their attack, and it was the obvious area for the redirected party to exercise its renewed commitment to 'a vigorous agitation'. But there were problems inherent in this approach. The question of land redistribution involved the interests of only minority sections of the population, and the party's decision to focus so directly on this agitation inevitably made it less relevant to the interests of most of those whom it purported to represent. Moreover, an active agitation to redistribute the land held by graziers proved deeply divisive for the nationalist movement, as Paul Bew has shown in his account of the ranch war and the practice of cattle-driving which came to characterise its methods.[46] Whereas anti-grazier sentiment had played a part in all the agitations before 1903, the importance of the major cleavage between the cultural majority and the ascendancy class had enabled the graziers to establish an ambience within rural society which enabled them to weather the ambiguous situation in which they found themselves. Now, however, with the landlords retreating from their ascendancy economic and social roles, the full thrust of this new agitation was directed against those who, in many cases, saw themselves as part of the nationalist establishment. And the cattle-driving which was the main method of this agitation was unusually cruel and vicious, albeit with animals taking the brunt of the physical violence. This was a most embarrassing campaign for Redmond, and one which gave to its leader on the ground, Laurence Ginnell, a power and an influence well beyond either his talents or the respect he held among his colleagues. Even David Sheehy and J. P. Farrell, two of those MPs who had gone out of their way to support O'Brien against the Davitt/Dillon/*Freeman's Journal* campaign in 1903, now felt constrained to play leading roles in the cattle-driving campaign,[47] while Dillon lent it encouragement, albeit from a distance and ambiguously.[48] This major part of the Nationalist Party's agitational strategy between 1906 and 1910 was damaging to the concept of a broad-based nationalism and divisive of the party still ostensibly pursuing that ideal.

The third area in which the failure of the Nationalist Party to rid itself of the incubus of the land question affected its continued viability was in its relationship to those who had acquired the ownership of their farms under the Wyndham Act or under earlier purchase provisions. A nation predominantly of farmers, Ireland was now dominated by small capitalist peasant proprietors, their interests distinctly different from when they had been tenants, and their outlook now generally freed from the traditional bane of their lives, rent-demanding and in other ways interfering landlords. Their concerns were now primarily focused on improving their agricultural efficiency and productivity. A party that aspired to represent their interests might have been expected to respond positively to initiatives such as those undertaken by the new Department of Agriculture and Technical Instruction, but this being another product of Conservative government and 'conciliationist' thought in Ireland, it received very little encouragement or endorsement from the party which represented its client farmers. Earlier still, many farmers had been badly let down because of the dissension over the conciliation policy, which directed United Irish League energies away from its role of advising farmers in their negotiations with their landlords; as George Crosbie, the editor of the *Cork Examiner*, had written after the campaign against the Land Act had already affected these negotiations, 'the best friends the landlords have had yet were the "fire-eaters" on our own side'.[49] What the new peasant proprietors in Ireland needed was a party able to address the practical agrarian problems which they faced in a way which matched how they now felt about their own futures. Such farmers were not going to abandon old political loyalties for the relatively alien political ideas and personnel of Sinn Féin, but they would have liked their own representatives to have moved further in the direction of that 'self-reliance' which would now, of necessity, come to characterise their own lives and work.

The outcome of the 1903 Land Act and the political adjustments which followed it were no more auspicious for those who stood on the other side of the great historical divide which had been formed around the question of land. Mark Bence-Jones has shown how the 'bonus', the 12 per cent of the purchase price paid to landlords selling estates under the provisions of the Wyndham Act, was largely squandered by those who happened to be the possessors at that time and who were therefore the recipients of the handsome and welcome cash sum paid as part of the settlement. What might have served to sow the seeds of a new economic viability, by investment in new types of business or in a home farm on the demesne retained under the purchase schemes, went instead on the gaming-tables of Monte Carlo, in expenditure on 'wine, women and song' or sport and motoring, or in other non-productive activities, like improving gardens and houses.[50] It is perhaps ironic that a class whose long demise had been haunted by the impossible demands of an encroaching *laissez-faire* economic philosophy should now find itself incapable of making effective use of what was now an entirely capitalist opportunity. It was, however, not surprising. The journey from the role of paternalist landlord, through ineffectual attempts at economic efficiency, to that of country gentleman deprived of social role and function was indeed a long one, and had incurred a suffering which had left many of the ascendancy class exhausted, confused and uncertain about their identity, in terms both of class and nation. Having failed to listen to the voices of members of their own class, those like Conner or Sharman Crawford or Butt—or even Parnell—who had mapped out what it was necessary for them to do in order to survive, the task assumed by a Shawe-Taylor or a Dunraven in the moment of final eclipse was probably an impossible one. The proffered embrace which would once have been readily taken up by their fellow-countrymen was now unwisely, but explicably, rejected by those who had fought so long on the battlefield that the enemy's continued existence had become essential to their own sense of identity. The resulting sense of universal rejection and disaffection, both from their own countrymen and within the British polity with which they had also identified, ensured that essentially private and individual pursuits would be more immediately attractive than larger interests, whether their own or those of the wider society.

In 1902 and 1903 the initiatives of Shawe-Taylor and of William O'Brien, both supported by large numbers of those whom they represented, promised to break the mould in which Irish politics had been set for at least a quarter of a century. The way in which each had chanced their arm to this end was in some ways reminiscent of the leadership displayed in more recent years in the dismantling of the communist regimes of eastern Europe and the ending of the apartheid system in South Africa. In retrospect, it can be seen that at stake in Ireland was the creation of a plural society, involving the dismemberment of a structure of society based upon a sharp political delineation between differing ethnic and religious groupings and the abandonment by the nationalist movement of a particular system of organisation and agitation—one which had served an important purpose but had also been too 'totalitarian' in its character to provide a continuing basis for a free and open society. The failure of these initiatives showed that the removal from Irish life of the major issue of agricultural land tenure had not ended the attitudes of mind which had been created in its service, and the bold concept of a plural society was to perish in more than half a century of deepening sectarian mono-cultures, the resonances of 1903 not being heard again until the advent of new attitudes and sympathies in the 1980s.

7

Postscript and Retrospect

The Irish land question had dominated the political relationship of Britain and Ireland during much of the nineteenth century, so much so that it had become almost the eye through which that relationship was seen. Now, even though very substantially resolved by the consequences of the 1903 Land Act, it was to cast a long shadow into the twentieth century. This was so in three major areas: in the inability of the political culture to free itself of the habits of mind and action created by the land issue; in the consequences of that tradition for the economic ethos and structure of twentieth-century Ireland; and in the direct impact of the land conflict and its legacy on social and community relations within Ireland, as well as between Ireland and Britain. The long journey from William Conner's plea in the 1830s and 1840s for a legal recognition of the traditional rights of the occupiers of the land to the highly developed political and social mobilisations of the land war had shaped Ireland in ways which could not easily be undone. This began to be evident in the immediate aftermath of the Wyndham Act of 1903, when effectively a new split occurred in the ranks of the mainstream nationalist movement, potential co-operation between nationalists and more moderate unionists was aborted, and a reversion occurred, through activities like cattle-driving, to a social disruption which now lacked any justification in terms of a wider national collective solidarity. These were all signs that the transition to an Ireland freed of landlordism would not mean an end to its pervasive legacy.

The claim that the Wyndham Act had finally solved the land question has by and large received the endorsement of history.

By 1921 most Irish farmers owned their holdings,[1] and the 1923 Land Act, the first such legislation to occur under the new juris- diction of the Irish Free State, speeded up the process for those who still remained as tenants. Landlordism, as historically understood in Ireland, no longer existed. This achievement had largely flowed from the 1903 act, although the working of that legislation ran into some practical difficulties, which were resolved by a new land act in 1909, put through by the Liberal government. This legislation mainly addressed problems that had arisen in relation to purchase, including the introduction of a limited element of compulsion, even though it followed upon the extensive peregrinations of the Dudley Commission inquiring into congestion in Ireland. That royal commission, the last of the great British inquiries into the Irish land system, had more than usually a political agenda. Notwithstanding the con- scientious and extensive work of its members, the reality was that it had been brought into existence in large part to get both the British Liberal government and the Irish Nationalist Party off the hook in terms of issues on which they were on the defensive. Its creation simultaneously served the interests of both.

While the Liberal Party had worked its way out of the apparent stranglehold upon its platform of the issue of Irish Home Rule, the sense of obligation and moral force associated with the Gladstonian legacy on Ireland continued to dictate to Liberals the need for a progressive policy on Ireland and a com- mitment to their Irish allies. Moreover, the more overtly hostile stance towards Ireland which had characterised Lord Rosebery's dominance in the leadership had, in the aftermath of the Boer War, evaporated and given way to a 'new liberalism' which sought to put as positive as possible an aspect on this commit- ment. With Home Rule acknowledged to be an impossibility, and with the first outcome of the substitute, gradualist 'step-by- step' policy, the Irish Council Bill, ultimately rejected by the Nationalists as inadequate, it was not easy to see a way for the Liberal government to oblige. This was a situation in which tokenism was likely to appeal, and the Nationalist Party led by Redmond and Dillon were themselves ready to accept almost anything which suggested that the relationship with the British Liberals, in which so much had been invested, was returning some dividend. The Dudley Commission was the result. It bought time, and held out at least a prospect of reform in an area which was acutely sensitive politically and socially in Ireland and which was attuned to the moral and social sensitivities of British Liberalism. Moreover, insofar as it appeared to reopen the land question it counteracted the notion that the Conservatives had successfully resolved that issue, gratifying some partisan sentiments among Liberals while also vindicating the action of those now in possession of the Nationalist Party in rejecting the achievements and processes associated with the Wyndham Act.

Achievement, however, eluded the Dudley Commission. The problem of congestion was indeed a very real one and was to remain so throughout the twentieth century. But it was not helped by its use as an ingredient in a nationalist strategy. Whereas the land question as understood in the nineteenth-century context had served as a metaphor for occupation and confiscation, the question of congestion was one which had to be resolved within an Irish context, because at its heart—as indeed the Dudley Commission discovered through its inquiries—was a competition between Irish people for that scarce resource of land, rather than between native occupier and the now vanquished, if still comfortable, descendants of the conquerors. This reality had to be, and was, faced by the revolutionary Dáil Éireann, when it issued the decree of 29 June 1920 against claimants for land redistribution, describing their actions as a 'stirring up of strife amongst our fellow countrymen'.[2] Where the question of agrarian congestion related to the longer history of the land issue was in the heightened expectations which had been raised in the consciousness of those who held very small holdings or, indeed, held no land at all.

Both the Land League and the United Irish League had been founded initially upon the plight of the poor smallholders in the west of Ireland. In both cases the purposes of the organisation were much wider than this, and eventually the issue upon which both were ostensibly established was lost in those other purposes. This is not to say that the founders of these bodies had cynically or hypocritically used the sufferings of the impoverished farmers for ulterior motives, but rather that many grievances were perceived to be caught up in the encompassing sense emerging from the Great Famine onwards that many—if not all—ills faced by various elements of Irish society were in one way or another traceable to the inappropriateness of government from London. But the status given to land as the symbol of liberation from oppression was such that those who had too little or no land were unable to see either their individual identity or their national and social identity in terms other than as landholders and farmers. The disappointment and frustration engendered by the failure to achieve significant alleviation in their condition even though they played so important a role in mobilising reform for those wealthier than themselves was consolidated into an expectation that something could be done for them. It was this expectation which fuelled the ranch war and a succession of smallholder revolts, culminating through the 1940s and 1950s in a political party, Clann na Talmhan, specifically devoted to the pursuit of their interests on the national political stage.

Politically, as evidence before the Dudley Commission shows, there were great problems in satisfying this hunger for land. Land added to the stock for redistribution was subject to claimants not only from among the impoverished western farmers but also from those in the locality of the newly available land wanting to enlarge their own farms or provide land for their sons or for other local men seeking land. In other words, the national myth about the land, etched so deeply into the national consciousness through the political struggle over landownership in the nineteenth century and which had itself helped to create the longing for viable farms, had also multiplied the claimants to the point where the demand could never be met.

For those farmers whose holdings were viable enough for them to purchase under the provisions of the various measures culminating in the 1903 act, the struggle over tenure had also left a powerful legacy. In George Bernard Shaw's *John Bull's Other Island* Larry complains that Matthew has changed:

He's not the same to me. He used to be very civil to Masther Larry: a deal too civil, I used to think. Now he's as surly and stand-off as a bear.

The change is explained by Aunt Judy:

Oh sure he's bought his farm in the Land Purchase. He's independent now.

And Nora's summary of this transformation drives the point home:

> It's made a great change, Larry. Youd harly know the old tenants now. Youd think it was a liberty to speak t'dhem— some of dhem.[3]

Shaw here captures the transition from a forced deference— conveyed by Larry a few lines later:

> Of course they all hated us like the devil. Ugh! Ive seen them in that office, telling my father what a fine boy I was, and plastering him with compliments, with your honor here and your honor there, when all the time their fingers were itching to be at his throat.[4]

—to a surly determination to redress the balance of the past; Shaw's use of the word 'independent' is intended as highly ironic, depicting the continued enslavement which is epitomised in the determination to draw the last ounce out of a status acquired painfully through a long and protracted struggle. While the reality of individual reactions was much more complex than this, Shaw's portrayal of the personal example is a useful parallel to what can be discerned as the legacy in economic and political terms of that struggle for the land.

W. E. Vaughan has argued that the real importance of the land question was that, as a result of the obsession with landlord–tenant relations, the whole issue of Irish land came to be viewed exclusively in terms of ownership and occupation, to the neglect both of agricultural improvement and of the claims of elements of the population other than farmers. 'As a result,' he concludes, 'when landlordism was abolished, it was replaced by a highly private system of ownership.'[5] Agriculture in the Ireland of a peasant proprietary was insufficiently subjected to wider social and economic influences, for its operations were circumscribed by a moral tradition rather than by either economic criteria or a perceived role within the plurality of a wider social identity. The maintenance of the status of the farmer as the transmitter of tradition and as the legitimate occupier of the soil took precedence over the exercise of skill and professionalism as an agriculturalist in a world in which the reality of international competition was impinging ever more forcefully upon the economics of Irish agriculture. Both the vigour and the frustrations evident in the history of the agricultural co-operative movement in Ireland attest to this. On the one hand, those like Sir Horace Plunkett who were trying to spread the co-operative concept as a means of compensating for the innate inefficiencies of a system of small farms were pressing the arguments derived from competition, but on the other they attempted to justify their concepts by reference to the same romanticised value system which did so much to uphold a tradition of farming fundamentally in conflict with their aspirations. For example, one of the most passionate proponents of agricultural co-operation in Ireland, the mystic, poet and writer George Russell (AE), underpinned his message with an argument that the 'rural exodus' could be stemmed by the 'miracle' of making the countryside 'a place where a man can enjoy the fullest and freest development of his spiritual, intellectual and social powers'.[6] And yet his underlying objective was to produce an Irish agriculture efficient enough to compete on the modern international market, able to rival the country projected as both the nearest model for Ireland and its most effective competitor, Denmark. This objective, however, may well have been hindered by the idealisation of a rural tradition which was self-satisfied and doggedly determined to hold on to the gains which had been made in terms of status even though at the cost of economic competitiveness.

Each of the three agrarian agitations of the late nineteenth century had arisen in the context of agricultural recession. In part at least, those recessions, especially that of the late 1870s, reflected a change in the competitive environment within which European agriculture had to operate. But the political and social imperatives at work within Ireland enabled that fundamental economic reality to be obscured by the issue of land tenure, closely integrated as that was with the entirely separate issue, in economic terms, of nationality. Not only had the question of tenure come to stand as the principal explanation of economic failure in Irish agriculture, but its solution was seen to carry with it the panacea for all the ills of agrarian life. This, unfortunately, closely coincided with significant changes in the world competition in agricultural products, thus immuring Irish agriculture from a realisation of the economic factors with which it had to contend. This greatly reinforced the sense of complacency represented by a culture defined so strongly in terms of the individual small farmer, working his land on the basis of tradition, resenting changes in the demands of the principal market for his goods, and constructing as alien and opposed to his own world-view forms of agriculture, such as grazing, which indicated response to these changes. The cattle-driving of the ranch war of 1907–9, deprived largely of political justification in terms of the substantive interests of the national-ist movement, was the ultimate expression of this defensive stance. It represented a battle, not by the struggling small farmers of the congested districts, but of middle-ranking farmers for the continuance of their particular culture of tillage farming against those more immediately exploiting the available market. It was an attitude of mind, however, which was to permeate in one way or another Irish attitudes to farming and government policy on agriculture until the late 1950s, when the reality of a deeply depressed economy and society began, partly through the efforts of the government of Seán Lemass, to bring Irish attitudes into a more international context.

The course that determined this outcome was set in concrete by the land war. In Dr Vaughan's view, there were two possible responses by the farmers to their fall in incomes from 1877: either to stabilise them by increasing production, or to rectify their losses by forcing the landlords to reduce their rents:

> In the conditions of the 'great depression' an increase of output based on greater investment in agriculture would have been a more rational solution to the problem of diminished incomes. But the preconditions for such a solution were absent in Ireland because landlords and tenants did not regard each other as partners in the business of agricultural production and because Irish landlords did not have the habit of investing in Irish agriculture. In the end, Irish tenants opted for the politically exhilarating policy of com-pensating themselves at the expense of the landlords.[7]

This, for Vaughan, is part of a project to reclaim the role of the landlord. While not hesitating to castigate landlords for their manifest failure effectively to defend that role, he sees the need to set the debate back into the context of the weaknesses of peasant proprietary as an alternative. Referring to the work of critics of that system, such as Raymond Crotty, Vaughan contends:

> Since we can look critically at peasant proprietary, we can look dispassionately at the system of land tenure which preceded it because the transition from landlordism to peasant proprietary need no longer be regarded as inevitable, desirable and logical.[8]

Moreover, he sees a substantial part of the justification for the system of peasant proprietary as the one drawn retrospectively from the fact that the land issue ceased to be a political question when the farmers became the owners of their land.[9] There is, however, another view as to how the economic legacy of the land question was shaped and determined, which sets a longer context than that created by the land war and more adequately explains the historical gestation of a culture so antipathetic to the economic competitiveness of Irish agriculture.

The whole history of the Irish land question occurred within the framework of the establishment and consolidation of the economic and ideological hegemony of *laissez-faire* capitalism in Europe and, indeed, more universally. There have been, and there remain, some powerful arguments against that dominance, in particular in relation to the impact on traditional social and moral values. But it would be a hardy opponent of that ideology who could not admit, particularly given the resurgence since the 1960s of market force economics and the dismantling of the communist regimes of eastern Europe, that the longer-term pattern of the past two hundred years has been the strengthening and expansion of capitalism as a universal economic ideology. In this context, Ireland does not look on the face of it to be a prime candidate for its rejection. Certainly in Ireland, as in many other European rural societies, the force of tradition has played a strong part in resisting the impact of economically driven change, but in twentieth-century terms it is a society clearly alienated from the main alternative to capitalism and unlikely, given its strong populist and democratic political tradition, to succumb to the anti-capitalist ideologies of the right. And yet at the centre of the Irish land question stands an attitude hostile to the impact of world capitalism on the practice and principles of agricultural production. The origins of this can be found more in the circumstances of pre- and post-Famine Ireland than in the land war, and the responsibility for it attaches more to the advocates of *laissez-faire*, especially in government and administration, and to the landlords, than to the tenant farmers themselves.

Capitalism requires clarity as to the rights of property, as indeed did a traditional society. But in asserting as essential to capitalism the particular form of land tenure practised in England, government, ideologues and landlords all contributed to a confusion, rather than a clarification, of property rights as they existed in Ireland. Those who understood best what was happening were commentators like William Conner, John Stuart Mill and—given an altered twist by the intervention of the Great Famine—James Fintan Lalor, for all of whom the reality of Irish custom and rights stood higher than a theory of capitalism distorted by the prism of English practice and colonising interest. In particular, what Conner sought was a legislative regulation of the practices by which landlords and tenants in Ireland had, since the plantations, worked to reconcile their coexistence in the Irish countryside. This had, of course, not been a comfortable process, but much of the evidence suggests a broad willingness of both tenants and landlords to accept the reality of each other's existence and to work towards arrangements which enabled the landlords to survive on the basis of a rent fixed not by the market but by valuation, which recognised the pre-existing property rights of the tenant by accepting his perpetuity of tenure (including, of course, his right to sell), and by allowing the market to operate in the context of such shared rights and common interests as would evolve out of the stabilisation of these arrangements. It was the failure of Conner's remedy, or something like it, which set on its course the polarising conflict over tenure which proved so damaging to the capacity of Irish agriculture to respond to the demands of capitalist competition.

Common law in England had helped to create a partnership between the landlord and the farmer, and the clarity in custom as well as in law as to the respective rights and obligations of each had facilitated, rather than hindered, the advance of capitalism. The very period from the 1850s to the 1870s which in Ireland saw rising agricultural prosperity but lack of resolution as to the relative roles of landlords and tenants, saw in England large new investment in agriculture on the part both of landlords and of tenant farmers; as one English economic historian has written of that period, 'Bold investment by both indicated a confident age.'[10] In Ireland the complication of relatively recent conquest made such economic co-operation inherently more difficult, for there it remained the case that resistance to custom by government and landlords was more likely to prevent, and recognition of it to create, the security and stability required for the development of capitalism. There were, of course, many other problems in Ireland with which English agriculture did not have to cope. Large-scale industrialisation had created livelihoods in England for those made redundant on the land by the advance of modern capitalist farming, whereas in Ireland the massive problem of over-population undermined the possibility of agricultural reform and modernisation. The Great Famine was a devastating remedy for this problem; but had the basic principles of tenure been already resolved along lines such as those proposed by Conner, it is possible that consolidation of farms and accumulation of ownership might have happened in a form which began the process of change along consensus lines rather than by brutal landlord eviction. In such a scenario, tenants and landlords would have shared responsibility for actions seen to be in the interests of both. Partnership on the land, the absence of which in the 1870s Vaughan decries, may have evolved had the issue of the rights of a subdued population been faced earlier and more comprehensively. In those circumstances, the Irish landlord may have been a very different creature from his English counterpart, but he might also have evolved his own distinctive role and identity, playing a positive part in holding together a more viable agrarian society through the transition to capitalism. Greater stability in the countryside, and an Irish agriculture geared to the market and sensitive to investment possibilities, might also have proved more of a stimulus to non-agricultural economic development. Some validity exists in the analysis of Lalor, who saw as a consequence of the Famine the dissolution of the civil society at the pinnacle of which the landlords had sat and the consequent need for a new social compact which recognised the extent of the breakdown which had occurred. The land question, more than any other issue, represented through the rest of the nineteenth century the outward sign of these unresolved questions of social order and legal right.

The dispute over tenure was thus of fundamental importance in determining the character of Irish agriculture in the nineteenth and twentieth centuries, not because of that issue in itself, but because capitalism had been discredited in the consciousness of Irish farmers by the use to which it had been put in justifying the deprivation of rights traditionally held and passionately defended. There were defenders of capitalism who saw the damage being done; J. S. Mill was one, and the majority of the members of the Bessborough Commission were others. But the fierce attachment of British political opinion to the form of property right with which it was familiar, and the constraints consequently imposed upon possible legislation, meant that too little recognition was given, usually too late, to the legitimate perceptions of Irish occupiers. Thus the Ulster custom, initially a token of rights Irish farmers believed they held, was diluted to compensation for improvement to reconcile it to the limitations of outlook of British legislators. The 'three Fs' granted a belated recognition of those rights, but in a context in which the pattern of conflict had been set firm and in which the machinery created was bound to be used as an adversarial weapon. Only purchase, and the elimination of landlordism, could now resolve the problem, and although it gave no more to the farmers than Conner or Mill had sought, it did so to the exclusion of any continuing political and social role for the landlords, who had in any case—as Vaughan has so impressively shown—already largely written themselves out of the action of the Irish rural economy. For the bulk of the population it opened up the prospect, not always effectively pursued, of a relatively strong control of the terms in which capitalism was applied, avoiding many of the disastrous outcomes faced by communities in the Scottish Highlands in the era of Thatcherite capitalism; there whole communities are held to ransom by the property developers who have acquired in the market-place the ownership of estates once the possession of former hereditary chiefs.[11]

Land purchase represented the *cul-de-sac* in which the Irish land tenure issue came to its end; it was the solution to which there was no alternative. It involved buying the landlords out, not only in terms of the ownership of their land, but also of the role they had historically seen themselves as fulfilling. Because in the end it was what they themselves wanted, and because the terms of purchase—especially under the 1903 act—were moderately generous to them, it held out for them the prospect of relative prosperity and influence within Ireland—for most of them the only country with which they could identify themselves. For the tenants it meant ownership of the land to which they believed they had always possessed a proprietary right, and at a cost below that of the rent they would otherwise have been paying, and which they would be liable to pay only for a fixed term of years. More broadly for them, both as tenants and as nationalists, there was a powerful symbolic importance in the fact that the process of purchase was being facilitated by a subsidy from the British Treasury; to that extent the conquest was being undone. The opportunities for reconciliation were not what they had been in the 1840s, but the change was an important one for social relations within Ireland and for the relationship between Ireland and Britain. But that too was to be subverted by the eventual rejection of the conciliation policy which evolved within the nationalist movement in the aftermath of the Wyndham Act. The gesture which symbolically offered incorporation in the nation in return for the undoing of the fruits of conquest may have strained the limits of what had occurred, but it was important to the evolving sense of nation, and its negation was therefore of great moment.

There was also a longer legacy in the form of the part that the annuities payable under the land purchase legislation were to play in the relationship of the newly established Irish Free State and Great Britain. Much of the argument for the 1903 act had turned around the fact that a substantial part of the cost of the transfer of land, and the necessary credit facilities, were being provided by the British exchequer—that being, of course, the exchequer of the United Kingdom, but its identification as British being useful in a political sense. With the formation of the Irish Free State, arrangements had to be made for the payment of the annuities by which the farmers were meeting their share of the costs of purchase. They were, of course, repaying a debt to the exchequer, but of a United Kingdom which no longer existed in the same form. The farmers' payments were now payable to the government of the Free State, but, as a result of negotiations in 1922 and 1923 pursuant to the Treaty, it was agreed that the Free State would pay land annuities of £3.13 million per annum to the British government.[12] While the technical obligation was a clear one, at least to the proportion of the national debt which still attached to the remaining United Kingdom, it might have been more sensitive and politic to have allowed this money to remain with the Irish exchequer (at least the component attaching to the area of the Free State) than to have provided the ammunition that this did for the opposition in the Free State. Given the role of conquest in the history of the land tenure issue and the degree to which land purchase was perceived as returning the land to its traditional owners, this provided a grievance which reopened the land issue in the politics of the new state and contributed to a poisoning of the in any case difficult process of normalisation of relationships between the two states and their governments. This was the more unfortunate in that, in the wider context of negotiations in 1925 over the splitting up of the national debt, there seems to have been some prospect that the Irish premier, W. T. Cosgrave, might have secured the remission of the land annuities.[13] As it was, they remained a grievance in Anglo-Irish relations—one greatly intensified once de Valera had come to office—until finally removed by a lump-sum payment of £10 million as part of a wider Anglo-Irish trade and financial agreement in April 1938.[14] But by that time they had served to add new fuel to the dying embers of the land issue, given great electoral advantage to de Valera, and aggravated Anglo-Irish relations on an issue on which public opinion in Britain inevitably, but unfairly, stereotyped the reaction in terms of traditional expectations of the Irish.

The Irish land question, both in its long history and in its resolution, had far-reaching implications in relation to the ethnic tensions of the country. This issue impinged in very different ways upon the majority Catholic Irish population and the two minorities, the Presbyterian Irish and the Anglican Irish. When it came to defending the traditional rights of land tenure, especially as in the post-Famine years and in the 1898–1903 period, there was a strong and natural alliance between Catholic and Presbyterian tenant farmers. However, whereas this issue of land tenure merged and integrated with nationalism for the majority, this was not so for the northern Presbyterian farmers, whose adjustment to capitalism was made easier on account of the north's location as hinterland to a thriving industrial centre, thus replicating some of the conditions of the transition to industrial capitalism observable in the British experience. But the main cleavage which the land question formed and accentuated was that between tenant farmers and the landlords, which meant—in most of the country—between the Catholic Irish and the Anglican Irish. The developing metaphor of land and nationalism, combined with the element of 'terror' which accompanied the collective mobilisation of the majority community, inevitably created a conflict with strong racial and ethnic undertones. The tradition of Smith O'Brien, of Isaac Butt and even, it should be said, of Charles Stewart Parnell was left little breathing-space in this environment, despite the abiding lip-service still paid to it. The dimension of reconciliation involved in the O'Brien–Dunraven-inspired initiatives after the 1903 Land Act were thus crucial in breaking the mould of the preceding quarter-century; the aborting of that 'new departure' cemented in place that divisive and ultimately anti-national pattern. It was ironic indeed that a crucial role in defeating the conciliation policy was played by the Catholic nationalists of Belfast from whose immediate circumstances the issue of the land could not have been more remote.

In the part played in this outcome by Joseph Devlin and his followers, in alliance with Dillon, Davitt and Sexton and the *Freeman's Journal*, is foreshadowed the later partition of Ireland. The land question had by the early twentieth century become so central to the social and political dynamic of Ireland that it had severely limited the potential for the very concept of a civil society. The implications of the finalisation of land purchase, as provided for under the Wyndham Act, had, however, opened up a new path. In fact, in economic and social terms a new potential existed for an alliance of interest between the 'strong' farmers, so central to the whole formation of a nationalist hegemony, and the now unambiguously capitalist former landlord class. The latter generally had retained possession of their demesne lands, in many cases substantial farms, and all of them were now, by reason of their purchase money, significant capitalist investors. The future of that class in modern Ireland was to a degree diminished by the circumstances and character of the Anglo-Irish conflict of 1917–21, but in 1903 there was an open prospect of a merging of interests of the most substantial class of Irish farmers and of their erstwhile landlords. Indeed, the later history of the relationship of these two groups, their historical distinctiveness determined by the land issue, by conquest and by ethnic and religious difference, shows that their roles economically, and to an extent socially, were to merge. The trivial, but symbolically revealing, example of fox-hunting illustrates this point. As Trollope's account of the fate of the hunt in the land war shows, there was no sharper symbolic definer of the division of interest between the hunters, as the elite, and the watching crowd—so easily turned from festive bystanders into bitter antagonists—as the conquered mass. And yet a cursory glance at the columns of the largely Catholic/nationalist *Irish Independent* in the 1930s or of the pastimes of the modern Irish elite (for example, Charles Haughey) shows how the hunt in modern Ireland has become a national and unifying factor between traditionally opposed cultures and a consolidator of the essential capitalist commonalty of the two leading contestant groupings of the land war. What happened in 1903–4 was that the political logic of this new economic and class reality was defied and the primacy of ethnic and sectarian division was asserted to the detriment of both capitalist interest and nationalist potential.

The specific environment and set of relationships which created the immediate circumstances of partition were deep and entrenched, and were likely to have been, and to have persisted in being, intractable in terms of any likely constitutional settlement in Ireland. What the opportunities of 1903–4 provided was the possibility that for the future and for the greater part of Ireland majorities and minorities might come to be defined in terms of class and economic interests and a break made with the pattern of the past, partly created because of the land question, in which major alignments were defined almost entirely in terms which correlated to ethnic and sectarian identities. Had such a realignment been carried through, it would necessarily have carried with it significant implications for how the Protestants in the north saw themselves, whether as an embattled regional majority, or as having diverse alliances and interests in relation to counterparts, whether defined in religious, class or economic terms, elsewhere in Ireland. Likewise, it would have avoided for the more nationally located minority, the so-called southern Unionists, the fate which awaited them of being dragged along in the wake of a political agenda devised by co-religionists with whom their sympathies were not absolute but to whom there was no longer any countervailing weight. The reassertion of the old lines of enmity by the official nationalist movement, as achieved by Dillon and others in the aftermath of the 1903 act, ensured that what had been an incidental, if central, consequence of the dispute over land tenure would be stereotyped into the politics of a new age. Those like William O'Brien who had sought a different path had perceived that a nation founded on ethnic and sectarian division could not be a complete nation, and that compromise with the symbols and structures of nationality might, in the end, provide the opportunity for a fuller national life. After all, what had the very concept of Home Rule been about, if not—unsuccessfully, as it transpired—to provide such a framework of compromise and accommodation. It was perhaps the land issue's identification with Home Rule which had wrecked that aspiration; it was its resolution which provided an opening for a new attempt, defined in terms and symbols untrammelled by that legacy.

If partition, and what it represented in terms of a national life, is the most tangible legacy of the land question, it is by no means an isolated one. It was part of the larger obstruction posed by the land question itself, and then by its lingering shadow, to Ireland's coming to terms with its place in an increasingly capitalist Europe. The end of the Union took Ireland, in both its parts, into a romanticised idyll of rurality, religiosity and sectarian triumphalism, drawn from a long historical legacy, but shaped in more recent times by rival constructions etched out through conflict over the possession and cultural meaning of the land. It was the beckoning call at the end of the 1950s of a new Union, then known as the European Economic Community, which helped to draw Ireland—or at least that part of it which constituted the Republic of Ireland—back into a wider economic, political and cultural environment and enabled an exceedingly claustrophobic relationship with a powerful neighbour, a relationship substantially shaped by conquest and appropriation of the land, to merge back into the variety and pluralism of a new multi-national entity; Ireland had, in the words of Fergal Tobin, 'abandoned an officially prescribed make-believe culture in favour of the noisy, vulgar but real charms of a freely available alternative'.[15] Was it no more than coincidence that this pulling away of the veil of the past was so quickly followed by a reopening of the issue of the constitutional forms which had stereotyped the ethnic and sectarian cleavage drawn in such stark terms by the land question? Or had the spectre of unrealised affinities of interest and aspiration been drawn from its uneasy grave to expiate, in a final and dreadful exorcism, the early twentieth-century failure properly and decently to lay to rest the ethnic and sectarian attributes of a substantively resolved issue?

In a capitalist world land is a commodity, but if its possession is in dispute, the rules that apply will not be capitalist ones. In Ireland that dispute created not only a conflict based on histori-cal ethnic and religious fault-lines, but it kept alive an ideal of the land which bedevilled a process of modernisation of which Ireland was inextricably a part. Joseph Lee has suggested that 'The Irish carry from their mother's womb not so much a fanatic heart as a begrudger one', that 'Status depended not only on rising oneself, but on preventing others from rising', and that 'For many, keeping the other fellow down offered the surest defence of their own position.'[16] Whether this is too universal a judgment to be fair or not, the circumstances of the long conflict over land, of the consequent idealisation of its pos-session, even in unsustainably small parcels, and of the rivalries generated by this between those whose interests in class and economic terms, whether at the bottom or the top, were essen-tially similar must have served to accentuate such a propensity. It was a conflict which was central in the shaping of modern Ireland, and one which has substantially influenced the forms, the attitudes and the problems of that society long after its cessation.

Appendix

LEGISLATION OF THE PARLIAMENT OF THE UNITED KINGDOM

Irish Incumbered Estates Act, 1848

'An Act to facilitate the Sale of Incumbered Estates in Ireland'. 11 & 12 Vict., c. 48 [14 August 1848]

To enable indebted estates to be sold free of encumbrance. Gave power to owner to contract to sell, subject to approbation of the High Court of Chancery in Ireland, despite encumbrance. Advertisement to find those with a claim on the estate. Purchase money paid to Bank of Ireland in name of the Accountant General, to be applied in payment of the encumbrances or otherwise to persons entitled under the act.

Incumbered Estates (Ireland) Act, 1849

'An Act further to facilitate the Sale and Transfer of Incumbered Estates in Ireland'. 12 & 13 Vict., c. 77 [28 July 1849]

Provided for appointment of Commissioners for Sale of Incumbered Estates in Ireland, to carry out the provisions of this and the previous act in place of the High Court of Chancery. Three commissioners, each appointed for a term of five years, to have the jurisdiction of a Court of Equity. (The Commission was also called the Incumbered Estates Court (Ireland).) Purchase money from sale of an estate now to be held in the name of the commissioners and, after costs, to be applied towards payment or satisfaction of encumbrances or charges on the property.

Incumbered Estates (Ireland) Act, 1852

'An Act to continue the Powers of Applying for a Sale of Lands under the Act for facilitating the Sale and Transfer of Incumbered Estates in Ireland'. 15 & 16 Vict., c. 67 [30 June 1852]

Provided for an extension of one year to the original three-year period within which application could be made for the sale of an estate under the legislation.

Incumbered Estates (Ireland) Act Continuance Act, 1853

'An Act for continuing and amending the Act for facilitating the Sale and Transfer of Incumbered Estates in Ireland'. 16 & 17 Vict., c. 64 [15 August 1853]

Provided for a further extension of one year within which application could be made under the legislation.

Incumbered Estates (Ireland) Act Continuance Act, 1855

'An Act to extend the period for applying for a Sale under the Acts for facilitating the Sale and Transfer of Incumbered Estates in Ireland'. 18 & 19 Vict., c. 73 [30 July 1855]

Provided for a further extension of one year.

Landed Estates Court (Ireland) Act, 1858

'An Act to facilitate the Sale and Transfer of Land in Ireland'. 21 & 22 Vict., c. 72 [2 August 1858]

Constituted a Landed Estates Court as a permanent court for the sale and transfer of land, whether encumbered or unencumbered, and invested it with other and more extensive powers. Replaced Commissioners for Sale of Incumbered Estates. Judges to hold office during good behaviour. The court was given the status of a Court of Equity, with appeals to be directly to the Court of Appeal in Chancery (Ireland).

The Landed Property (Ireland) Improvement Act, 1860 [Cardwell's Act]

'An Act to amend the Law relating to the Tenure and Improvement of Land in Ireland'. 23 & 24 Vict., c. 153 [28 August 1860]

Provided for compensation for improvements made by tenants where prior consent of the owner had been obtained.

The Landlord and Tenant Law Amendment Act (Ireland), 1860 [Deasy's Act]

'An Act to consolidate and amend the Law of Landlord and Tenant in Ireland'. 23 & 24 Vict., c. 154 [28 August 1860]

Provided that the relation of landlord and tenant in Ireland 'shall be deemed to be founded on the express or implied Contract of the Parties, and not upon Tenure or Service'.

Landlord and Tenant (Ireland) Act, 1870 [Gladstone's First Land Act]

'An Act to amend the Law relating to the Occupation and Ownership of Land in Ireland'. 33 & 34 Vict., c. 46 [1 August 1870]

Made enforceable at law the tenant right custom where it existed in the province of Ulster or in cases of like practices elsewhere in Ireland. Provided for compensation for disturbance by the landlord of a tenant not enjoying a tenant right practice. Gave compensation for improvements made by a tenant or his predecessors where the tenant was quitting his holding and was not claiming under the other provisions of this act. Established provision for the sale of a holding by the tenant through the Landed Estates Court and with advances from the Commissioners of Public Works (the 'Bright clauses'). For an exposition of the working of the act and its consequences, see W. E. Vaughan, *Landlords and Tenants in Mid-Victorian Ireland*, Oxford: Clarendon Press, 1994, pp. 93–102.

Landlord and Tenant (Ireland) Act, 1872

'An Act to explain and amend the Landlord and Tenant (Ireland) Act, 1870, so far as relates to the Purchase by Tenants of their Holdings'. 35 & 36 Vict., c. 32 [18 July 1872]

Enacted regulations for the purchase by tenants of their holdings, and enabled sale to proceed in certain cases where advances had been paid, notwithstanding forfeiture.

Land Law (Ireland) Act, 1881 [Gladstone's Second Land Act]

'An Act to further amend the Law relating to the Occupation and Ownership of Land in Ireland, and for other purposes relating thereto'. 44 & 45 Vict., c. 49 [22 August 1881]

Provided for right of tenant to sell his tenancy. Gave power to civil bill courts to fix rent (termed a judicial rent), with provision for referral to a Land Commission, established under the act and comprising a judicial and two other commissioners. Provided for conversion of ordinary tenancies to fixed tenancies. (These provisions constituted what were commonly called the 'three Fs'). Extended facilities for purchase by tenants of their holdings.

Arrears of Rent (Ireland) Act, 1882

'An Act to make provision respecting certain Arrears of Rent in Ireland'. 45 & 46 Vict., c. 47 [18 August 1882]

Provided for settlement by Land Commission of arrears of rent antecedent to the 1881 act.

Purchase of Land (Ireland) Act, 1885 [Ashbourne Act]

'An Act to provide greater facilities for the Sale of Land to occupying Tenants in Ireland'. 48 & 49 Vict., c. 73 [14 August 1885]

Gave the power to the Land Commission to make advances to the tenants for the purchase of their holdings, whether directly from their landlords or from the Land Commission. Empowered the Commission to purchase whole estates for resale.

Land Law (Ireland) Act, 1887

'An Act to amend the Land Law (Ireland) Act, 1881, and the Purchase of Land (Ireland) Act, 1885, and for other purposes consistent therewith'. 50 & 51 Vict., c. 33 [23 August 1887]

Extended the benefits of the 1881 act to leaseholders and made changes to the procedures for the purchase of holdings.

Purchase of Land (Ireland) Amendment Act, 1888

'An Act further to facilitate the Purchase of Land in Ireland by increasing the amount applicable for that purpose by the Land Commission'. 51 & 52 Vict., c. 49 [24 December 1888]

Increased the limit of advances which were permitted to be made by the Land Commission.

Land Law (Ireland) Act, 1888, Amendment Act, 1889

'An Act to amend "The Land Law (Ireland) Act, 1888", with regard to Leaseholders'. 52 & 53 Vict., c. 59 [30 August 1889]

Clarified the 1888 act with respect to certain categories of lease-holders.

Purchase of Land (Ireland) Act, 1891 [Balfour Act]

'An Act to provide further Funds for the Purchase of Land in Ireland, and to make permanent the Land Commission; and to provide for the Improvement of the Congested Districts in Ireland'. 54 & 55 Vict., c. 48 [5 August 1891]

Provided for payment to vendor in land stock. Established permanency of the Land Commission. Made provision to ensure that an adequate proportion of the available funds was reserved for the purchase of farms for which the valuation was under £50. Constituted a Congested Districts Board, with powers and resources to enable it to amalgamate holdings and to aid migration and emigration, agriculture and industry in the areas defined as congested.

Congested Districts Board (Ireland) Act, 1893

'An Act to amend the power of the Congested Districts Board so far as respects the Purchase and Holding of Property'. 56 & 57 Vict., c. 35 [24 August 1893]

Gave additional powers to the Board to acquire and hold property in order to achieve its purposes.

Congested Districts Board (Ireland) Act, 1894

'An Act to make further provision with respect to the Congested Districts Board for Ireland'. 57 & 58 Vict., c. 50 [25 August 1894]

Provided for guarantee for deposits and purchaser's insurance money, and other matters relating to the Congested Districts Board.

Purchase of Land (Ireland) Amendment Act, 1895, Session 2

'An Act to re-enact Section Thirteen of the Purchase of Land (Ireland) Act, 1891'. 59 Vict., c. 4 [5 September 1895]

Re-enacted, with modification, the specified clause.

Land Law (Ireland) Act, 1896

'An Act to further amend the Law relating to the Occupation and Ownership of Land in Ireland, and for other purposes relating thereto'. 59 & 60 Vict., c. 47 [14 August 1896]

Comprised five main parts, providing for: (1) changes to the law regarding the determination of fair rents; (2) alterations to the functioning of the Land Commission; (3) changes to the provisions for land purchase; (4) amendments to the procedures for the purchase and sale of land by the Congested Districts Board; and (5) provisions for the reinstatement of, or purchase of a holding by, an evicted tenant.

Congested Districts Board (Ireland) Act, 1899

'An Act to amend certain provisions of the Land Law (Ireland) Act, 1896, affecting the Congested Districts Board, and to make further provision for the expenses of that Board out of money provided by Parliament'. 62 & 63 Vict., c. 18 [1 August 1899]

Purchase of Land (Ireland) Act, 1901

'An Act to amend subsection (1) of section nine of the Purchase of Land (Ireland) Act, 1891, and subsection (2) of section forty-three of the Land Law (Ireland) Act, 1896'. 1 Edw. VII, c. 3 [2 July 1901]

Provided for the exceeding of the specified maximum amount for an advance towards the purchase of land.

Purchase of Land (Ireland) (No. 2) Act, 1901

'An Act to extend the Purchase of Land (Ireland) Amendment Act, 1889'. 1 Edw. VII, c. 30 [17 August 1901]

Congested Districts Board (Ireland) Act, 1901

'An Act to amend the Congested Districts Board (Ireland) Acts'. 1 Edw. VII, c. 34 [17 August 1901]

Provided for facilitation of resale of land by the Congested Districts Board and the extension of the powers of the Board to enable it to purchase land outside the defined congested districts.

Irish Land Act, 1903 [Wyndham Act]

'An Act to amend the Law relating to the occupation and ownership of land in Ireland and for other purposes relating thereto and to amend the Labourers (Ireland) Acts'. 3 Edw. VII, c. 37 [14 August 1903]

New provisions for purchase and resale of whole estates to the occupying tenants, with substitution of cash payments for guaranteed land stock. Establishment of a Land Purchase Aid Fund for funding of Land Commission purchases. Provision for the jurisdiction, powers and duties of the Land Commission in relation to this act to be exercised and performed by three members of the Commission, designated the Estates Commissioners. For a fuller exposition of this act see above, pp. 153–8.

Irish Land Act, 1904

'An Act to explain and amend Section forty-eight of the Irish Land Act, 1903, with respect to the payment and application of the percentage provided by the said section'. 4 Edw. VII. c. 34 [15 August 1904]

Irish Land Act, 1907

'An Act to make provision with respect to the Disposal of Mining

Rights under section thirteen of the Irish Land Act, 1903, and to amend section fifty-four of that Act'. 7 Edw. VII. c. 38 [28 August 1907]

Evicted Tenants (Ireland) Act, 1907

'An Act to facilitate the provision of Land for certain Evicted Tenants in Ireland and for other purposes connected therewith, and to make provision with respect to the tenure of office by the Estates Commissioners'. 7 Edw. VII. c. 56 [28 August 1907]

Gave power to the Estates Commissioners to acquire land compulsorily for evicted tenants, but excluding land held by a tenant 'cultivating the same as an ordinary farmer in accordance with proper methods of husbandry' and land being purchased under the Land Purchase Acts.

Evicted Tenants (Ireland) Act, 1908

'An Act to amend section one of the Evicted Tenants (Ireland) Act, 1907, with respect to the compulsory acquisition of tenanted land'. 8 Edw. VII. c. 22 [1 August 1908]

Irish Land Act, 1909 [Birrell Act]

'An Act to amend the law relating to the Occupation and Ownership of Land in Ireland, and for other purposes relating thereto.' 9 Edw. VII. c. 42 [3 December 1909]

Altered the financial provisions of the 1903 Act. Limited the amount of an advance to a non-resident occupier. Changed the definition of a congested estate. Provided for compulsory purchase of an estate where agreement could not be reached with the vendor through the processes of the 1903 Act. Gave corporate status to the Congested Districts Board and reconstituted the Board.

Irish Land (Provision for Sailors and Soldiers) Act, 1919

'An Act to facilitate the provision of land in Ireland for men who have served in the Naval, Military, or Air Forces of the Crown in the present war, and for other purposes incidental thereto'. 9 & 10 Geo. V. c. 82 [23 December 1919]

Extension of the benefits of the Land Purchase Acts to men who had served in the forces, subject to fitness and suitability, as if they had been tenants or proprietors.

Irish Free State Land Purchase (Loan Guarantee) Act, 1924

'An Act to authorise the Treasury to guarantee a loan to be raised by the Government of the Irish Free State for the purposes of Land Purchase in that State'. 15 Geo. V. c. 3 [18 December 1924]

Northern Ireland Land Act, 1925

'An Act to amend the Law relating to the Occupation and Ownership of Land in Northern Ireland; and for other purposes relating thereto'. 15 & 16 Geo. V. c. 34 [28 May 1925]

Altered the rate of purchase annuity, provided for automatic sale of remaining tenanted land in Northern Ireland and abolished the power to fix judicial rents.

Northern Ireland Land Act, 1929

'An Act to amend the Northern Ireland Land Act, 1925'. 19 Geo. V, c. 14 [27 March 1929]

Northern Ireland Land Purchase (Winding Up) Act, 1935

'An Act to make provision for the winding up of the system of land purchase in Northern Ireland established by the Land Purchase Acts and other enactments in that behalf, for the abolition of the Land Purchase Commission, Northern Ireland, and the transfer of functions exercisable under the said Acts and other enactments, and for purposes incidental to the purposes aforesaid and consequential thereon'. 25 & 26 Geo. V, c. 21 [6 June 1935]

LEGISLATION OF THE IRISH OIREACHTAS

Land Law (Commission) Act, 1923

'An Act to amend the law relating to the Irish Land Commission and to dissolve the Congested Districts Board for Ireland and transfer its functions to the Irish Land Commission, and for other purposes connected therewith'. No. 27 of 1923 [24 July 1923]

Reconstituted the Irish Land Commission and dissolved the Congested Districts Board, transferring its functions, funds and staff to the Land Commission.

Land Act, 1923

'An Act to amend the law relating to the occupation and ownership of land and for other purposes relating thereto'. No. 42 of 1923 [9 August 1923]

Abolished remaining elements of dual ownership and put the machinery for making tenants owners, and for expropriating land to relieve congestion, on an entirely compulsory basis. For a fuller exposition of this Act see C. F. Kolbert and Timothy O'Brien, *Land Reform in Ireland: A Legal History of the Irish Land Problem and its Settlement*, Cambridge: Department of Land Economy, 1975, pp. 47–9.

Land Bond Act, 1925

'An Act to make further and better provision in relation to the issue of Land Bonds under the Land Act, 1923, and the guarantee and redemption thereof and payment of interest thereon and for the disposal of purchase annuities paid under that Act'. No. 25 of 1925 [3 July 1925]

Land Act, 1926

'An Act to confirm and, for the purpose of such confirmation, to declare the extent of the application of the Land Act, 1923, to tenanted land and to define more fully the land which is tenanted land for the purposes of that Act'. No. 11 of 1926 [11 March 1926]

Averted the possibility that a landlord prior to the passing of the 1923 Act could become entitled to the land by reason of the expiration of a tenancy.

Land Act, 1927

'An Act to amend the law relating to the occupation and ownership of land and for other purposes relating thereto'. No. 19 of 1927 [21 May 1927].

Extensive procedural provisions in relation to the functioning of the Land Commission, the financial provisions for land purchase, and other aspects of managing land occupation issues.

Land Act, 1929

'An Act to give to the Irish Land Commission power in certain cases to appoint limited administrators to deceased persons, to fix the standard purchase annuity in respect of holdings subject to rents other than judicial rents, to explain and amend the provisions of the Land Act, 1923, in relation to fisheries and fishing rights, and to give to the Irish Land Commission power to purchase certain fisheries and fishing rights'. No. 31 of 1929 [24 July 1929]

Land Act, 1931

'An Act to make provision for the early vesting of holdings in the purchasers thereof under the Land Purchase Acts and for that and other purposes to amend those Acts and the Local Registration of Title (Ireland) Act, 1891, and also to make provision in respect of the variation of certain tithe rent-charges and variable rents'. No. 11 of 1931 [30 April 1931]

Land (Purchase Annuities Fund) Act, 1933

'An Act to make provision for the disposal of the moneys now or hereafter to the credit of the Purchase Annuities Fund'. No. 2 of 1933 [30 March 1933]

Allowed surpluses in the fund, not required for the Guarantee Fund, to be made available to the Exchequer as the Minister of Finance should direct.

Land Bond Act, 1933

'An Act to make provision in relation to the payment of certain purchase money and the making of certain advances under the Land Act, 1923, and subsequent Land Purchase Acts by means of an issue of bonds, and in relation to the creation, issue, and redemption of bonds for that purpose, and in relation to other matters connected with the matters aforesaid, and to amend in certain respects the law relating to Land Purchase Finance'. No. 33 of 1933 [29 September 1933]

Land Act, 1933

'An Act to amend generally the law, finance, and practice relating to land purchase, and in particular to make further and better provision for the execution of the functions of the judicial and lay commissioners of the Land Commission and to provide for the revision of purchase annuities and certain other annual payments and for the funding of arrears thereof, and to provide for other matters connected with the matters aforesaid'. No. 38 of 1933 [13 October 1933]

Land Bond Act, 1934

'An Act to make further provision for the creation and issue of Land Bonds for the purpose of the payment of purchase moneys and the making of advances under the Land Purchase Acts and to provide for the payment of interest on and the redemption of such Land Bonds and for other matters connected therewith'. No. 11 of 1934 [23 March 1934]

Land Act, 1936

'An Act to amend and extend the Land Purchase Acts in divers respects'. No. 41 of 1936 [14 August 1936]

Land Act, 1939

'An Act to amend and extend the Land Purchase Acts in divers respects and to amend the law in relation to the application of the Increase of Rent and Mortgage Interest (Restrictions) Acts, 1923 to 1930, to dwelling-houses of which the Land Commission is the landlord'. No. 26 of 1939 [8 August 1939]

Land Act, 1946

'An Act to amend and extend the Land Purchase Acts'. No. 12 of 1946' [11 June 1946]

Gave power to the Land Commission to direct purchasers to reside on their holdings.

Land Reclamation Act, 1949

'An Act to authorise the Minister for Agriculture to carry out land reclamation, field drainage and other works for the improvement of agricultural holdings and to provide for the payment by the occupiers of a contribution towards the cost of those works and for other matters relating to the matters aforesaid'. No. 25 of 1949 [30 July 1949]

Extended the use of annuities as provided under the Land Purchase Acts for the purposes of this legislation.

Land Act, 1950

'An Act to amend and extend the Land Purchase Acts'. No. 16 of 1950 [19 June 1950]

Land Act, 1953

'An Act to amend and extend the Land Purchase Acts'. No. 18 of 1953 [7 July 1953]

Land Act, 1954

'An Act to amend section 15 of the Land Act, 1950'. No. 21 of 1954 [13 July 1954]

The sole purpose of this Act was to amend the retirement age of Lay Commissioners of the Land Commission from 65 years to 67 years.

Land Bond Act, 1964

'An Act to amend the Land Bond Act, 1934'. No. 13 of 1964 [30 June 1964]

Increased the limit on the creation and issue of land bonds for land purchase from £15 million to £25 million.

Land Act, 1965

'An Act to amend and extend the Land Purchase Acts'. No. 2 of 1965 [9 March 1965]

Land Bond Act, 1969

'An Act to amend the Land Bond Act, 1934, to provide for the alteration of existing land bonds to unnumbered units of one pound, and to provide for other matters connected with the matters aforesaid'. No. 24 of 1969 [30 July 1969]

Increased the limit on the creation and issue of land bonds for land purchase from £25 million to £40 million; provided that land bonds already issued and those issued in future should be in denominations of £1; transferred the registers of land bonds to the Bank of Ireland.

Land Bond Act, 1975

'An Act to amend the Land Bond Act, 1934'. No. 5 of 1975 [5 May 1975]

Increased the limit on the creation and issue of land bonds for land purchase to £60 million.

Land Bond Act, 1978

'An Act to amend the Land Bond Act, 1934'. No. 22 of 1978 [5 July 1978]

Increased the limit on the creation and issue of land bonds for land purchase to £80 million.

Land Bond Act, 1980

'An Act to amend the Land Bond Act, 1934'. No. 5 of 1980 [13 May 1980]

Increased the limit on the creation and issue of land bonds for land purchase to £105 million.

Land Bond Act, 1983

'An Act to amend the Land Bond Act, 1934'. No. 9 of 1983 [31 March 1983]

Increased the limit on the creation and issue of land bonds for land purchase to £130 million.

Land Act, 1984

'An Act to amend and extend the Land Purchase Acts'. No. 24 of 1984 [16 December 1984]

Excluded leases of agricultural land from certain enactments in the Land Acts of 1860, 1870, 1881, 1887 and 1896; dissolved the Purchase Annuities Fund set up under the act of 1923; dissolved the Irish Church Temporalities Fund established under the Irish Church Act of 1869; and amended section 46 of the 1923 Land Act so as to extend its application from the registered owner of a holding to a person having an interest in it.

Land Bond Act, 1992

'An Act to amend and extend the Land Purchase Acts and to make provision with respect to other matters connected with the aforesaid'. No. 4 of 1992 [18 March 1992]

Provided for the dissolution of the Land Bond Fund established under the act of 1923 and the Guarantee Fund established under the Act of 1891, and for the redemption of land bonds.

Sources: United Kingdom Statute Books; Acts of the Oireachtas; C. F. Kolbert and Timothy O'Brien, *Land Reform in Ireland: A Legal History of the Irish Land Problem and its Settlement*, Cambridge: Department of Land Economy, 1975.

References

Introduction (pp. 1–4)
1. R. Barry O'Brien, *The Parliamentary History of the Irish Land Question from 1829 to 1869, and the Origin and Results of the Ulster Custom*, London, 1880.
2. John E. Pomfret, *The Struggle for Land in Ireland, 1800–1923*, repr., New York: Russell & Russell, 1969.
3. J. S. Donnelly, *The Land and the People of Nineteenth-Century Cork: The Rural Economy and the Land Question*, London: Routledge & Kegan Paul, 1975.

Chapter 1: Landlords, Tenants and Agrarian Change (pp. 5–26)
1. W. C. Sellar and R. J. Yeatman, *1066 and All That*, London: Methuen, 1930, p. 107.
2. Patrick O'Farrell, *Ireland's English Question*, London: Batsford, 1971.
3. Thomas A. Boylan and Timothy P. Foley, *Political Economy and Colonial Ireland: The Propagation and Ideological Function of Economic Discourse in the Nineteenth Century*, London: Routledge & Kegan Paul, 1992, p. 117.
4. R. D. Collison Black, *Economic Thought and the Irish Question, 1817–1870*, Cambridge: Cambridge University Press, 1960, p. 24.
5. Harold Perkin, *The Origins of Modern English Society, 1780–1880*, London: Routledge & Kegan Paul, 1969, pp. 38–56.
6. T. C. Foster, *Letters on the Condition of the People of Ireland*, London, 1847, pp. 30–31.
7. H. D. Inglis, *Ireland in 1834: Journey throughout Ireland during the spring, summer, and autumn of 1834*, London, 1834, I, p. 64.
8. Foster, *Letters*, p. 28.

9. Ibid., pp. 110–13.
10. Ibid., p. 216.
11. Ibid., pp. 116–128.
12. Mr & Mrs S. C. Hall, *Ireland: Its Scenery, Character, &c*, London, 1843, III, pp. 261–2.
13. J. L. and Barbara Hammond, *The Village Labourer*, London: Longmans, Green, 1948, I, pp. 83–92.
14. J. H. Clapham, *An Economic History of Modern Britain*, Cambridge: Cambridge University Press, 1932, Bk 2, p. 259.
15. E. A. Currie, 'Land Tenures, Enclosures and Field-Patterns in Co. Derry in the Eighteenth and Nineteenth Centuries', *Irish Geography*, ix (1976), pp. 50–53.
16. Ibid.
17. Ralph Gibson and Mark Blinkhorn, Introduction to *Landownership and Power in Modern Europe*, London: Harper Collins, 1991, p. 14.
18. Ibid.
19. Quoted in C. F. Kolbert and Timothy O'Brien, *Land Reform in Ireland: A Legal History of the Irish Land Problem and its Settlement*, Cambridge: Department of Land Economy, 1975, p. 12.
20. K. Theodore Hoppen, 'Landownership and Power in Nineteenth-Century Ireland: The Decline of an Elite' in Gibson and Blinkhorn (eds), *Landownership and Power*, p. 176.
21. Pastoral address of Abp John Thomas Troy, 1798, quoted in A. C. Hepburn, *The Conflict of Nationality in Modern Ireland*, London: Edward Arnold, 1980, pp. 13–14.
22. W. E. Vaughan, *Landlords and Tenants in Mid-Victorian Ireland*, Oxford: Clarendon Press, 1994; idem, 'A Study of Landlord and Tenant Relations in Ireland between the Famine and the Land War, 1850–78' (Ph.D. thesis, Trinity College, Dublin, 1973).
23. Barbara L. Solow, *The Land Question and the Irish Economy, 1870–1903*, Massachusetts: Harvard University Press, 1971.
24. See *The Irish Journals of Elizabeth Smith, 1840–1850*, ed. David Thomson with Moyra McGusty, Oxford: Clarendon Press, 1980.
25. E. Estyn Evans, Introduction to *Facts from Gweedore, compiled from the notes of Lord George Hill*, Belfast: Queen's University, 1971, p. xvi.
26. J. Michael Hill, 'The Origins of the Scottish Plantations in Ulster to 1625: A Reinterpretation', *Journal of British Studies*, xxxii, no. 1 (Jan. 1993), pp. 24–43.

27. Michael Beames, Peasants and Power: *The Whiteboy Movements and their Control in Pre-Famine Ireland*, Brighton: Harvester, 1983, pp. 128–39.
28. L. M. Cullen, *An Economic History of Ireland since 1660*, London: Batsford, 1976, p. 115.
29. Thomas Bartlett, 'An End to Moral Economy: The Irish Militia Disturbances of 1793', *Past and Present*, no. 99 (May 1983), pp. 41–64.
30. Elizabeth Smith, *Irish Journals*, pp. 157–8.
31. Ibid., p. 6.
32. Evans, *Facts from Gweedore*, pp. v–vi.
33. Elizabeth Batt, *The Moncks and Charleville House: A Wicklow Family in the Nineteenth Century*, Dublin: Blackwater Press, 1979, p. 233.
34. Vaughan, *Landlords and Tenants in Mid-Victorian Ireland*, p. 85.

Chapter 2: Pressure for Reform (pp. 27–53)

1. Black, *Economic Thought and the Irish Question*, p. 24.
2. William Conner, *Two Letters to the Editor of the Times on the Rackrent Oppression of Ireland, its Source, its Evils and its Remedy*, Dublin, 1846. The two letters constituting the main body of this pamphlet were a response to the reports of the *Times* commissioner, T. C. Foster, sent to report on conditions in Ireland (see above, pp. 12–14).
3. Ibid., p. iv.
4. See Black, *Economic Thought and the Irish Question*, p. 24.
5. David N. Buckley, *James Fintan Lalor: Radical*, Cork: Cork University Press, 1990, pp. 29ff.
6. Ibid., pp. 34–5.
7. J. S. Mill, *The Principles of Political Economy*, 3rd ed., London, 1852, I, p. 401.
8. Mill uses the term 'cottier' to apply to small farmers and 'generally all peasant farmers whose rents are determined by competition' (*Principles*, p. 383); but see Michael Beames, 'Cottiers and Conacre in Pre-Famine Ireland', *Journal of Peasant Studies*, ii (1975), pp. 351–4 for an explanation of diverse meanings attaching to this term in the Irish context; see also Oliver MacDonagh, 'The Economy and Society, 1830–45' in W. E. Vaughan (ed.), *A New History of Ireland*, V: *Ireland under the Union, 1801–70*, Oxford: Clarendon Press, 1989, pp. 218–19, for a more general definition.
9. Mill, *Principles*, p. 401.
10. Ibid., p. 402.

11. Ibid., pp. 398–9.
12. J. S. Mill, *England and Ireland*, London, 1868, pp. 12–13.
13. Black, *Economic Thought and the Irish Question*, pp. 24–5.
14. E. D. Steele, 'J. S. Mill and the Irish Question: The Principles of Political Economy', *Historical Journal*, xiii (1970), pp. 220–34; idem, 'J. S. Mill and the Irish Question: Reform, and the Integrity of the Empire, 1865–1870', *Historical Journal*, xiii (1970), pp. 419–50; idem, *Irish Land and British Politics: Tenant-Right and Nationality, 1865–1870*, Cambridge: Cambridge University Press, 1974, pp. 48–55.
15. Lynn Zastoupil, 'Moral Government: J. S. Mill on Ireland', *Historical Journal*, xxvi (1983), pp. 707–17; Bruce L. Kinzer, 'J. S. Mill and Irish Land: A Reassessment', *Historical Journal*, xxvii (1984), pp. 111–27.
16. Mill, *Principles*, p. 402.
17. Conner, *Two Letters*, pp. x, xv, xviii, xxvi–xxvii.
18. Steele, *Irish Land and British Politics*, p. 35.
19. William Shee, *Papers, Letters and Speeches in the House of Commons on the Irish Land Question, with a Summary of its Parliamentary History, from the General Election of 1852 to the Close of the Session of 1863*, London, 1863, p. viii.
20. J. S. Donnelly, 'Landlords and Tenants' in Vaughan (ed.), *New History of Ireland*, V, pp. 338–43.
21. J. H. Whyte, *The Independent Irish Party, 1850–9*, Oxford: Oxford University Press, pp. 7–8.
22. Ibid., pp. 14–38.
23. Ibid., p. 88.
24. Charles Gavan Duffy, *The League of North and South*, London, 1886.
25. Shee, *Papers, Letters and Speeches*, p. 3.
26. Paul Bew, *Land and the National Question in Ireland, 1858–82*, Dublin: Gill & Macmillan, 1978, pp. 38–45.
27. R. V. Comerford, *The Fenians in Context: Irish Politics and Society, 1848–82*, Dublin: Wolfhound Press, 1985, p. 105.
28. E. R. Norman, *The Catholic Church and Ireland in the Age of Rebellion, 1859–1873*, London: Longmans, Green, 1965, p. 157.
29. For Cullen's view see ibid., p. 386.
30. Comerford, *Fenians in Context*, pp. 106–7: Norman, *Catholic Church*, p. 170.
31. Comerford, *Fenians in Context*, pp. 213–15.
32. Oliver MacDonagh, *States of Mind: A Study of Anglo-Irish Conflict, 1780–1980*, London: Allen & Unwin, 1983, pp. 35–6.

33. Steele, *Irish Land and British Politics.*
34. Robert Lowe's phrase, quoted ibid., p. 254.
35. Ibid., p. 201.
36. Batt, *The Moncks and Charleville House*, pp. 230–31.
37. Duke of Argyll, quoted in Steele, *Irish Land and British Politics*, p. 287.
38. For a succinct statement of the provisions of the bill, the public discussion of it, the lines of the parliamentary debates on it, and the amendments incorporated into the final act, see ibid., pp. 277–312.
39. Ibid., p. 315.
40. Ibid., p. 298.
41. Ibid., p. 293.
42. Black, *Economic Thought and the Irish Question*, pp. 53–5.
43. George Campbell, *The Irish Land, London*, 1869, pp. 5–6.
44. Ibid., pp. 6–7.
45. Ibid.
46. Ibid., pp. 30–31.
47. Steele, *Irish Land and British Politics*, p. 309.

Chapter 3: Land and Nationalism (pp. 54–93)
 1. W. Neilson Hancock, *Report on the Landlord and Tenant Question in Ireland from 1860 till 1866*, Dublin, 1866, p. xxi.
 2. *The Times*, 2 Jan. 1868.
 3. Ibid.
 4. Ibid.
 5. Comerford, *Fenians in Context*, p. 178.
 6. Ibid., p. 216.
 7. David Thornley, *Isaac Butt and Home Rule*, London: MacGibbon & Kee, 1964, pp. 15–21.
 8. Isaac Butt, *Land Tenure in Ireland: A Plea for the Celtic Race*, Dublin, 1866, p. 9.
 9. Ibid., p. 52.
10. Ibid., p. 53.
11. Ibid., p. 57.
12. Ibid., p. 58.
13. Ibid., p. 64.
14. Isaac Butt, *The Irish People and the Irish Land: A Letter to Lord Lifford; with comments on the publications of Lord Dufferin and Lord Rosse*, Dublin, 1867, p. 297.
15. Quoted in Black, *Economic Thought and the Irish Question*, p. 70.
16. T. W. Moody, *Davitt and Irish Revolution, 1846–82*, Oxford: Clarendon Press, 1981, pp. 117ff.

17. *Connaught Telegraph*, 3 June 1876.
18. Ibid.
19. Ibid.
20. Ibid.
21. Gerard Moran, 'James Daly and the Rise and Fall of the Land League in the West of Ireland, 1879–82', *Irish Historical Studies*, xxix, no. 114 (Nov. 1994), p. 190. For another account of Daly's significance see J. J. Lee, *The Modernisation of Irish Society, 1848–1918*, Dublin: Gill & Macmillan, 1973, pp. 69–70.
22. Moran, 'James Daly', pp. 192–200.
23. Ibid., p. 192.
24. See, for example, correspondence between Matthew Harris and Thomas Brennan, Charles J. Kickham and Michael Davitt, Oct. 1877 – July 1880 (NLI, W. G. Fallon Papers, MS 22704).
25. Moody, *Davitt and Irish Revolution*, chs 7–8.
26. *Connaught Telegraph*, 1 July 1876.
27. Moody, *Davitt and Irish Revolution*, pp. 283ff.
28. N. D. Palmer, *The Irish Land League Crisis*, New Haven: Yale University Press, 1940.
29. T. W. Moody, 'The New Departure in Irish Politics, 1878–9' in H. A. Cronne, T. W. Moody and D. B. Quinn (eds), *Essays in British and Irish History in honour of James Eadie Todd*, London: Muller, 1949.
30. Moody, *Davitt and Irish Revolution*.
31. J. S. Donnelly, *The Land and the People of Nineteenth-Century Cork: The Rural Economy and the Land Question*, London: Routledge & Kegan Paul, 1975.
32. Solow, *The Land Question and the Irish Economy*.
33. Samuel Clark, *Social Origins of the Irish Land War*, Princeton: Princeton University Press, 1979; also his articles 'The Social Composition of the Land League', *Irish Historical Studies*, xvii, no. 68 (Sept. 1971), pp. 447–69; 'The Political Mobilisation of Irish Farmers', *Canadian Review of Sociology and Anthropology*, xii, no. 4, pt 2 (1975), pp. 483–99; 'Agrarian Class Conflict and Collective Action in Nineteenth-Century Ireland', *British Journal of Sociology*, xxix, no. 1 (Mar. 1978), pp. 22–40.
34. Bew, *Land and the National Question*.
35. Vaughan, *Landlords and Tenants in Mid-Victorian Ireland*; idem, 'A Study of Landlord and Tenant Relations in Ireland between the Famine and the Land War, 1850–78'; idem, *Landlords and Tenants in Ireland, 1848–1804*, Dublin: Economic and Social History Society of Ireland, 1984.

36. Moody, *Davitt and Irish Revolution*, p. 295.
37. *Connaught Telegraph*, 15 Feb. 1875.
38. Donnelly, *Land and People*, p. 250.
39. Ibid.
40. Clark, *Social Origins*, pp. 11–12.
41. Ibid., pp. 129–32, 231–2, 234–5, 266–7.
42. Vaughan, *Landlords and Tenants in Mid-Victorian Ireland*, pp. 55–66.
43. Vaughan, 'Landlord and Tenant Relations', p. 11. For a summary of a developing alternative reading of the economic data see K. Theodore Hoppen, *Ireland since 1800: Conflict and Conformity*, London: Longman, 1989, pp. 90–94.
44. Vaughan, 'Landlord and Tenant Relations', pp. 122ff.
45. Ibid., p. 142.
46. Quoted in Fergus O'Ferrall, *Catholic Emancipation: Daniel O'Connell and the Birth of Irish Democracy, 1820–30*, Dublin: Gill & Macmillan, 1985, p. 17.
47. Clark, *Social Origins*, esp. chs 8–9.
48. Quoted in J. C. Beckett, *The Making of Modern Ireland*, 2nd ed., London: Faber, 1981, p. 304.
49. David Seth Jones, 'Agrarian Capitalism and Rural Social Development in Ireland' (Ph.D. thesis, Queen's University, Belfast, 1977), pp. 27–8.
50. See David Seth Jones, *Graziers, Land Reform, and Political Conflict in Ireland*, Washington: Catholic University of America Press, 1995, p. 180; Moran, 'James Daly', pp. 191, 204–6.
51. Bew, *Land and the National Question*, pp. 223–4.
52. Vaughan, *Landlords and Tenants, 1848–1904*, p. 33.
53. Ibid.
54. Moody, *Davitt and Irish Revolution*, p. 326.
55. Margaret O'Callaghan, *British High Politics and a Nationalist Ireland: Criminality, Land and the Law under Forster and Balfour*, Cork: Cork University Press, 1994, p. 9.
56. *Report of Her Majesty's Commissioners of Inquiry into the Working of the Landlord and Tenant (Ireland) Act, 1870, and the acts amending the same* [Bessborough Commission], [C 2779], H.C. 1881, xviii, 269, p. 5.
57. Ibid., p. 19.
58. *Florence Arnold-Forster's Irish Journal*, ed. T. W. Moody and Richard Hawkins, with Margaret Moody, Oxford: Clarendon Press, 1988, p. 321.

Chapter 4: The Land as Metaphor (pp. 94–115)

1. Michael Davitt, *The Fall of Feudalism in Ireland; or the Story of the Land League Revolution*, London: Harper, 1904, pp. 150–51.
2. See, for example, Donnelly, *Land and People*, pp. 275ff.
3. Quoted in Davitt, *Fall of Feudalism.* pp. 149–50.
4. Ulick Canon Bourke to Parnell, 18 Oct. 1879 (TCD, Davitt Papers, MS 9369, f. 845).
5. Comerford, *Fenians in Context*, p. 70.
6. W. T. Thornton, *A Plea for Peasant Proprietors: with the Outlines of a Plan for their Establishment in Ireland*, London, 1848.
7. *Florence Arnold-Forster's Irish Journal*, p. 19.
8. Anna Parnell, *The Tale of a Great Sham*, ed. Dana Hearne, Dublin: Arlen House, 1986.
9. Janet K. TeBrake, 'Irish Peasant Women in Revolt: The Land League Years', *Irish Historical Studies*, xxviii, no. 109 (May 1992), pp. 63–80.
10. Davitt to Dillon, [24 Aug. 1882] (TCD, Davitt Papers, MS 9403, f. 1556).
11. Laurence M. Geary, *The Plan of Campaign, 1886–1891*, Cork: Cork University Press, 1986, p. 6.
12. Ibid., p. 12.
13. See Emmet Larkin, *The Roman Catholic Church and the Plan of Campaign in Ireland, 1886–1888*, Cork: Cork University Press, 1978, pp. 4–10.
14. Conor Cruise O'Brien, *Parnell and his Party, 1880–90*, Oxford: Clarendon Press, 1957, p. 202.
15. Ibid.
16. William O'Brien, *Christmas on the Galtees: An Inquiry into the Condition of the Tenantry of Mr Nathaniel Buckley*, Dublin, 1878, published originally as a series of articles in the *Freeman's Journal*, first publicly identified O'Brien in terms of the land issue.
17. Davitt–Dillon correspondence, July–Aug. 1887 (TCD, Davitt Papers, MS 9403, ff. 1564, 1565, 1566).
18. For an extended account of the divergencies in attitude to the handling of Irish issues—especially as between Hicks Beach, Salisbury and Lord Randolph Churchill—in the period preceding Balfour's appointment see L. P. Curtis, *Coercion and Conciliation in Ireland, 1880–92: A Study in Conservative Unionism*, Princeton: Princeton University Press, 1963, pp. 120–73, although with conclusions differing in some important respects from those given above.

19. Ibid., p. 169.
20. O'Callaghan, *British High Politics*, p. 20.
21. Ibid., pp. 104–21.
22. Northcote to Gibson, 18 Dec. 1880 (House of Lords Record Office, Ashbourne Papers, B71/9).
23. Ibid.
24. Gibson to Northcote, 21 Dec. 1880 (copy) (ibid., B71/10)
25. Ibid.
26. Graham D. Goodlad, 'The Liberal Party and Gladstone's Land Purchase Bill of 1886', *Historical Journal*, xxxii, no. 3 (Sept. 1989), p. 641.
27. Allen Warren, 'Gladstone, Land and Social Reconstruction in Ireland, 1881–1887', *Parliamentary History*, ii (1983), pp. 153–73.
28. *The Times*, 13 Apr. 1882.
29. Lord Waterford to Lord Ashbourne, 20 Apr. 1890 (House of Lords Record Office, Ashbourne Papers, B154/12).
30. For a more detailed account of the northern agitation see Alvin Jackson, *The Ulster Party: Irish Unionists in the House of Commons, 1884–1911*, Oxford: Clarendon Press, 1989, pp. 158–64.
31. Alvin Jackson, 'Irish Unionism and the Russellite Threat', *Irish Historical Studies*, xxv, no. 100 (Nov. 1987), pp. 376–404.
32. For the origins of the United Irish League see Philip Bull, 'The Reconstruction of the Irish Parliamentary Movement, 1895–1903: An Analysis with special reference to William O'Brien' (Ph.D. thesis, University of Cambridge, 1972), pp. 105–39.
33. Lord Salisbury, 'Disintegration', *Quarterly Review*, clvi, no. 312 (Oct. 1883), pp. 559–95.
34. William O'Brien, *An Olive Branch in Ireland and its History*, London, 1910, p. 89.

Chapter 5: Land Agitation and a Proto-State (pp. 116–142)
1. Quoted in Moody, *Davitt and Irish Revolution*, p. 399.
2. *Freeman's Journal*, 25 July 1899.
3. *Irish People*, 7 Sept. 1901.
4. Davitt to Dillon, 6 May 1902 (TCD, Dillon Papers, MS 6728, f. 117)
5. Bartlett, 'An End to Moral Economy'.
6. Anthony Trollope, *The Macdermots of Ballycloran* (1847), London: Penguin, 1993, p. 364.

7. J. W. Mackail and Guy Wyndham, *Life and Letters of George Wyndham*, London: Hutchinson, n.d., II, p. 411.
8. Salisbury to the King, 9 Apr. 1902 (PRO, CAB/41/27/8).
9. *Mayo News*, 26 Feb. 1898; Irish Office Records, PRO, CO 903/8/1, p. 10; *Hansard*, 4th series, liii, 1535–63 (24 Feb. 1898).
10. *The Times*, 1 Mar. 1898.
11. Irish Office Records PRO, CO 903/8/1, p. 18.
12. Ibid., pp. 36–7; William O'Brien's diary, 16 Oct. 1898 (*Irish People*, 23 Mar. 1907); Sophie O'Brien, 'Recollections of a Long Life' (NLI, MS 4214, Vol. II, p. 33).
13. William O'Brien's diary, 17 Oct. 1898 (*Irish People*, 23 Mar. 1907).
14. L. P. Curtis, 'Stopping the Hunt, 1881–1882: An Aspect of the Irish Land War' in C. H. E. Philpin (ed.), *Nationalism and Popular Protest in Ireland*, Cambridge: Cambridge University Press, 1987, pp. 349–402.
15. Anthony Trollope, *The Land-leaguers* (1883), London: Penguin, 1993, pp. 59–65.
16. Curtis, 'Stopping the Hunt', pp. 363–4.
17. Waterford to Gibson, 9 Oct. 1881 (House of Lords Record Office, Ashbourne Papers, B154/3).
18. Ibid.
19. Mark Bence-Jones, *Twilight of the Ascendancy*, London: Constable, 1987, p. 39.
20. For studies of Conservative policy on Ireland in this period see Curtis, *Coercion and Conciliation*; Catherine Shannon, 'Local Government in Ireland: The Politics and Administration' (M.A. thesis, University College, Dublin, 1963); eadem, *Arthur J. Balfour and Ireland, 1874–1922*, Washington: Catholic University of America Press, 1988; Andrew Gailey, *Ireland and the Death of Kindness: The Experience of Constructive Unionism, 1890–1905*, Cork: Cork University Press, 1987.
21. *Irish People*, 8 June 1901.
22. Irish Crimes Records, PRO CO 903/9, p. 310; *The Times*, 28 Apr. 1902.
23. *Irish People*, 5 July 1902.
24. O'Brien to Harrington, 14 May 1898 (NLI, Harrington Papers, MS 8576 (32)).
25. *Mayo News*, 16 July 1898.
26. Ibid., 30 July 1898.
27. Inspector-General's monthly confidential report, July 1898 (Irish Office Records, PRO CO 904/68).

28. *Hansard*, 4th series, lxxii, 880–88 (12 June 1899).
29. Ibid., lxxiii, 306–54 (22 June 1899).
30. Salisbury to the King, 11 Mar. 1902 (PRO CAB/41/27/8).
31. Richard Davis, *The Young Ireland Movement*, Dublin: Gill & Macmillan, 1987, p. 39.
32. Charles Gavan Duffy, *Four Years of Irish History, 1845–9*, London, 1883, pp. 487–9.
33. For a fuller exposition of this idea see Philip Bull, 'A Fatal Disjunction, 1898–1905: Sinn Féin and the United Irish League' in Rebecca Pelan (ed.), *Irish-Australian Studies: Papers of the Seventh Irish Australian Conference*, Sydney: Crossing Press, 1994, pp. 37–51.
34. *Florence Arnold-Foster's Irish Journal*, p. 423.
35. *Irish People*, 23 June 1900.
36. *Freeman's Journal*, 12 Dec. 1900.
37. *Irish People*, 4 Jan. 1902.
38. *Mayo News*, 14 May 1898.
39. Irish Office Records, PRO CO 903/8/1, p. 41.
40. Ibid. The police believed that a Father Coen had been behind this move, but that he had been too 'wary' to leave himself open to prosecution or ecclesiastical censure.
41. Irish Office Records, PRO CO 903/8/2, pp. ix–xi.
42. Ford to O'Brien, 12 June 1898 (UCC, William O'Brien Papers, AIA/83).
43. Davitt to O'Brien, 23 June 1898 (NLI, Davitt Letters, MS 913).
44. Irish Office Records, PRO, CO 903/8/1, p. 38.
45. *Mayo News*, 16 July 1898.
46. See Philip Bull, 'The United Irish League and the Reunion of the Irish Parliamentary Party, 1898–1900', *Irish Historical Studies*, xxvi, no. 101 (May 1988), pp. 51–78.
47. See William L. Feingold, *The Revolt of the Tenantry: The Transformation of Local Government in Ireland, 1872–1886*, Boston: Northeastern University Press, 1984.
48. *Hansard*, 4th series, lxxx, 1322–3 (20 Mar. 1900).
49. O'Brien's diary, 14 Aug. 1898 (*Irish People*, 26 Jan. 1907).
50. O'Brien to P. Moclair (draft), 10 Jan. 1899 (UCC, William O'Brien Papers, AJA/25–6).
51. Mandeville to O'Brien, 4 July 1899 (ibid., AJB/82–3).
52. Donald E. Jordan, *Land and Popular Politics in Ireland: County Mayo from the Plantation to the Land War*, Cambridge: Cambridge University Press, 1994, p. 219.
53. Ibid., pp. 255–6.

54. Ibid., p. 256.
55. For more detailed studies of this important Mayo figure and his complex relationship with the Land League see Jordan, *Land and Popular Politics*, pp. 265–77, and Gerard Moran, 'James Daly and the Rise and Fall of the Land League in the West of Ireland, 1879–82', *Irish Historical Studies*, xxix, no. 114 (Nov. 1994), pp. 189–207.
56. Correspondence between James Daly and William O'Brien, 4 Jan. – 3 Feb. 1898 (UCC, William O'Brien Papers, AIA/2, 7, 17, 22, 124); *Independent*, 26 Jan. 1898; *Freeman's Journal*, 18 Jan. 1898.
57. 'The United Irish League, its origins and history', report by Assistant Inspector Allan Cameron, 10 Oct. 1898 (N.A.I., Crime Branch Special Papers, 17425/S).
58. Ibid.
59. Jordan, *Land and Popular Politics*, pp. 222–6, 237–44.
60. Larkin, *Roman Catholic Church and the Plan of Campaign*, p. xiii.
61. For an exposition of the interests and concerns of the graziers see David S. Jones, 'The Cleavage between Graziers and Peasants in the Land Struggle, 1890–1910' in Samuel Clark and J. S. Donnelly (eds), *Irish Peasants: Violence and Political Unrest, 1780–1914*, Manchester, 1983, pp. 374–417; idem, 'Agrarian Capitalism and Rural Social Development in Ireland'; idem, *Graziers, Land Reform, and Political Conflict in Ireland*.
62. Michael D. Higgins and John P. Gibbons, 'Shopkeeper-Graziers and Land Agitation in Ireland, 1895–1900' in P. J. Drudy (ed.), *Ireland: Land, Politics and People*, Cambridge: Cambridge University Press, 1982, pp. 93–118.
63. Liam Kennedy, 'Farmers, Traders and Agricultural Politics in Pre-Independence Ireland' in Clark and Donnelly (eds), *Irish Peasants*, p. 369.
64. Donald Jordan, 'Merchants, "Strong Farmers" and Fenians: The Post-Famine Elite and the Irish Land War' in Philpin (ed.), *Nationalism and Popular Protest*, pp. 320–48.
65. See David Fitzpatrick, 'The Disappearance of the Irish Agricultural Labourer, 1841–1912', *Irish Economic and Social History*, vii (1980), pp. 66–92.
66. Paul Bew, 'The Land League Ideal: Achievements and Contradictions' in Drudy (ed.), *Ireland: Land, Politics and People*, pp. 77–92.
67. Samuel Clark, 'The Importance of Agrarian Classes: Agrarian

Class Structure and Collective Action in Nineteenth-Century Ireland', ibid., p. 31.

68. Vaughan, *Landlords and Tenants, 1848–1904*, p. 33.

Chapter 6: 'Chancing an Arm' (pp. 143–175)

1. Richard Stanihurst, 'Historie of Ireland' in *Holinshed's Irish Chronicle*, p. 323.
2. Letter of Lord Barrymore to the *Daily Express*, reported in *The Times*, 22 Sept. 1902.
3. Timothy McCarthy to O'Brien, 6 Sept. 1902 (UCC, William O'Brien Papers, AM/178).
4. William O'Brien, *Olive Branch*, p. 142.
5. Shawe-Taylor to O'Brien, 12 Sept. 1902 (UCC, William O'Brien Papers, AM/185).
6. *The Times*, 22 Sept. 1902.
7. Newspaper notice dated 16 Oct. 1902, preserved in minute book of the Land Conference Committee (NLI, MS 10907).
8. Ibid.
9. Minutes of Provisional Committee, 17 Nov. 1902 (ibid.).
10. G. de L. Willis to Lord Mayo, 28 Nov. 1902 (ibid.).
11. The O'Conor Don to Lord Dunraven, 30 Nov. 1902 (ibid.).
12. Minutes of Land Conference Committee, 28 Nov. 1902 (ibid.).
13. Minutes of Land Conference Committee, 12 Dec. 1902 (ibid.).
14. Lord Mayo to the Executive Committee of the Landowners' Convention, 28 Nov. 1902, newscutting (ibid.).
15. Minutes of Land Conference Committee, 12 Dec. 1902 (ibid.).
16. Ibid.
17. Harrington to Lord Mayo, 17 Nov. 1902 (ibid.).
18. Lord Mayo to Harrington, 17 Nov. 1902 (copy) (ibid.).
19. Harrington to Lord Mayo, 18 Nov. 1902 (ibid.).
20. Ibid.
21. Lord Dunraven to Harrington, fragment of letter [beginning and date missing, but after that of 27 Dec. 1902] (NLI, Harrington Papers, MS 8587).
22. Lord Dunraven to Harrington, 27 Dec. 1902 (ibid.).
23. Ibid.
24. Curtis, *Coercion and Conciliation*, p. 354.
25. Wilfrid Scawen Blunt, *My Diaries*, London, 1922, II, p. 56.
26. Condon to O'Brien, 8 Apr. 1903 (UCC, William O'Brien Papers, AN/24–5).
27. See F. S. L. Lyons, *The Irish Parliamentary Party, 1890–1910*, London: Faber, 1951, p. 103; Blunt, *My Diaries*, p. 56.

28. George Crosbie to O'Brien, 14 Nov. 1903 (UCC, William O'Brien Papers, AN/100).

29. Davitt to Dillon, 'Wednesday' [probably 26 Aug. 1903] (TCD, Dillon Papers, MS 6728, f. 150).

30. O'Brien to Timothy McCarthy, 16 Feb. [1902] (copy) (UCC, William O'Brien Papers, AM/4–5); Redmond to O'Brien, 21 Feb. 1902, (ibid., AM/10); see also Sally Warwick-Haller, *William O'Brien and the Irish Land War*, Dublin: Irish Academic Press, 1990, pp. 213–14.

31. O'Connor to O'Brien, 12 Aug. 1902 (UCC, William O'Brien Papers, AM/139–43). For discussion of this letter and its implications see Bull, 'The Reconstruction of the Irish Parliamentary Movement', pp. 354–9; Warwick-Haller, *William O'Brien*, pp. 218–20; J. V. O'Brien, *William O'Brien and the Course of Irish Politics, 1881–1918*, Berkeley: University of California Press, 1976, pp. 134–7.

32. William O'Brien, 'The Lost Opportunities of the Irish Gentry' (1887) in *Irish Ideas*, London: Longmans, 1893, pp. 13–29.

33. Redmond to Dillon, 25 Sept. 1903 (copy) (NLI, Redmond Papers, MS 15182 (4)).

34. O'Brien, *Olive Branch*, p. 184.

35. Davitt to Dillon, 'Wednesday' [probably 16 Sept. 1903] (TCD, Dillon Papers, MS 6728, f. 155a). F. S. L. Lyons (*John Dillon: A Biography*, London: Routledge & Kegan Paul, 1968, p. 238) dates this letter as probably 15 Sept. 1903, and (following him) so does the annotation on the actual manuscript, but as the 16th was a Wednesday that is the more probable date.

36. *Freeman's Journal*, 26 Aug. 1903.

37. Ibid.

38. McHugh to Dillon, 12 Sept. 1903 (TCD, Dillon Papers, MS 6757, f. 1128).

39. Paul Bew, *Conflict and Conciliation in Ireland, 1890–1910: Parnellites and Radical Agrarians*, Oxford: Clarendon Press, 1987, pp. 55–6.

40. See above, p. 114.

41. *Freeman's Journal*, 24 May 1889.

42. Michael Davitt, 'The Irish Social Problem', *To-day*, new series, i, no. 4 (Apr. 1884), pp. 241–55.

43. Curtis, *Coercion and Conciliation*, p. 352.

44. See Philip Bull, 'The Significance of the Nationalist Response to the Irish Land Act of 1903', *Irish Historical Studies*, xxviii, no. 111 (May 1993), pp. 295–6.

45. D. G. Boyce, *Nationalism in Ireland*, London: Croom Helm, 1982, p. 277.
46. Bew, *Conflict and Conciliation*, pp. 133ff.
47. Sheehy to O'Brien, 12 Oct. 1903 (UCC, William O'Brien Papers, AN/69); Farrell to O'Brien, 15 Oct. 1903 (ibid., AN/70); Bew, *Conflict and Conciliation*, pp. 79–83, 152–8.
48. Bew, *Conflict and Conciliation*, p. 206.
49. Crosbie to O'Brien, 13 July [1904] (UCC, William O'Brien Papers, AN/42).
50. Bence-Jones, *Twilight of the Ascendancy*, pp. 91–138.

Chapter 7: Postscript and Retrospect (pp. 176–192)

1. J. J. Lee, *Ireland 1912–1985: Politics and Society*, Cambridge: Cambridge University Press, 1989, p. 71.
2. Quoted in M. A. G. Ó Tuathaigh, 'The Land Question, Politics and Irish Society, 1922–1960', *Irish Studies*, ii (1982), pp. 170–71.
3. George Bernard Shaw, *John Bull's Other Island* (1907), London: Penguin, 1984, Act III, p. 110.
4. Ibid., p. 111.
5. Vaughan, *Landlords and Tenants, 1848–1904*, p. 41.
6. George W. Russell (AE), *Co-operation and Nationality: A Guide for Rural Reformers from This to the Next Generation*, Dublin, 1912, p. 6.
7. Vaughan, 'Landlord and Tenant Relations', pp. 147–8.
8. Ibid., p. 7.
9. Ibid.
10. W. H. B. Court, *A Concise Economic History of Britain*, Cambridge: Cambridge University Press, 1954, p. 163.
11. John Hancox, 'Still Clearing the Scottish Highlands', *Guardian Weekly*, 26 Apr. 1992, p. 23.
12. Lee, *Ireland 1912–1985*, p. 110.
13. Ibid., p. 145.
14. Mary Daly, *Industrial Development and Irish National Identity, 1922–1939*, Dublin: Gill & Macmillan, 1992, p. 163.
15. Fergal Tobin, *The Best of Decades: Ireland in the Nineteen-Sixties*, Dublin: Gill & Macmillan, 1984, p. 229.
16. Lee, *Ireland 1912–1985*, p. 646.

Bibliography

I. MANUSCRIPT SOURCES:
IRELAND

National Library of Ireland
  John Redmond Papers
  William O'Brien Papers
  Sophie O'Brien, manuscript of *Recollections of a Long Life*, MS 4214
  Davitt Letters, MS 913 [part of the William O'Brien Papers]
  T. C. Harrington Papers
  Land Conference Committee minute book, MS 10907

Library of Trinity College, Dublin
  John Dillon Papers
  Michael Davitt Papers

Library of University College, Cork
  William O'Brien Papers

National Archives, Dublin
  Crime Branch Special Papers

ENGLAND

British Library
  W. E. Gladstone Papers
  A. J. Balfour Papers
  Carnarvon Papers

Bodleian Library
  Harcourt Papers
  Kimberley Papers

House of Lords Record Office
  Ashbourne Papers

Public Record Office, Kew
  Cabinet Papers
  Irish Office Records
  Irish Crimes Records, 1902

II. OFFICIAL PUBLICATIONS

Hansard

Parliamentary Papers, *Report and Minutes of Evidence from Her Majesty's Commissioners of Inquiry into the State of the Law and Practice in respect to the Occupation of Land in Ireland,* 1845 [Devon Commission]

Parliamentary Papers, *Report and Minutes of Evidence from Her Majesty's Commissioners of Inquiry into the Working of the Landlord and Tenant (Ireland) Act, 1870, and the acts amending the same,* 1881 [Bessborough Commisssion]

Parliamentary Papers, *Report and Minutes of Evidence from His Majesty's Commissioners appointed to Inquire into and Report upon the Operation of the Acts dealing with Congestion in Ireland,* 1906–8 [Dudley Commission]

Law Reports: The Public General Statutes, London, 1848–1935

Acts of the Oireachtas, Dublin, 1923–1992

III. NEWSPAPERS

  Connaught Telegraph
  Freeman's Journal
  Independent
  Irish People
  Mayo News
  The Times

IV. WORKS BY CONTEMPORARIES

Arnold-Forster, Florence, *Florence Arnold-Forster's Irish Journal*, ed.
T. W. Moody and Richard Hawkins, with Margaret Moody,
Oxford: Clarendon Press, 1988

Blunt, Wilfrid Scawen, *My Diaries*, 2 vols, London, 1922

Butt, Isaac, *Land Tenure in Ireland: A Plea for the Celtic Race*, Dublin,
1866

——*The Irish People and the Irish Land: A Letter to Lord Lifford; with
comments on the publications of Lord Dufferin and Lord Rosse*,
Dublin, 1867

Cairnes, J. E., 'Ireland in Transition' [a series of articles], *Economist*,
9 Sept. – 4 Nov. 1865

Campbell, George, *The Irish Land*, London, 1869

Conner, William, *Two Letters to the Editor of The Times on the Rackrent
Oppression of Ireland, its Source, its Evils and its Remedy*, Dublin,
1846

Davitt, Michael, 'The Irish Social Problem', *To-day*, new series, i, no.
4 (Apr. 1884), pp. 241–55

——*The Fall of Feudalism in Ireland; or the Story of the Land League
Revolution*, London, 1904

Duffy, Charles Gavan, *Four Years of Irish History, 1845–9*, London,
1883

——*The League of North and South*, London, 1886

Errington, George, *The Irish Land Question: A Letter to the Rt. Hon.
H. C. E. Childers, M.P.*, Dublin, 1880

Forster, William, 'A Series of Printed Letters bound together and
which give a Narrative of William Forster's Visits to Ireland,
December 1846 – April 1847' in *Distress in Ireland: Narratives of
Visits made in 1846 and 1847 by Members of the Society of Friends, in
the Distressed Districts*, London [1846–7], nos 1–5

Foster, T. C., *Letters on the Condition of the People of Ireland*, London,
1847

Hall, Mr & Mrs S. C., *Ireland: Its Scenery, Character, &c*, 3 vols,
London, 1841–3

Hancock, W. Neilson, *Report on the Landlord and Tenant Question in
Ireland from 1860 till 1866*, Dublin, 1866

Hill, Lord George, *Facts from Gweedore, compiled from the notes of Lord
George Hill*, intro. & ed. E. Estyn Evans, Belfast: Queen's
University, 1971

Humphreys, David, *The Justice of the Land League*, London, 1880

Inglis, H. D., *Ireland in 1834: Journey throughout Ireland during the
spring, summer, and autumn of 1834*, 2 vols, London, 1834

Lewis, George Cornewall, *On Local Disturbances in Ireland, and on the Irish Church Question*, London, 1836

Mill, J. S., *The Principles of Political Economy*, 3rd ed., 2 vols, London, 1852

——*England and Ireland*, London, 1868

O'Brien, R. Barry, *The Parliamentary History of the Irish Land Question from 1829 to 1869, and the Origin and Results of the Ulster Custom*, London, 1880

O'Brien, William, *Christmas on the Galtees: An Inquiry into the Condition of the Tenantry of Mr Nathaniel Buckley*, Dublin, 1878

——'The Lost Opportunities of the Irish Gentry'(1887) in William O'Brien, *Irish Ideas*, London, 1893, pp. 13–29

—— 'Diary', as published in the *Irish People* newspaper between 5 Jan. and 1 June 1907

——*An Olive Branch in Ireland and its History*, London, 1910

Parnell, Anna, *The Tale of a Great Sham*, ed. Dana Hearne, Dublin: Arlen House, 1986

Richey, Alexander, *The Irish Land Laws*, London, 1880

Russell, George W.(AE), *Co-operation and Nationality: A Guide for Rural Reformers from This to the Next Generation*, Dublin, 1912

Salisbury, Marquis of, 'Disintegration', *Quarterly Review*, clvi, no. 312, (Oct. 1883), pp. 559–95

Shee, William, *Papers, Letters and Speeches in the House of Commons on the Irish Land Question, with a Summary of its Parliamentary History, from the General Election of 1852 to the Close of the Session of 1863*, London, 1863

Smith, Elizabeth, *The Irish Journals of Elizabeth Smith, 1840–1850*, ed. David Thomson with Moyra McGusty, Oxford: Clarendon Press, 1980

Thornton, W. T., *A Plea for Peasant Proprietors: with the Outlines of a Plan for their Establishment in Ireland*, London, 1848

Trollope, Anthony, *The Macdermots of Ballycloran* (1847), London: Penguin, 1993

—— *The Land-leaguers* (1883), London: Penguin, 1993

Tuke, James H., *Irish Distress and its Remedies: A Visit to Donegal and Connaught in the spring of 1880*, London, 1880

Wyndham, George, *Life and Letters of George Wyndham*, ed. J.W. Mackail and Guy Wyndham, 2 vols, London, n.d.

V. LATER WORKS

Aalen, Frederick H. A., 'Constructive Unionism and the Shaping of

Rural Ireland, *c.* 1880–1921', *Rural History*, iv, no. 2 (1993), pp. 137–64

Akenson, D. H., *Between Two Revolutions: Islandmagee, County Antrim, 1798–1920*, Ontario: P. D. Meany, 1979

Bartlett, Thomas, 'An End to Moral Economy: The Irish Militia Disturbances of 1793', *Past and Present*, no. 99 (May 1983), pp. 41–64

Batt, Elizabeth, *The Moncks and Charleville House: A Wicklow Family in the Nineteenth Century*, Dublin: Blackwater Press, 1979

Beames, Michael, 'Cottiers and Conacre in Pre-Famine Ireland', *Journal of Peasant Studies*, ii (1975), pp. 351–4

——*Peasants and Power: The Whiteboy Movements and their Control in Pre-Famine Ireland*, Brighton: Harvester, 1983

Beckett, J. C., *The Making of Modern Ireland*, 2nd ed., London: Faber, 1981

Bence-Jones, Mark, *Twilight of the Ascendancy*, London: Constable, 1987

Bew, Paul, *Land and the National Question in Ireland, 1858–82*, Dublin: Gill & Macmillan, 1978

——*Conflict and Conciliation in Ireland, 1890–1910: Parnellites and Radical Agrarians*, Oxford: Clarendon, 1987

Black, R.D. Collison, *Economic Thought and the Irish Question, 1817–1870*, Cambridge: Cambridge University Press, 1960

Boyce, D. G., *Nationalism in Ireland*, London: Croom Helm, 1982

Boylan, Thomas A., and Foley, Timothy P., *Political Economy and Colonial Ireland: The Propagation and Ideological Function of Economic Discourse in the Nineteenth Century*, London: Routlege & Kegan Paul, 1992

Buckley, David N., *James Fintan Lalor: Radical*, Cork: Cork University Press, 1990

Bull, Philip, 'The Reconstruction of the Irish Parliamentary Movement, 1895–1903' (Ph.D. thesis, University of Cambridge, 1972)

——'The United Irish League and the Reunion of the Irish Parliamentary Party, 1898–1900', *Irish Historical Studies*, xxvi, no. 101 (May 1988), pp. 51–78

——'The Significance of the Nationalist Response to the Irish Land Act of 1903', *Irish Historical Studies*, xxviii, no. 111 (May 1993), pp. 295–6

——'A Fatal Disjunction, 1898–1905: Sinn Féin and the United Irish League' in Rebecca Pelan (ed.), *Irish-Australian Studies: Papers of the Seventh Irish-Australian Conference*, Sydney: Crossing Press, 1994, pp. 37–51

Burn, W. L., 'Free Trade in Land: An Aspect of the Irish Question', *Transactions of the Royal Historical Society*, 4th series, xxxi (1949), pp. 61–74

Clark, Samuel, 'The Social Composition of the Land League', *Irish Historical Studies*, xvii, no. 68 (Sept. 1971), pp. 447–69

—— 'The Political Mobilisation of Irish Farmers', *Canadian Review of Sociology and Anthropology*, xii, no. 4, pt 2 (1975), pp. 483–99

—— 'Agrarian Class Conflict and Collective Action in Nineteenth-Century Ireland', *British Journal of Sociology*, xxix, no. 1 (Mar. 1978), pp. 22-40

—— *Social Origins of the Irish Land War*, Princeton: Princeton University Press, 1979

—— and Donnelly, J. S. (eds), *Irish Peasants: Violence and Political Unrest, 1780–1914*, Manchester: Manchester University Press, 1983

Comerford, R. V., *The Fenians in Context: Irish Politics and Society, 1848–82*, Dublin: Wolfhound Press, 1985

Cullen, L. M., *An Economic History of Ireland since 1660*, London: Batsford, 1976

Currie, E. A., 'Land Tenures, Enclosures and Field-Patterns in Co. Derry in the Eighteenth and Nineteenth Centuries', *Irish Geography*, ix (1976), pp. 50–62

Curtis, L. P., *Coercion and Conciliation in Ireland, 1880–92: A Study in Conservative Unionism*, Princeton: Princeton University Press, 1963

—— 'Incumbered Wealth: Landed Indebtedness in Post-Famine Ireland', *American Historical Review*, lxxxv, no. 2 (Apr. 1980), 332–67

—— 'On Class and Class Conflict in the Land War', *Irish Economic and Social History*, viii (1981), 86–94

—— 'Stopping the Hunt, 1881–1882: An Aspect of the Irish Land War' in Philpin (ed.), *Nationalism and Popular Protest*, pp. 349–402

Daly, Mary, *Industrial Development and Irish National Identity, 1922–1939*, Dublin: Gill & Macmillan, 1992

Davis, Richard, *The Young Ireland Movement*, Dublin: Gill & Macmillan, 1987

Donnelly, J. S., *The Land and the People of Nineteenth-Century Cork: The Rural Economy and the Land Question*, London: Routledge & Kegan Paul, 1975

Drudy, P. J. (ed.), *Ireland: Land, Politics and People*, Cambridge: Cambridge University Press, 1982

Elliott, Marianne, 'Ireland and the French Revolution' in H.T. Dickinson (ed.), *Britain and the French Revolution, 1789–1815*, London: Macmillan, 1989

Evans, E. Estyn, *Irish Folk Ways*, London: Routledge & Kegan Paul, 1957

——*The Personality of Ireland: Habitat, Heritage and History*, Belfast: Blackstaff, 1981

Feingold, William L., 'The Tenants' Movement to Capture the Irish Poor Law Boards, 1877–1886', *Albion*, vii (fall 1975), 216–31

——*The Revolt of the Tenantry: The Transformation of Local Government in Ireland, 1872–1886*, Boston: Northeastern University Press, 1984

Fitzpatrick, David, 'The Disappearance of the Irish Agricultural Labourer, 1841–1912', *Irish Economic and Social History*, vii (1980), pp. 66–92

Gailey, Andrew, *Ireland and the Death of Kindness: The Experience of Constructive Unionism, 1890–1905*, Cork: Cork University Press, 1987

Geary, Laurence M., *The Plan of Campaign, 1886–1891*, Cork: Cork University Press, 1986

Gibbon, Peter, and Higgins, M. D., 'Patronage, Tradition and Modernisation: The Case of the Irish "Gombeenman"', *Economic and Social Review*, vi, no. 1 (1974), pp. 27–44

——,——'The Irish "Gombeenman": Reincarnation or Rehabilitation?', *Economic and Social Review*, viii, no. 4 (1977), pp. 313–20

Gibson, Ralph, and Blinkhorn, Mark (eds), *Landownership and Power in Modern Europe*, London: Harper Collins, 1991

Goodlad, Graham D., 'The Liberal Party and Gladstone's Land Purchase Bill of 1886', *Historical Journal*, xxxii, no. 3 (Sept. 1989), pp. 627–641

Hammond, J. L., *Gladstone and the Irish Nation*, London: Longmans, 1938

Hill, J. Michael, 'The Origins of the Scottish Plantations in Ulster to 1625: A Reinterpretation', *Journal of British Studies*, xxxii, no. 1 (Jan. 1993), pp. 24–43

Hoppen, K. Theodore, *Ireland since 1800: Conflict and Conformity*, London: Longman, 1989

Jackson, Alvin, 'Irish Unionism and the Russellite Threat', *Irish Historical Studies*, xxv, no. 100 (Nov. 1987), pp. 376–404

——*The Ulster Party: Irish Unionists in the House of Commons, 1884–1911*, Oxford: Clarendon Press, 1989

Jones, David Seth, 'Agrarian Capitalism and Rural Social Development in Ireland' (Ph.D. thesis, Queen's University, Belfast, 1977)

——'The Cleavage between Graziers and Peasants in the Land Struggle, 1890–1910' in Clark and Donnelly (eds), *Irish Peasants*, pp. 374–417

——*Graziers, Land Reform, and Political Conflict in Ireland*, Washington: Catholic University of America Press, 1995

Jordan, Donald, 'Merchants, "Strong Farmers" and Fenians: The Post-Famine Elite and the Irish Land War' in Philpin (ed.), *Nationalism and Popular Protest*, pp. 320–48

——*Land and Popular Politics in Ireland: County Mayo from the Plantation to the Land War*, Cambridge: Cambridge University Press, 1994

Kennedy, Liam, 'A Sceptical View of the Reincarnation of the Irish "Gombeenman"', *Economic and Social Review*, viii, no. 3 (1977), 213–22

——'Farmers, Traders and Agricultural Politics in Pre-Independence Ireland' in Clark and Donnelly (eds), *Irish Peasants*, pp. 339–73

Kinzer, Bruce L., 'J. S. Mill and Irish Land: A Reassessment', *Historical Journal*, xxvii (1984), pp. 111–27.

Knott, J. W., 'Land, Kinship and Identity: The Cultural Roots of Agrarian Agitation in Eighteenth- and Nineteenth-Century Ireland', *Journal of Peasant Studies*, xii, no. 1 (1984), pp. 93–109

Kolbert, C. F., and O'Brien, Timothy, *Land Reform in Ireland: A Legal History of the Irish Land Problem and its Settlement*, Cambridge: Department of Land Economy, 1975

Larkin, Emmet, *The Roman Catholic Church and the Plan of Campaign in Ireland, 1886–1888*, Cork: Cork University Press, 1978

Lee, J. J. *The Modernisation of Irish Society, 1848–1918*, Dublin: Gill & Macmillan, 1973

——*Ireland 1912–1985: Politics and Society*, Cambridge: Cambridge University Press, 1989

Lowe, W. J., 'Landlord and Tenant on the Estate of Trinity College, Dublin, 1851–1903', *Hermathena*, cxx (1976), pp. 5–24

Lyons, F.S.L., *The Irish Parliamentary Party, 1890–1910*, London: Faber, 1951

——*John Dillon: A Biography*, London: Routledge & Kegan Paul, 1968

——*Charles Stewart Parnell*, London: Collins, 1977

MacDonagh, Oliver, *States of Mind: A Study of Anglo–Irish Conflict, 1780–1980*, London: Allen & Unwin, 1983

Mansergh, Nicholas, *The Irish Question, 1840–1921: A Commentary on Anglo-Irish Relations and on Social and Political Forces in Ireland in the Age of Reform and Revolution*, 3rd ed., London: Allen & Unwin, 1975

Moody, T. W., 'The New Departure in Irish Politics, 1878–9' in H. A. Cronne, T. W. Moody and D. B. Quinn (eds), *Essays in British and Irish History in honour of James Eadie Todd*, London: Muller, 1949

——*Davitt and Irish Revolution, 1846–82*, Oxford: Clarendon Press, 1981

Moran, Gerard, 'James Daly and the Rise and Fall of the Land League in the West of Ireland', *Irish Historical Studies*, xxix, no. 114 (Nov. 1994), pp. 189–207

Moriarty, Daniel Patrick, 'The Transformation of Rural Ireland: The Irish Land Purchase Policy of the Conservative Party in Britain, 1885–1923' (Ph.D. thesis, University of North Carolina, 1988)

Nolan, William, *Fassadinin: Land, Settlement and Society in South-East Ireland, 1600–1850*, Dublin: Geography Publications, 1979

Norman, E. R., *The Catholic Church and Ireland in the Age of Rebellion, 1859–1873*, London: Longmans, 1965

O'Brien, Conor Cruise, *Parnell and his Party, 1880–90*, Oxford: Clarendon Press, 1957

O'Brien, J. V., *William O'Brien and the Course of Irish Politics, 1881–1918*, Berkeley: University of California Press, 1976

O'Callaghan, Margaret, 'Crime, Nationality and the Law: The Politics of Land in Late Victorian Ireland' (Ph.D. thesis, University of Cambridge, 1989)

——*British High Politics and a Nationalist Ireland: Criminality, Land and the Law under Forster and Balfour*, Cork: Cork University Press, 1994

O'Farrell, Patrick, *Ireland's English Question*, London: Batsford, 1971

O'Ferrall, Fergus, *Catholic Emancipation: Daniel O'Connell and the Birth of Irish Democracy, 1820–30*, Dublin: Gill & Macmillan, 1985

Ó Tuathaigh, M. A. G., 'The Land Question, Politics and Irish Society, 1922–1960', *Irish Studies*, ii (1982), pp. 170–71

Palmer, N. D., *The Irish Land League Crisis*, New Haven: Yale University Press, 1940

Perkin, Harold, *The Origins of Modern English Society, 1780–1880*, London: Routledge & Kegan Paul, 1969

Philpin, C. H. E. (ed.), *Nationalism and Popular Protest in Ireland*, Cambridge: Cambridge University Press, 1987

Pomfret, John E., *The Struggle for Land in Ireland, 1800–1923* (1930), New York: Russell & Russell, 1969

Shannon, Catherine, 'Local Government in Ireland: The Politics and Administration' (M.A. thesis, University College, Dublin, 1963)

—— *Arthur J. Balfour and Ireland, 1874–1922*, Washington: Catholic University of America Press, 1988

Solow, Barbara, *The Land Question and the Irish Economy, 1870–1903*, Cambridge, Mass.: Harvard University Press, 1971

Steele, E. D., 'Ireland and the Empire in the 1860s: Imperial Precedents for Gladstone's First Irish Land Act', *Historical Journal*, xi (1968), pp. 64–83

—— 'J. S. Mill and the Irish Question: The Principles of Political Economy', *Historical Journal*, xiii (1970), pp. 220–34

—— 'J. S. Mill and the Irish Question: Reform and the Integrity of the Empire, 1865–1870', *Historical Journal*, xiii (1970), pp. 419–50

—— *Irish Land and British Politics: Tenant-Right and Nationality, 1865–1870*, Cambridge, 1974

TeBrake, Janet K., 'Irish Peasant Women in Revolt: The Land League Years', *Irish Historical Studies*, xxviii, no. 109 (May 1992), pp. 63–80

Thornley, David, *Isaac Butt and Home Rule*, London: MacGibbon & Kee, 1964

Tobin, Fergal, *The Best of Decades: Ireland in the Nineteen-Sixties*, Dublin: Gill & Macmillan, 1984

Vaughan, W. E., 'A Study of Landlord and Tenant Relations in Ireland between the Famine and the Land War, 1850–78' (Ph.D. thesis, Trinity College, Dublin, 1973)

—— 'Farmer, Grazier and Gentleman: Edward Delany of Woodtown, 1851–99', *Irish Economic and Social History*, ix (1982), pp. 53–72

—— *Landlords and Tenants in Ireland, 1848–1904*, Dublin: Economic and Social History Society of Ireland, 1984

—— *Landlords and Tenants in Mid-Victorian Ireland*, Oxford: Clarendon Press, 1994

—— (ed.), *A New History of Ireland, V: Ireland under the Union, 1801–70*, Oxford: Clarendon Press, 1989

Warren, Allen, 'Gladstone, Land and Social Reconstruction in Ireland, 1881–1887', *Parliamentary History*, ii (1983), pp. 153–73

Warwick-Haller, Sally, *William O'Brien and the Irish Land War*, Dublin: Irish Academic Press, 1990

Whyte, J. H., *The Independent Irish Party, 1850–9*, Oxford: Oxford University Press, 1958

Winstanley, Michael J., *Ireland and the Land Question, 1800–1922*, London: Methuen, 1984

Zastoupil, Lynn, 'Moral Government: J. S. Mill on Ireland', *Historical Journal*, xxvi (1983), pp. 707–17

Index